# Prophet of Purpose

# Prophet of Purpose

*The Life of*

## Rick Warren

## JEFFERY L. SHELER

DOUBLEDAY

*New York   London   Toronto   Sydney   Auckland*

Published in the United States by Doubleday Religion, an imprint of
the Crown Publishing Group, a division of Random House, Inc., New York.

www.crownpublishing.com

DOUBLEDAY and the DD colophon are registered trademarks of Random House, Inc.

Library of Congress Cataloging-in-Publication Data

Sheler, Jeffery L.
Prophet of purpose : the life of Rick Warren / by Jeffery L. Sheler.—1st ed.
        p.        cm.
1. Warren, Richard, 1954– 2. Christian biography. 3. Baptists—United States—
Clergy—Biography. 4. Life—Religious aspects—Christianity.
5. Evangelicalism—United States. I. Title.
BX6495.W37S44 2009
286'.1092—dc22
[B]
2009024050

ISBN 978-0-385-52395-0

PRINTED IN THE UNITED STATES OF AMERICA

DESIGN BY LEONARD W. HENDERSON

1  3  5  7  9  10  8  6  4  2

First Edition

To Jonah, Bryan, and Sean

*Be strong and courageous.*
*Do not be afraid . . . for the LORD your God goes with you;*
*He will never leave you nor forsake you.*

DEUTERONOMY 31:6

# Contents

# Contents

# Prophet of Purpose

.

# *America's Pastor*

THEY BEGAN ARRIVING AT ANGEL STADIUM in Anaheim early in the morning in a steady stream of shiny SUVs and sport sedans that lined up in neat rows and quickly disgorged their passengers—a decidedly upscale mix of young families, middle-aged couples, and singles of all ages, most of them appropriately attired for a balmy spring day in colorful shorts and T-shirts or tan-revealing sundresses, flip-flops, baseball caps, and sunglasses. Some hurried inside to stake out the better seats next to the dugouts and behind home plate. Others lingered in the parking lot and clustered around barbeque grills and coolers or tossed Frisbees or lounged in beach chairs and sipped sodas in the warm Southern California sun.

It was a picture perfect day for the ballpark, and the Orange County suburbanites were out in force. But it was not to see their hometown Angels, who happened to be playing in Oakland that afternoon. On this particular Sunday—April 17, 2005—baseball was giving way to worship and to the twenty-fifth anniversary celebration of probably the largest, easily the fastest-growing, and arguably the most influential evangelical congregation in the country, Saddleback Church in nearby Lake Forest.

Renting Angel Stadium had been the idea of Saddleback's fifty-one-year-old founder and senior pastor, Rick Warren, a man well-known for thinking big. It was Warren, after all, who in 1980, fresh out of a Southern Baptist seminary, audaciously announced to a handful of worshipers that the church they were starting from scratch in his tiny apartment would one day number 20,000 and would occupy a 50-acre campus. In 2004 they surpassed that goal. What began with two families as "a church for people who hate church" had grown to a congregation of more than 22,000 regular attenders on a 120-acre campus with an annual operating budget of more than $30 million.

# Prophet of Purpose

It was Warren, too, who, thinking that other pastors might benefit from the lessons he had learned about church growth, began conducting training seminars in the late 1980s to promote a biblical model of ministry based on what he saw as "God's purposes." In 1995, he explained that model in a book for pastors entitled *The Purpose-Driven Church*. It sold over a million copies and helped launch the Purpose-Driven Network, a global alliance of now more than 10,000 congregations in 162 countries. Seven years later he wrote a spin-off, a book intended for laypeople called *The Purpose-Driven Life*. It became the best-selling nonfiction hardcover of all time—more than 25 million copies sold in the first three years alone.

The resulting fame and fortune catapulted Warren onto the national and international stage. Suddenly he found himself deluged with media interview requests and with calls from leaders in government, business, academia, the sports world, and the entertainment industry—even from foreign heads of state—seeking personal spiritual guidance or offering speaking invitations. At a time when many evangelical leaders were enlisting in the culture wars and aligning themselves with narrow partisan causes, Warren used his new public platform to call attention to the plight of the poor and the powerless, especially to AIDS victims in Africa.

At the same time, Warren and his wife, Kay, were determined that their sudden wealth would not alter their lifestyle. They became "reverse tithers," giving away 90 percent of their income and keeping just 10 percent. Most of the proceeds from *The Purpose-Driven Life* went to establish nonprofit foundations for AIDS relief and for pastoral training. Warren gave back the salary that his church had paid him over twenty-five years and began working for free. The Warrens stayed in the same unpretentious house in a hillside subdivision and continued driving the same Ford SUV. There would be no yachts, no vacation homes, no expensive wardrobes.

All of this, of course, was seriously abnormal behavior, and the world soon took notice. Here was an evangelical leader—a Southern Baptist, no less—who simply did not fit the stereotype of the dour Religious Right activist or of the money-grubbing TV preacher that so often seemed to dominate media portraits of evangelical Christians and their leaders. Instead Warren represented a new and more winsome breed of evangelical: theologically and socially conservative, yes, but far less political and far more positive in engaging the broader culture. Suddenly Warren was on the media's radar screen and he quickly became a familiar face on *Larry King Live*, *Good Morning America*, and other national TV news and public-affairs talk shows where he affably offered a fresh evangelical perspective on topics ranging from euthanasia and the Terri Schiavo case to the meaning of Christmas and the role of faith in the aftermath of 9/11. Warren was on his way to becoming, as *Fortune* magazine would describe him, "secular America's favorite evangelical Christian."

Perhaps more important was Warren's growing stature among his fellow evangelicals. The evangelical movement—some 50 million Americans who describe themselves as "born again" and espouse biblical values—had emerged as a potent political and cultural force in the final quarter of the twentieth century. Now it stood at a crossroads with the aging and passing of an older generation of leaders and no shortage of competing younger voices vying to succeed them. Warren stepped ahead of the pack in 2002 when the evangelical flagship magazine *Christianity Today* declared him "America's most influential pastor"— a reflection of the broad reach of his Purpose-Driven Network and of the tens of thousands of church leaders who looked to him for guidance. Two years later, a nationwide survey of pastors found that only the legendary evangelist Billy Graham, long the most revered figure in American Protestantism, was regarded as having greater influence on evangelical churches and church leaders. In the minds of preachers and pundits alike there appeared to be little doubt that if anyone was capable of succeeding the aging Graham in the honorific role of "America's Pastor," it was Rick Warren.

And yet Warren was not without detractors. Vocal critics within the movement questioned his "seeker-sensitive" approach to ministry, accusing him of promoting "feel-good" religion over the often rigorous demands of traditional Christianity. His therapeutic message and market-driven techniques, they argued, emphasized church growth over true discipleship. And in his eagerness to address international social ills such as AIDS and poverty, said his more conservative critics, Warren had become a fellow traveler with political and theological liberals—sworn enemies of the Religious Right. In many respects, Warren had emerged as a pivotal figure in a struggle for the soul of American evangelicalism.

YET EVIDENCE OF SUCH CONTROVERSY was nowhere in sight on this sunny Sunday afternoon. On this day Warren was fully immersed in the only role he had ever really aspired to in his twenty-five years of ministry—that of a local-church pastor. For this special celebration he wanted his entire Saddleback flock, which normally attends services spread over a weekend in multiple venues, to gather together in one place for the very first time, and Angel Stadium was the only facility in Orange County large enough to accommodate them.

A few minutes after 1 p.m. the 45,000-seat stadium was nearly full, and it was rocking. From a wide, elevated stage built over second base, an ensemble of guitars, drums, and assorted wind instruments cranked out the opening bars of an upbeat praise song and the crowd came to its feet, clapping, swaying, and singing along. The lead singer and Saddleback's worship director, Rick Muchow, a fiftyish-looking man with a shaved head and wire-rimmed glasses, danced and bobbed about the stage while a video cameraman scurried around the edges, capturing the energetic performance from various angles and flashing it to the stadium's JumboTron screens. Over the stage, a long banner formed a proscenium arch in big block letters—God's Purposes. God's Church. God's Plan.

After a few more songs, the crowd settled into their seats and Muchow moved to center stage to make an introduction. "To the rest of the planet he's the best-selling author in the world . . . and this week *Time* magazine named him one of the hundred most influential people in the world. But to us and to me he is our pastor. Let's give a warm Saddleback welcome to Pastor Rick!"

The crowd jumped to its feet as Warren loped onto the stage big and bear-like, looking his usual laid-back self in an untucked rose-colored sport shirt, black slacks, wraparound sunglasses, spiky hair, and signature goatee. His fleshy and slightly sun-burned face—a face once famously compared in its ordinariness to that of a "friendly butcher"— filled the giant screens in right and left fields. Warren acknowledged the ovation with a broad smile and a spirited "Woo-*hoo*!"

"You know," he said, grabbing the microphone, "there are two things I've always wanted to do in a stadium." Turning toward the band, he broke into the first lines of Jimi Hendrix's "Purple Haze," punctuating it with a riff on the air guitar. "The other thing I've always wanted to do," he said when the laughter and applause subsided, "is the wave. So let's start over here." Pointing down the first-base line at the grandstands he directed the rising and falling of his cheering congregation, around and around the stadium, laughing with glee at the spectacle as Muchow and the band struck up a musical accompaniment. "What I want to say about that," Warren said when it finally ended, "is that the wave is just starting. For twenty-five years it's been building . . . You are the most amazing church, and *I love you!*"

FOR ALL OF HIS ACCOMPLISHMENTS and stature, there is something disarmingly approachable about Rick Warren that audiences and interviewers pick up on almost immediately. He comes across as an average guy—genial, gregarious, quick with a self-deprecating joke—someone you would more expect to be captain of a bowling team than a megachurch pastor. He laughs easily and often with a loud and hearty Robert De Niro kind of laugh—head tilted back, chin jutted out, the corners of his mouth tipped slightly downward. He prefers hugs to handshakes, wrapping his arms around even the most casual of acquaintances as though they were family. He eats copious amounts of food and has the girth to prove it. His personal sense of fashion, he likes to say, is clothes that don't itch.

In one of the first national-media profiles of Warren late in 2002, *Christianity Today* explored his "regular guy" appeal and found that, to a large extent, it was rooted in his rural upbringing as the son of a Southern Baptist minister who launched and pastored tiny churches in small Northern California towns. "Warren remains a small-town personality," the magazine observed, "a class president and class clown rolled together." Warren's wife, Kay, put it more bluntly: "He's not sophisticated in any way. This is a man who will come out in an Elvis costume. He's a ham. He's a goofball."

Yet there is far more to Warren than a small-town, fun-loving everyman. In attempting to explain his success, those closest to him and those who have studied him from afar tend to use very similar terms to describe him: he is a "management genius" and a "spiritual entrepreneur" who understands business principles and organizational dynamics better than many MBAs. Peter Drucker, the late legendary management consultant and a longtime Warren mentor, once described Warren as "the inventor of perpetual revival" and Saddleback's organizational model as "the most significant sociological phenomenon of the second half of [the twentieth] century." Indeed, no modern church pastor has matched Warren's success as a motivator and mobilizer of Christian workers. Each week some 9,500 Saddleback members participate in more than 200 local projects, from feeding the homeless and leading neighborhood Bible studies to cleaning and maintaining the church grounds. Thousands more have gone overseas on short-term mission trips. Most of the work is organized through the more than 3,200 small groups who meet weekly in private homes for prayer and Bible study and form the backbone of Saddleback's organizational structure.

Others have attributed Warren's pastoral success to his celebrated skills as a communicator. Alan Wolfe, a noted Boston College political scientist, once referred to Warren as "not only the best preacher, but simply the best public speaker I have ever heard." A big part of what impressed Wolfe and others is Warren's knack for simplifying and clarifying complex subjects. Both in the pulpit and in his books he prefers conversational storytelling to lofty oratory or scholarly exegesis and is fond of using lists and easy-to-remember alliterations to communicate a point. The purpose of life, for example, as he explained in *The Purpose-Driven Life*, may be easily summed up in five bullet points: "You were planned for God's pleasure. You were formed for God's family. You were created to become like Christ. You were shaped for serving God. You were made for a mission." In one sermon on missionary outreach, Warren sought to reassure his flock that there was nothing to fear about working as missionaries. "It's not about location; it's about dedication. It's not about where you are; it's about whom you serve. It's not about crossing the sea; it's about seeing the cross." It was classic Warren-speak.

To his family and staff, what accounts most for Warren's success is his strong personal faith—an attribute one might reasonably expect in a member of the clergy. But in Warren's case, earnestly believing the mantra that "God's work done God's way will not lack God's support" has produced a bold sense of confidence that his aides often find inspiring but also nerve-wracking at times. "If Rick believes God is in it— a vision, a plan, a program—he will not let go of it even if there is no other reason, humanly speaking, to believe it's going to work," says Glen Kreun, Saddleback's chief administrative pastor and Warren's longest-serving associate. "In the early years, people would say to him all the time, 'You'll never reach twenty thousand. You'll never be able to afford fifty acres. What are you thinking?' But Rick doesn't quit. And when you're riding with somebody who is that positive, you can't help but be positive." Warren's faith has proved contagious, and out of it has sprung a church and a worldwide movement.

As THE AFTERNOON WORE on at Angel Stadium, the celebratory mood continued to build with energetic performances by Christian pop artist Michael W. Smith and a colorfully costumed dance troupe from Rwanda. Hundreds of church staff members and volunteers marched from the dugouts and onto the infield to receive recognition and were greeted with a fireworks display.

There to offer a personal greeting was the president of Rwanda, Paul Kagame, tall and pencil thin in a dark blue suit and red tie. Warren welcomed him to the stage with a hug. A year earlier, Kagame had invited Warren to work with churches in Rwanda to help turn the tiny east African country, wracked by poverty and genocide, into the first Purpose-Driven nation. He had come to California to congratulate "my friends, Rick and Kay Warren" on Saddleback's twenty-fifth anniversary and to thank them for the work they were about to undertake in his country. "We in Rwanda understand the great need for good leaders," Kagame said in a quiet, almost inaudible voice as he nodded to Warren, "because we have witnessed the destruction that self-serving leadership can cause."

Next came a message from President George W. Bush, read by Peace Corps director Gaddi Vasquez, an Orange County native, calling Saddleback's ministry milestone "a tribute to your dedication and service . . . I applaud your compassion and your commitment to your faith." Then there was Larry Ross, longtime spokesman for Billy Graham, who delivered the ailing evangelist's personal greetings and his regrets that he could not be present. There was Charles Colson, a former Watergate figure and now a Christian commentator and elder statesman of the evangelical movement, praising Warren for his work on behalf of the marginalized of society. "Over the years I've come to know the great, the near great, and the would-be great," Colson said. "But this guy, Rick Warren, is the real deal."

And then there was Warren himself, finally alone in the pulpit, and in his element. Looking out over the sun-drenched stadium he reminded his flock of his very first Saddleback sermon, delivered in a high school auditorium at a dress rehearsal for the first service in 1980. It had included a vision statement spelling out in amazingly prophetic detail what the then twenty-seven-year-old Warren believed his start-up church would accomplish and become—the 20,000 members, the land, the training and commissioning of thousands of lay ministers and short-term missionaries, hundreds of thousands of Orange County residents reached with the Gospel, and so on.

"Friends," Warren's tenor voice echoed through the stadium's public address system, *that vision has been fulfilled! God is faithful! And you ain't seen nothin' yet!"*

When the cheering and applause quieted, Warren continued. "During the last couple of years I've been quietly asking the Lord, 'What do you want to do next, Lord? What is your plan for the next twenty-five years?' And God says this in the book of Isaiah, chapter 43, verses 18 and 19: 'Do not cling to events of the past or dwell on what happened long ago. Watch for the new thing I am going to do. It is happening already—you can see it now!'

"And so I stand before you today to share with you the next vision. It is a dream of global expansion. It is a dream of total mobilization. And it is a dream of radical devotion. *God is going to use you to change the world!"*

For the next thirty minutes or so Warren unveiled his latest and undoubtedly his most ambitious project to date: a worldwide Saddleback-led campaign to battle the "global giants" of poverty, disease, ignorance, egocentric leadership, and spiritual emptiness. He called it the PEACE plan—an acronym based on five strategies he said were drawn from the teachings of Christ: planting churches, equipping servant-leaders, assisting the poor, caring for the sick, and educating the next generation. In the months ahead, Saddleback members would study the strategies and begin applying them, first locally and then globally. This was to be the "beta version" of the PEACE plan, and after a period of testing and adjusting, it would be rolled out as an international campaign involving thousands of churches and millions of Christians around the world. Warren predicted it would spark "a global revolution" that would ignite "a new Reformation in the church of God" and a worldwide spiritual awakening.

"Now I know you may be sitting there saying, 'But it just seems so big and so overwhelming. Why us?' I would say to you the same thing Jesus Christ said in Matthew 19:26. 'Humanly speaking it is impossible. But with God everything is possible.' I would rather attempt something great and fail than attempt to do nothing and succeed. Throughout the history of the world, in God's timing there are always three phases: impossible, possible, and done. Everything is considered impossible until somebody does it. And God wants to use you."

IT WAS TIME TO CLOSE the deal. If it had been a Billy Graham crusade, the choir would have begun singing "Just as I Am," and thousands of seekers would be called from their seats to gather in front of the stage to commit their lives to Christ. But Warren was about to ask his congregation to make a life-changing commitment of a different sort.

"There is no doubt in my mind that for the past twenty-five years God has been setting us up—you, me, everybody in this stadium, and the ten thousand Purpose-Driven churches—to bless the entire world. First he has blessed us, and now he is making us a blessing. If you are willing to commit yourself to this, if you will say, 'Rick, I'm in. I'm willing to serve God's purposes in my generation, whatever it takes,' I want you to stand up. Stand up quietly right now where you are, and hold up the signs that you have been given."

All around the hushed stadium tens of thousands of the Saddleback faithful came to their feet, men and women of all ages, teenagers and children, waving bright red placards emblazoned with bold yellow letters: Whatever it takes!

Warren silently surveyed the fluttering ocean of red surrounding him for what seemed like several minutes. There was no movement. The only sound in the stadium was a breeze rumbling across a microphone, a jet plane passing overhead.

When Warren finally continued, his voice cracked. "You know, the great nineteenth-century evangelist D. L. Moody once said that the world is yet to see what God can do through one person who is totally committed to Him. Well, I'm looking at a stadium full of people who are saying, 'Whatever it takes, God. Whatever it takes,' and I believe we are making history . . . So I'll just say this from the bottom of my heart: I love you. I mean, *I really, really do love you!* And the world has not yet seen what's going to happen in the next twenty-five years. But it's going to be a wild ride, *so buckle up!*"

The revolution was under way.

CHAPTER TWO

# "A Peculiar People"

*But ye are a chosen generation, a royal priesthood, a holy na-*
*tion, a peculiar people; that ye should show forth the praises*
*of Him who hath called you out of darkness into His mar-*
*velous light.*

— I PETER 2:9

WHEN THE UNIQUE BRAND OF CHRISTIAN faith practiced by
Rick Warren, his Saddleback flock, and tens of millions of others who
call themselves evangelicals emerged as a robust movement late in the
twentieth century, it was widely regarded with puzzlement and
apprehension—and occasionally with disdain—in some of the more
secular quarters of American society. To some media commentators
who chronicled the rise of the Religious Right in the early 1980s,
evangelical Christianity seemed a strange and rustic religion that
appealed mainly to rural folk in the South and Midwest—people a
*Washington Post* writer would snidely describe as "largely poor,
uneducated, and easy to command." It was a brand of faith that
appeared to outsiders as highly politicized and largely disconnected
from the more refined traditions of mainline Protestantism and the long
historic arc of Roman Catholicism. And if the broadcasts of some
popular televangelists were any indication, it was a movement led by
pugnacious preachers in cheap suits and bad haircuts with an uncanny
knack for fund-raising and melodrama. So, at least, were the
unflattering stereotypes that seemed to define evangelicals as they first
appeared, as if out of nowhere, on the national media's radar screen in
the final decades of the century.

Yet evangelicals were hardly newcomers to the American religion scene. Theirs was a rich and diverse tradition that stretched back nearly four hundred years. Rooted in the spiritual stirrings of post-Reformation Europe, it was planted in the American colonies with the arrival of New England's Puritans in the seventeenth century and was fortified and disseminated in the Great Awakening revivals of the eighteenth and nineteenth centuries.

Indeed, those who would march under the evangelical banner came from a wide variety of Protestant backgrounds, from conservative Baptists and Dutch Reformed Calvinists to pacifist Mennonites and tongues-speaking Pentecostals. Some bore familiar denominational labels like Methodist, Presbyterian, Congregationalist, and Lutheran. Others were part of lesser known bodies like the Evangelical Free Church or the Christian and Missionary Alliance, and vast numbers were associated with independent and nondenominational churches of assorted shapes and sizes. Their worship styles would run the gamut from traditional and liturgical to casual "contemporary praise." And they often differed with one another, sometimes vehemently, on doctrinal matters such as modes of baptism, rules of ordination, the validity of charismatic "gifts" such as speaking in tongues and faith healing, and the meaning of the Lord's Supper.

Yet what loosely united them and set them apart from other Christian traditions was a shared set of convictions and emphases—defining features often summarized as *conversionism*, an emphasis on being "born again," which evangelicals believe occurs when a person accepts Christ as savior and enters into a personal relationship with God; *biblicism*, a reliance on the Bible, as opposed to church tradition or the pronouncements of church officials, as the ultimate religious authority; *activism*, the responsibility of all believers, including laypeople, to be engaged in sharing the Gospel and converting others to the Christian faith; and *crucicentrism*, a focus on the redemptive death and resurrection of Jesus Christ as the only source of eternal salvation. While other Christian traditions embraced at least some of those characteristic beliefs, the combination represented a distinctly evangelical outlook and formed the gravitational center for a family of churches and religious enterprises that together made up the modern evangelical movement—and the spiritual home of Rick Warren.

IN A SENSE, THE HISTORY of evangelicalism has been an almost continuous process of revival and reform, of a people carving out and maintaining a religious identity separate from some other group or set of beliefs that they considered to be out of synch with a proper understanding of Scripture. It is a corrective impulse that goes back to the start of the Protestant Reformation in the early 1500s and to even earlier purifying movements in Christian history.

The spark that ignited the Reformation was Martin Luther's personal "rediscovery of the Gospel"—his embrace of essential New Testament teachings that he believed had been obscured in the Roman Catholic Church. In nailing his Ninety-five Theses to the cathedral door at Wittenberg, Luther had staked out the revolutionary view that God's grace was the sole basis of salvation for the sinner and was to be appropriated through faith alone (*sola fide*), unmediated by the church, as revealed through the Bible alone (*sola scriptura*), the only infallible authority on matters of faith. Those central tenets of the Reformation also would become key elements of modern evangelical belief.

Over the next two centuries, the theological uprising launched by Luther would sweep across Europe, spawning new movements and denominations that increasingly emphasized personal piety and individual accountability over church tradition and authority. In the American colonies, that egalitarian message would be fanned into a roaring fire in the 1740s by the revivalist preaching of Methodism founder John Wesley, Congregationalist minister Jonathan Edwards, and Anglican evangelist George Whitefield—key figures in what would become known as the Great Awakening. In churches and meeting halls and in outdoor gatherings from New England to Georgia, seekers by the thousands enthusiastically came to embrace a populist gospel that emphasized the necessity of the "new birth"—the belief that salvation was a gift from God, to be received with assurance by repenting of sin and placing one's faith in Jesus Christ as savior, rather than by engaging in church rituals.

## Prophet of Purpose

The Great Awakening would have a lasting impact on evangelicalism and on the course of Christianity in general in the United States. Beyond the theological innovations, the eighteenth-century revivals promoted what University of Notre Dame historian Mark Noll describes as "a new style of leadership—direct, personal, popular, and dependent much more on a speaker's ability to draw a crowd than upon that speaker's place in an established hierarchy." It is a style that would be emulated by modern stars of the evangelical pulpit, from itinerant evangelists Billy Sunday in the early 1900s and Billy Graham a half century later to broadcast personalities like Jimmy Swaggart, Jerry Falwell, and Pat Robertson, and finally to Warren—all of whom would use their formidable skills as communicators and media innovators to build a religious following independent of denominational ties.

The early revivals also undercut traditional church authority by simplifying the essentials of the Christian faith into a message with mass appeal that could be easily disseminated beyond the confines of the churches and without their approval. While "ecclesiastical life remained important" to evangelicals, says Noll, it became "not nearly as significant as the decision of the individual" to hear and accept the good news of salvation. That democratization of Protestant Christianity resonated powerfully in the colonies during the decades leading up to the American Revolution and would continue to be a defining characteristic of evangelicalism.

A second wave of revivals later in the eighteenth century would bring even more changes. The Second Great Awakening, as it would become known, erupted on three fronts—New England, the Cumberland Valley, and western New York—between the mid-1780s and the 1820s. In the Cumberland and in eastern Kentucky, the revivals grew out of a series of camp meetings where thousands gathered for several days of spirited and sometimes raucous preaching services. Where the first awakening had been led by Congregational and Anglican clergy, the camp-meeting preachers were mostly Baptists and Methodists, and the fervor they inspired helped to establish those denominations in the South.

In New England, the revival was more cerebral, sparked in part by a renewal of biblical commitment against the perceived heresies of Unitarianism and universalism, new religious movements that denied the doctrine of the Trinity and the necessity of salvation in Christ. It also gave rise to new missionary agencies and to church involvement in social causes such as abolition, temperance, child welfare, and prison reform—demonstrating a concern for the betterment of society that would characterize evangelical Protestantism through most of the nineteenth century.

The awakening in western New York, meanwhile, was largely the work of revivalist preacher Charles Grandison Finney, a Presbyterian minister whose carefully staged services produced thousands of converts in Rochester and other cities. Unlike Edwards, who had considered revival "a surprising work of God," Finney believed revival could be deliberately induced with careful planning, innovation, and publicity—strategies that would become commonplace in modern evangelistic crusades. Finney also emphasized the role of human volition in the salvation process, that individuals had the ability to "choose God" and thereby take control of their own spiritual destiny. That view would become a standard feature of modern American evangelicalism.

Out of the two Great Awakenings, American Protestantism emerged as a powerful culture-shaping force in the nineteenth century. While there were pockets of liberal dissent and some important doctrinal and regional differences—slavery being the most divisive—nearly all of the major Protestant denominations and their institutions were guided with varying degrees of intensity by a commitment to conversion, biblical authority, missionary outreach, and benevolent activism—all hallmarks of evangelicalism. It was a type of evangelicalism, as Noll describes it, "infused with postmillennial optimism"—a mindset that considered social reform to be an important part of the church's mission. Both by saving souls and by fighting social ills, evangelicals believed they could make the world a better place and thereby usher in the Second Coming of Christ. Their outlook was considered postmillennial because it was based on the popular belief that Christ would return after the biblical millennium, a one-thousand-year period of divinely ordered peace described in the Book of Revelation. Largely as a result of that social-reforming impulse, the number of charitable organizations in New England exploded during this period—growing from about fifty at the time of the War of Independence to nearly two thousand in 1820. Most of them were founded by Protestants, many of them of the evangelical variety.

But by mid-century, evangelical optimism found itself facing supreme challenges. The slavery debate had opened deep fissures in antebellum Protestantism. Many northern evangelicals had become zealous abolitionists, and many of their southern counterparts were staunch defenders of the "peculiar institution." Both sides appealed to Scripture to make their cases. The sectional conflict split several denominations, creating institutional rifts that in some cases still exist. None would be more consequential than the schism that divided the nation's Baptists and gave birth to the Southern Baptist Convention—the denominational home of Rick Warren.

THE HISTORY OF BAPTISTS in America is a rich and dramatic saga unto itself. From their roots among English Separatists in the early 1600s to the establishment of the first Baptist congregation in the colonies by Rhode Island founder Roger Williams in 1636, the early Baptists were fiercely independent churchmen who rejected the Church of England's authority and doctrines, especially its practice of infant baptism, and often were persecuted as a result. Yet their congregations continued to multiply, from Pennsylvania to the Carolinas, and after forming a constellation of loose-knit associations and missionary agencies, by the early nineteenth century they had emerged as a vibrant nationwide denomination.

While there would be disagreements over some doctrinal fine points and matters of church polity, a broad consensus quickly emerged within the churches over a core set of convictions that seemed to define what it meant to be Baptist. Those included the necessity of personal conversion through faith in Christ and repentance from sin; belief in the Bible as God's inspired and authoritative word; the priesthood of all believers, which meant that every Christian had direct access to God without need of a human mediator; the baptism of believers, by immersion only, as an outward sign of faith; the Lord's Supper as a memorial of the death and resurrection of Christ, not as a grace-imparting sacrament; religious freedom for all; separation of church and state; and the complete autonomy of the local church.

But by the 1840s, the slavery issue had so polarized the nation along sectional lines that it drove a wedge between Baptists of the North and South. As early as 1835, southern churches began to complain that missionaries who were slaveholders or who supported the institution were treated with contempt by the American Baptist Home Mission Society, which was dominated by northern abolitionists. In 1844, the Society threw off any pretense of neutrality and rejected the appointment of a Georgia slaveholder as a missionary. For southern churchmen that was the final straw. A year later, 328 delegates from nine states gathered in Augusta, Georgia, to organize the Southern Baptist Convention, a new denomination that eventually would become the nation's largest Protestant body. It would take the denomination 150 years after its founding to officially and publicly apologize for supporting slavery.

Meanwhile, as the sectional conflict erupted into a bloody and protracted Civil War, Baptists and other embattled evangelicals in the South turned increasingly inward, focusing more on personal spiritual matters and less on broad social concerns and embracing a cultural insularity that foreshadowed the rise of the fundamentalist movement just a few decades later.

THE DECADES AFTER THE WAR brought seismic changes to the American social and economic landscape that would shake the optimism and supremacy of evangelical Protestants. Industrialization and immigration hastened the nation's shift from an agrarian to an urban society, creating both new diversity and intractable social problems. Crowded cities blighted by crime, poverty, and disease posed a vexing challenge to the Protestants' belief that they were establishing the biblical millennium. By the 1880s, notes Columbia University professor Randall Balmer, "teeming, squalid tenements populated by immigrants, most of them non-Protestant, hardly looked like the precincts of Zion" that evangelicals had previously envisioned. So they adjusted their theology to reflect what was becoming a decidedly more pessimistic cultural reality.

From about 1870 onward, evangelicals began to embrace a theology known as premillennial dispensationalism. It was an imaginative and apocalyptic belief system that held, among other things, that the Second Coming would occur prior to the millennium, rather than after, and that world conditions until then would grow steadily worse. The theology was based on the teachings of John Nelson Darby, a nineteenth-century English churchman who believed that history was divided into seven ages, or dispensations, that would culminate in the Final Judgment and the end of the world. Based on a literalistic reading of the Old Testament prophecy books of Ezekiel, Zechariah, and Daniel and the New Testament Book of Revelation, Darby came up with a vivid end-times scenario that would be embellished and updated over the years by his theological successors.

According to dispensationalist belief, Christians one day would be suddenly snatched out of the world in an event called the Rapture, leaving nonbelievers behind to face the Great Tribulation, a seven-year period of turmoil and suffering during which the world would be ruled by the Antichrist. At the end of that period, the world's major powers would be drawn into a war in Israel and face off in the Battle of Armageddon. At the climax of the battle, Christ would return to defeat the evil forces and to set up his earthly kingdom of one thousand years—the biblical millennium.

That dispensationalist view of the Second Coming would become the default position for a wide swath of evangelicals in the twentieth century and would be popularized in the best-selling *Left Behind* novels in the 1990s. For many it simply offered a common-sense explanation for what they saw as a rampant moral decline and rejection of godliness in the world around them. The founding of the modern state of Israel in 1948 would fan their apocalyptic fervor by restoring the geographical setting for the end-times drama after an absence of nearly two thousand years. With the United Nations chartering of Israel, dispensationalists exulted, the final countdown had begun.

But, late in the nineteenth century, the theology's growing appeal had an important twofold impact. The belief that the Rapture could occur at any moment prompted many Protestant churches to redouble their missionary efforts in order to save as many souls as possible before time ran out. Meanwhile, for many evangelicals, the conviction that the world was beyond human repair and would continue to degenerate until Christ's return made social reform seem futile. While some conservative Christians would continue battling social ills with no less fervor than before, the motivation for doing so had changed. As religion historian George Marsden explains: "No longer was the goal to build a 'perfect society.' At best it was to restrain evil until the Lord returned."

The wrenching cultural changes that gave rise to premillennial pessimism sparked an altogether different kind of response among liberal Protestants. Rather than abandoning social reform, some northern critics of evangelical revivalism saw the dismal plight of the cities as reason to expand efforts on behalf of the poor and downtrodden. For them, sinful institutions—greedy corporations that abused workers and corrupt governments that permitted slumlords and sweatshop owners to operate with impunity—were as much in need of salvation as were sinful individuals. By the end of the century, their renewed dedication to social progress acquired distinct theological underpinnings that emphasized ethics and social action over spiritual conversion. The Social Gospel, as it became known, attracted a strong following in New York and other major northern cities, giving voice to a growing liberal movement that soon would challenge the evangelical dominance of most Protestant denominations.

Even before the rise of the Social Gospel movement, the stage was set for a clash between theological liberals and conservatives by two paradigm-shifting developments in Europe in the middle of the nineteenth century. The publication of Charles Darwin's *On the Origin of Species* in London in 1859 had gone virtually unnoticed by American churchmen during the run-up to the Civil War. After the war, however, the theological implications of Darwin's evolutionary theory began to sink in, and many evangelicals saw it as an attack on the truth of the Bible and its account of creation. Meanwhile, a more direct assault on the Scriptures had come across the Atlantic in the form of "higher criticism"—a body of mainly German scholarship that used rationalistic arguments and scientific methods to challenge the Bible's origins, historical accuracy, and accounts of the supernatural. As the century neared its end, the antiliteralist and antisupernaturalist claims of the higher critics found a growing audience among liberal Protestants and, along with the Social Gospel, gained a firm foothold in the major denominations.

Finally aroused from their complacency, evangelicals reacted with passion. By the 1880s, conservative theologians were fiercely defending the inspiration and "inerrancy" of Scripture against the skeptical arguments of the "modernists," who were seen as questioning not only the Bible's inspiration but such core Christian doctrines as the divinity of Jesus, the Virgin Birth, and the Resurrection. In virtually every major denomination, conservative leaders rose up in an attempt to enforce orthodoxy. Liberals at several prominent seminaries were brought up on heresy charges, trials were held, and some were dismissed. In the South, modernist tendencies at places like Methodist-run Vanderbilt University in Nashville and the Southern Baptist Seminary at Louisville, Kentucky, were quickly snuffed out. But in the North, as historian Marsden observes, "Conservative victories turned out to be largely illusory. Liberalism continued to grow as if the trials had never taken place." By the turn of the century, it was clear that the era of evangelical hegemony in American Protestantism had come to an end.

But the battle was far from over. In 1909, two California oil tycoons put up $250,000 to publish a twelve-volume series of booklets entitled *The Fundamentals* to enunciate what conservatives saw as essential Christian doctrines and to draw a line in the sand against the modernists. Between 1910 and 1915, some 3 million copies were printed and distributed to Protestant churchmen throughout the English-speaking world. Although the massive publishing effort would do little to slow the modernist advance, within a few years it would give rise to a militant conservative movement that would draw both its name and its theological bearings from the contentious pamphlets.

By the end of World War I, growing alarm over liberal influence in the churches and moral degeneracy in the culture prompted evangelical dissenters to begin to forge new alliances. In 1919, the World Christian Fundamentals Association met in Philadelphia to rally resistance to "the Great Apostasy [that] was spreading like a plague throughout Christendom." At the same time, coalitions of "fundamentalists"—as they had begun to call themselves—were organizing within the northern Baptist, Presbyterian, and other denominations to defend biblical orthodoxy in the churches and to battle the "false apostles" of "false science" who were promoting evolution and other "damnable heresies."

While not all evangelicals accepted the fundamentalist label, and while internal disputes prevented it from becoming as effective and cohesive a movement as it might have been, fundamentalism soon came to represent the evangelical vanguard in the battle against religious modernism. Through the early 1920s, fundamentalist preachers railed against doctrinal error and crumbling social mores, which, in their estimation, went hand in hand. Condemnation of "worldly" habits and amusements—smoking, drinking, dancing, card playing, and attending movies—became commonplace in fundamentalist pulpits and publications. As a pastor in Michigan declared at the time: "The people who indulge in these worldly things are always loose in doctrine . . . The two go together."

No subject illustrated that connection more dramatically to fundamentalists than Darwinism. To them, the theory of evolution was a "lie of Satan" that encouraged atheism and moral degeneracy by denying the literal truth of Scripture: that God created man in his image. If humans were no more than evolved animals, they reasoned, what need was there for God? Liberal Protestants, who rejected biblical literalism, had much less difficulty accepting Darwin's theory.

As the power struggles in the northern denominations intensified—and as the tide increasingly shifted against them—fundamentalist leaders threw themselves into a roiling national debate over whether evolution should be taught in public schools. Modeling their efforts on the successful campaign for Prohibition a few years before, they mobilized their flocks and lobbied state legislatures to pass laws banning evolution from the classroom. Between 1923 and 1928, five southern states adopted such laws, and bills were introduced in at least eleven other states. But it was a hollow and short-lived victory. The apparent show of fundamentalist strength set the stage for a dramatic legal confrontation that would seal the movement's ultimate decline as a potent cultural force.

In July 1925, John T. Scopes, a twenty-four-year-old high school science teacher, was put on trial in Dayton, Tennessee, accused of violating the state's recently enacted prohibition against teaching evolution. There was never any real doubt that Scopes had broken the law. He had done so deliberately at the suggestion of the American Civil Liberties Union in order to test the statute. After a theatrical eight-day trial that pitted Clarence Darrow, an acerbic and irreverent defense lawyer of national renown, against the famed orator William Jennings Bryant, a fundamentalist and three-time Democratic nominee for president, Scopes was convicted and fined $100, although his conviction was overturned later on a technicality. But in the court of public opinion, Bryant and the fundamentalists had suffered a humiliating defeat. Throughout the trial, Darrow and the assembled press succeeded in portraying them as narrow-minded bumpkins whose literalistic religion defied rational thinking. The unflattering caricature would stick in the public mind, and "fundamentalist" would become for many a derogatory label.

In the aftermath of the Scopes trial, the political momentum to prohibit the teaching of evolution collapsed. Having lost the denominational battles and perceiving that the culture had turned against them, fundamentalists withdrew from public life and from the Protestant mainstream. For the next two decades, largely unnoticed by the media, they began pouring their energy and resources into building their own subculture of churches, denominations, Bible colleges, missionary societies, publishing houses, and broadcast stations. For fundamentalists in the 1930s, note professors David Gushee and Dennis Hollinger, "the good life was the separated life hunkered down against a corrupt world, and a rancorous spirit was targeted toward the perceived evils of their day: liberalism, the Social Gospel, Communism, and general worldliness in lifestyle and morals." At the same time, a renewed focus on revivalism and missionary work saw conservative denominations like the Southern Baptist Convention, the Assemblies of God, and the Church of the Nazarene grow more rapidly than the country's population.

Yet discontent was brewing within the fundamentalist ranks. By the end of the 1930s, observes Christian Smith, sociology professor at the University of North Carolina–Chapel Hill, it was clear that "much of conservative Protestantism—under the banner of fundamentalism—had evolved into a somewhat reclusive and defensive version of its 19th-century self." And while the movement continued to grow organizationally, some participants began to see its "factionalist, separatist, judgmental character" as "an insurmountable impediment" to spreading the Gospel. "The conditions were ripe," says Smith, "for a countermovement from within."

As the nation went off to war in Europe and the Pacific, the desire for a more irenic, cooperative, and culturally engaged evangelicalism began to take hold. In New England, Philadelphia, the Upper Midwest, and California during the 1940s, a new generation of leaders stepped forward to chart a new and more moderate course. Among them were the Rev. Harold Ockenga of Park Street Church in Boston, theologian and journalist Carl F. H. Henry, and a young evangelist named Billy Graham. Although they were mostly fundamentalist in doctrine, the "neo-evangelicals"—as they would call themselves—sought to counteract the anti-intellectualism and insularity associated with militant fundamentalism. As a result of their efforts, a new constellation of organizations and alliances soon would arise that would help bring about an evangelical resurgence in the final third of the twentieth century.

An important first step came in 1942 when Ockenga spearheaded a drive to organize the National Association of Evangelicals. Conceived as an alternative to the liberal Federal Council of Churches (later to become the National Council of Churches), it brought together a diverse mix of traditions and, for the first time, provided moderate fundamentalists the means by which to speak with a unified voice to the broader culture. The Southern Baptist Convention, however, with its tradition of sectional pride and denominational self-sufficiency, opted to stand apart. Without them and a handful of other conservative denominations that also decided to stay out, the NAE would fall short of becoming the voice of a united movement.

———

# Prophet of Purpose

AFTER THE WAR, THE NEW EVANGELICAL MOVEMENT gathered momentum on other fronts. In 1946, Carl Henry, newly ordained as a northern Baptist minister, published *Remaking the Modern Mind*, which argued that evangelicalism should engage the intellectual life and the larger culture. A year later, Ockenga and popular California radio evangelist Charles Fuller teamed up to found Fuller Theological Seminary in Pasadena, California. It was to be, in the words of the founders, the "Cal Tech of modern evangelicalism," producing first-rate scholarship and Christ-centered theological training. Within a few decades it would become the evangelical flagship and the largest nondenominational seminary in the world.

Meanwhile, Billy Graham, who catapulted to national prominence as a crusade evangelist in the early 1950s, had begun sounding the call for a new evangelical periodical to rival the liberal Protestant journal *The Christian Century*. Graham envisioned a magazine that would "restore intellectual respectability" to evangelical Christianity while reaffirming with an irenic spirit "the power of the Word of God to redeem and transform" lives. In 1956, with the financial support of petroleum magnate J. Howard Pew, he launched *Christianity Today* and lured Henry, a former newspaper reporter, away from Fuller seminary to be its first editor. The magazine would become the leading voice of mainstream evangelicalism.

Graham's crusade ministry was just one of several "parachurch" organizations to sprout and flourish during the postwar years. Independent, entrepreneurial, innovative, and singularly focused on evangelism, they set a pattern for successful evangelical ministries for the remainder of the century. But no one among his contemporaries would match Graham's personal stature as both a symbol and guiding light of the modern evangelical movement. In many respects, his rise to prominence paralleled that of the movement itself.

After graduating from Wheaton College, a small Christian liberal arts school near Chicago, in 1943, and after a brief stint as a pastor in a Chicago suburb, Graham signed on as an itinerant evangelist with Youth for Christ, a parachurch ministry aimed at converting high school students. He traveled the country, honing his preaching skills at youth rallies and citywide revival meetings. In 1949, at the age of thirty, he launched a three-week tent crusade in Los Angeles, where his dynamic style and simple Bible message, tinged with anti-Communist rhetoric, caught the attention of newspaper publisher William Randolph Hearst, who instructed his editors to "puff Graham." The results, says Noll, were spectacular: "The rallies extended for another nine weeks, crowds jammed the 6,000-seat 'Canvas Cathedral,' and a new star had arisen on the nation's religious horizon."

Graham put that star status to good use. He organized the Billy Graham Evangelistic Association to plan and finance his preaching ministry, which soon would go international with radio and television broadcasts, movies, books, and a syndicated newspaper column. "He came to prominence at a moment when there was an emergence of media technologies, and he jumped on them and exploited them brilliantly," observes Balmer of Columbia University.

Graham's national stature grew even further as he struck up a friendship with President Dwight Eisenhower, setting what would become a career pattern as a confidant of presidents. Seeing Graham at the White House became a source of tremendous pride for evangelicals, as did his annual appearance on the Gallup Poll's list of "Ten Most Respected Men in the World." What kept Graham in such a position of high esteem, according to Noll and others, was the simplicity of his message (he avoided potentially divisive doctrinal discourses), the integrity of his ministry (he received a flat salary and never handled ministry finances), and the ability to resist the temptations that brought down other religious luminaries, especially during the "televangelist scandals" of the 1980s. Graham had become, in Noll's estimation, "the most attractive public face that evangelical Protestantism has offered to the wider world" since World War II.

While Graham's popular image was a key factor in rallying evangelicals and defining them in the public mind, it was the election of Jimmy Carter, a Southern Baptist, to the White House in 1976 that produced their great cultural coming out. Through media coverage of Carter's religious behavior—he taught Sunday school and prayed and read his Bible daily—the nonevangelical world was introduced to what until then had been to many an all but invisible subculture of born-again Christians.

# Prophet of Purpose

The 1980s saw many conservative evangelicals venturing as a group into the political arena, first under the banner of the Moral Majority, founded in 1979 by fundamentalist Baptist preacher Jerry Falwell, and later under the Christian Coalition, which grew out of TV broadcaster Pat Robertson's unsuccessful 1988 presidential campaign. At their zenith, the two groups would claim between 2 and 4 million active members between them, although those figures would later be disputed. While influential, their attempts at harnessing and brokering the evangelical vote produced mixed results as evangelicals—an estimated 50 million potential voters—proved not to be the conservative monolith or the hotbed of political activism that some had expected. Nearly a quarter tended to vote Democratic in presidential elections and relatively few signed on as campaign workers or donors. Still, the efforts succeeded in energizing a conservative bloc of voters who previously had put little stock in electoral politics or political solutions. By the 1990s, the Religious Right had become a key constituency of the Republican Party and played an important role in helping to elect George W. Bush twice to the presidency. With the White House and other high offices occupied by some of their own, American evangelicals were no longer cultural outsiders. They had reasserted themselves as the dominant voice of American Protestantism.

One of several important manifestations of that evangelical resurgence late in the twentieth century was a sudden explosion of megachurches—new and fast-growing congregations of two thousand or more attendees—in cities and suburbs throughout the country. While it had not been unusual previously to find a few stately old churches with thousands on their membership rolls, especially in Southern Baptist strongholds like Dallas, Atlanta, and other major cities of the Bible Belt, the new megachurches tended to be less denominational in their orientation and more contemporary in style, generally reflecting the tastes and spiritual migration of the baby boomers who made up their core. Beginning in the late 1970s the number of megachurches began to surge, growing from about 50 nationwide in 1970 to some 350 in 1990 and to more than 1,200 by the end of 2005.

Even though most evangelical Christians would continue to worship in churches of fewer than four hundred members, the burgeoning megachurches would become trendsetters in music and worship styles and in devising new approaches to ministry. While they seldom followed an identical formula, they shared some common characteristics. Virtually all offered a conservative biblical theology, an informal "seeker-sensitive" style of worship with lots of up-tempo music, a variety of social and outreach ministries, and a comfortable modern facility that more resembled a concert arena or a shopping mall—complete with food courts and information kiosks—than a traditional church. More than just places of worship, they often functioned as community centers, providing a wide range of opportunities for social networking, recreation, community service, counseling and support groups, and other programs.

Most evangelical megachurches were led by charismatic founding pastors who had set out to emulate the success of church-growth pioneers like Robert Schuller, who launched his 12,000-member Crystal Cathedral at a California drive-in theater in the 1950s, and Southern Baptist pastor W. A. Criswell, who built the First Baptist Church in Dallas to more than 25,000 members during his fifty years as its leader. The ambitious young pastors selected their church sites carefully, usually opting for upscale neighborhoods in fast-growing suburbs of major metropolitan areas—locations that could easily accommodate sprawling campuses and provide a rich source of well-educated and affluent congregants. Consequently, some of the most successful megachurches would sprout in places like South Barrington, Illinois, a wealthy suburb of Chicago; Longwood, Florida, an exclusive residential area near Orlando; and Peoria, Arizona, a fast-growing suburb of Phoenix.

One of the largest and most influential of this new breed of supersized congregations would take root in the Saddleback Valley of southern Orange County, California, where a young purpose-driven pastor would devote his entire ministry to pursuing an improbable vision of reaching unchurched suburbanites by the thousands with the Gospel of Jesus Christ. Yet the young preacher's phenomenal success, and the national renown that would come his way as a result, would originate in a setting far removed from the rarefied world of megachurches and the tony environs of Southern California.

## Prophet of Purpose

The vision and purpose that would impel Rick Warren to prominence would begin to take shape in a small-town parsonage amid a people of simple faith at a time when the evangelical movement was taking its first tentative steps out of the cultural shadows and onto the national stage.

# CHAPTER THREE

# Roots of Faith

ON A COOL, OVERCAST JANUARY MORNING IN 1954, a young Baptist preacher sat alone in a bustling hallway outside the delivery room at O'Connor Hospital in San Jose, California, and offered a silent prayer for his wife and the child she was about to deliver. James and Dorothy Warren—Jimmy and Dot to all who knew them—had rushed to the hospital in the middle of the night with the first signs of labor. The due date was still weeks away, and even though the doctors had assured them there was no real cause for alarm, Jimmy and Dot were worried.

They had every reason to be. On a similar night three years earlier, the young couple had raced to the same hospital after Dot's water broke seven months into her second pregnancy. Doctors induced labor, but the fully developed baby boy she delivered was stillborn. The Warrens were told that the fetus probably had been dead for some time. Dot later would adopt the opinion that her unborn child had become entangled in the umbilical cord, but they never knew for certain how he died.

Jimmy and Dot were devastated by the tragic loss. They named the infant Wayne and gave him a Christian burial. Their only other child at the time, three-year-old Jimmy Clyde, took the death especially hard. He had been so looking forward to having a brother or sister and could not understand why Jesus had taken the baby to heaven. The aching sadness in the Warren household would linger for many months.

As the young preacher replayed those events in his mind, he bowed his head and continued praying with renewed urgency. His prayers were interrupted by the sound of the delivery room door swinging open. A smiling doctor stepped quickly across the tiled hall and extended his hand, offering his congratulations and the welcome news that Dot had given birth to a healthy baby boy. Both mother and child were fine. Jimmy breathed a prayer of thanksgiving. Many years later he would write that the arrival of Richard Duane Warren on that January 28 would "forever change the Warren household . . . and later all of Christendom."

THAT RICK WARREN WOULD GROW UP to become an evangelical pastor is hardly surprising considering the strong Baptist lineage on both sides of the family. Though he would later insist that he was not groomed to be a preacher—"My parents never assumed or expected that I would go into the ministry"—it clearly was in his genes.

His great-grandfather on his mother's side, Ebenezer McCoy Armstrong, according to family lore, was a circuit-riding preacher in Illinois and Kansas who had been saved under the ministry of the famous nineteenth-century British Baptist preacher Charles H. Spurgeon, pastor of the largest church in London at the time. An old photograph of Armstrong and an original manuscript of one of Spurgeon's sermons, complete with handwritten notations, are prominently displayed in Warren's Saddleback office. Armstrong's son, Warren's maternal grandfather, Chester Moody Armstrong, was an ordained Baptist deacon and church planter, and most of Warren's aunts and uncles on both sides of the family were devout Baptist laypeople.

But it was Warren's father, Jimmy, who would have the greatest direct influence—not only on his decision to go into the ministry but on the trademark "Purpose-Driven" direction his ministry eventually would take.

JAMES RUSSELL WARREN WAS THE TENTH of twelve children born to Thomas and Martha Warren, poor sharecroppers in Nacogdoches County, Texas. By the time Jimmy came along in 1919, Thomas Warren was sixty-five years old. He would go on to sire twenty children in all—the last when he was seventy-one. His first wife, with whom he had eight children, had died in childbirth, as would Martha when Jimmy was just six years old.

Like most families in the Deep South in those days, the Warrens were regular churchgoers, although old Tom was not known to be particularly devout. For him, attending Sunday services at the local Baptist church was just part of the natural rhythm of life—as much as plowing, planting, and tending the dusty cotton fields day after day, week after week. It was the only life he knew. Going to the little country church provided a welcome respite from the week's labors and a chance to socialize with neighbors who struggled, as the Warrens did, to coax a meager living from the hardscrabble Texas soil.

As the widowed Tom got on in age and the farm began to fail during the Great Depression, the younger children were taken in by their adult siblings who had long since moved away. Jimmy, then a freckle-faced twelve-year-old with a mop of blond hair, went to live with a sister and her husband near Shreveport, Louisiana. When it was time for high school, he was sent to Acadia Baptist Academy, a small rural boarding school run by Southern Baptists near Eunice, about ninety miles west of Baton Rouge in the heart of Cajun country. It was there that he came to embrace the Christian faith in a personal way. Having come from a "mildly Christian home," as one family member later would put it, Jimmy "probably accepted Christ a few years earlier." But at Acadia his faith "caught fire and he really began to grow spiritually." He read the Bible voraciously and drank in the spirited sermons at the school's daily chapel services. Before long, he would feel that God was calling him to the ministry.

Jimmy wasted little time answering the call. By his senior year he was preaching on weekends at a tiny Baptist mission on a south Louisiana bayou. Week after week, Bible in hand, the lanky young preacher did his best to mimic the fervor of the chapel orators as he exhorted the rough-hewn Cajun farmers to give their hearts to Jesus. He began to relish the idea of one day pastoring his own congregation. But his enthusiasm for the ministry was suddenly dampened when an elderly pastor pulled him aside one Sunday after hearing him preach and remarked that Jimmy spoke with a slight stutter. Perhaps it would be better, the pastor suggested, if he considered another line of work.

Though disappointed, Jimmy accepted the minister's advice as having come from an obviously experienced and discerning man of God. Reluctantly he set aside any thought of full-time Christian ministry but continued on in the faith with no less passion, believing that God had a plan for his life even if it wasn't being a pastor. Meanwhile, he applied himself to his studies and took on a part-time job in the school's maintenance shop to help pay his tuition. Working side by side with the chief custodian, he learned how to do basic carpentry, plumbing, and electrical work—skills that he would put to productive use throughout his life.

Between his studies and his job, Jimmy found little time for dating—not that there was much to do at the isolated campus surrounded by rice fields and cattle farms. Eunice, the nearest town with a picture show and other amusements, was nine miles away and few students had automobiles. Occasional parties held in the fellowship hall of the Pilgrim Rest Baptist Church on the edge of campus were sternly chaperoned affairs conducted in strict compliance with Baptist rules of conduct, which meant no dancing, no worldly music, and no public displays of affection. On Friday nights when he wasn't out preaching, Jimmy sometimes joined other students in the parlor of the girls' dormitory for board games and hymn singing around a piano. On one such occasion, he and some friends were perusing a student yearbook from Dodd College, a Baptist-run two-year school for women in Shreveport. One particular photograph had caught their eye. It was a full-page picture of a young woman with thick dark hair, sparkling eyes, and a bright, winsome smile. Jimmy was love-struck. "Now there is the girl I'm going to marry!" he suddenly announced to his companions. They laughed derisively at his wishful thinking.

After graduating in 1941, Jimmy headed to Southern California, where two of his older siblings lived and where work was said to be more plentiful than in the Depression-ravaged South. Almost immediately he landed a job at a tree nursery and moved in with a sister and her family in Pasadena. When the Japanese attack on Pearl Harbor pushed the nation into World War II later that year, he quit his job and enlisted in the army. Initially he was assigned to a military police unit guarding a weapons laboratory in the Mojave Desert. A few months later, he volunteered for a newly formed K-9 corps and was transferred to a training facility in the San Francisco area, where he was promoted to sergeant. Life was changing fast for Jimmy, and the changes were only beginning.

A few days before Thanksgiving in 1943, he went to the Southern Pacific Railroad station in Redwood City to buy a train ticket back to

Louisiana for Christmas. He struck up a conversation with the ticket agent, a friendly young woman who he discovered also had Louisiana connections and a good Baptist background. She invited him to church and he accepted. After church that following Sunday, the young woman's mother invited the soldier home for dinner. He went, and while Mom was busy in the kitchen, Jimmy and the young woman visited in the living room. As they talked, he casually picked up a book from the coffee table. Suddenly his face turned crimson. It was the same college yearbook that he and his Acadia friends had examined in the girls' dormitory several years earlier, and sitting across from him was the girl in the photograph. "What on earth is the matter?" she asked, having noticed his dramatic change of hue. "I'll—I'll tell you later," he stammered.

When he returned to California after Christmas he called on the young woman, and on the first weekend of January 1944, Jimmy Warren and Dorothy Nell Armstrong had their first date—during which he told her the story of the picture. This time it was she who blushed. The young soldier obviously made an impression. They continued dating, became engaged on Valentine's Day, and were married three weeks later on the fourth of March. He was twenty-four. She was twenty-one. Six weeks later Jimmy's unit shipped out to the South Pacific.

No sooner had he left the country than Dot began to hear from her friends what a mistake she had made. She and Jimmy had known each other for all of three months. What did she really know about the young soldier who had swept her off her feet? Chances were she would never see him again, her friends insisted, and waiting for him would be a waste of time. But Dot felt at peace. She believed that the love she and Jimmy had professed for one another was authentic and that God had brought them together for a reason. She would wait for her husband and to discover God's plan for their lives.

Unlike Jimmy's upbringing, there was nothing "mildly Christian" about the home in which Dorothy Armstrong had been raised. Her parents were staunch Baptist laypeople who were actively engaged in church work. Her father, Chester, had grown up in a Baptist parsonage in Illinois and had seen his parents devote their lives to serving God and tending their flock. Her mother, Nellie, was raised in the Cherokee Strip in western Oklahoma by devout Baptist parents. In the 1940s, after Dot was grown, the Armstrongs started a Southern Baptist congregation in their Redwood City home. From their example, she learned early on that living a Christian life meant more than just going to church once or twice a week. It was an all-encompassing commitment that involved reaching out to share one's faith and to serve the needs of others.

Dot was born in 1922 in Vaughn, New Mexico, a small desert town near the center of the state where her father worked for the railroad as a telegraph operator. The youngest of five children, she spent most of her growing-up years on an apple farm in northwest Arkansas, just outside of Bentonville, where the family had moved in 1930. She was a happy and fun-loving child who also demonstrated a decidedly serious side. She had accepted Christ at a young age, and while other children fidgeted or fell asleep in church, she often would sit quietly and listen intently to the preacher's sermons. She enjoyed school and did well in her studies. She sometimes spoke of becoming a teacher. She also was musically inclined, having learned the piano at home, and frequently played and sang at church. As a teenager her social life centered mainly on church youth activities, which were aimed at providing a safe haven against the taint of "worldly amusements." By the time she graduated from high school in 1940 she had sensed that God was calling her to some form of ministry—although to exactly what, she was not sure. She went off to Dodd College in Louisiana in hopes of finding out.

Two years at the junior college did not bring much clarity to the call. When she finished school she moved back with her parents, who by then had sold the farm in Arkansas and had moved to Northern California. There she took a job with the Southern Pacific Railroad, joined the local Baptist church, and began teaching a Sunday school class for high school girls. She remained convinced that God was beckoning her to full-time service, so she went to her pastor for guidance. The pastor advised her to pray and to wait; the Lord would reveal his plan in his good timing. So she prayed and she waited. And then she met and married Jimmy Warren and she waited some more.

JIMMY CAME HOME IN MARCH of 1946, six months after the war ended and nearly two years after he had left his new bride. Even though he and Dot had written often during their separation, they were little more than strangers. Getting reacquainted would take some time.

They moved into an apartment in Redwood City, California. Jimmy picked up where he left off before the war and went to work for a nursery. Dot continued working for the railroad. Within a few months the nursery went up for sale and Jimmy and Dot decided to buy it and work the business together. They pulled together what resources they could find and made the purchase. Almost immediately they discovered that the business was in trouble and apparently had been for some time. They struggled to keep it afloat, but the struggle soon began to wear on them and the business continued to flounder.

One Sunday morning early in the fall of 1946, Jimmy and Dot were attending a worship service at a new church her parents had helped organize. Dot was the church pianist and Jimmy was a newly ordained deacon. The speaker that morning was a visiting Baptist missionary to China. At the end of his message the missionary gave an invitation imploring young people in the congregation to come forward and dedicate their lives to full-time Christian service. Dot got up from the piano in the middle of the invitation hymn and went to the front of the church. Jimmy came up the aisle behind her and they embraced. Quietly, Jimmy confessed to Dot for the first time that he had felt God's call to preach some years earlier but had been running away from it. Dot confessed that she, too, had felt a call and had come to believe that God wanted her to marry a preacher and perhaps to become a missionary, but instead God had sent Jimmy into her life. Now she understood why.

Standing at the front of the church that morning, Jimmy and Dot recommitted their lives to the Lord and to full-time ministry. The following January they enrolled at Oklahoma Baptist University to begin formally preparing for a life of Christian service together.

By the time they arrived at the Shawnee, Oklahoma, campus Dot was two months pregnant, and on July 12, 1947, she gave birth to their first child, James Clyde Warren. She continued to take classes part-time while she cared for the baby. Jimmy, meanwhile, carried a full course load, worked a part-time job, and preached on weekends at a small country church for five dollars a week plus all the meat, milk, eggs, butter, and produce he could load into his car. It usually was enough food to get the family through the week even after sharing a major portion with their married student neighbors.

Jimmy and Dot graduated together in June 1950 and accepted the pastorate of a struggling new church just outside of San Jose, California, not far from Dot's parents. They were eager to get back to California and begin their life's work. But that fall, when they caught their first glimpse of the San Tomas Baptist Church in the tree-lined residential community of Campbell, their hearts sank. The building was an unfinished shell and the lot was cluttered with construction debris. A sign posted on the door by the Santa Clara County Department of Health declared the site "unfit for human occupancy." Inside walls were only roughed in and electrical wiring and plumbing were exposed. There were no bathrooms.

Jimmy and Dot knew they had accepted a difficult assignment, but this was more than they had bargained for. They felt a bit overwhelmed but they refused to be discouraged. They were determined to build the church—literally, by hand, if necessary. For the next several weeks Jimmy worked feverishly, applying the construction skills he had learned as a teenager in Louisiana, in order to make the building habitable. On Sundays he preached to a congregation of fewer than thirty people and Dot played the piano and taught Sunday school. Meanwhile, in what little spare time they had, they both began taking classes at the Golden Gate Baptist Theological Seminary in nearby Berkeley. Jimmy squeezed in a few hours a week working for the seminary's buildings and grounds department to earn extra money since his congregation was unable to pay a full-time salary.

Little by little the church began to grow. By the end of the first year, it had grown enough that it was able to lend Jimmy and Dot a small down payment on the house next door. They moved in and almost immediately gave their garage and a shop building over to the church's use. On Sundays they also gave over use of their living room, dining room, and kitchen for the church's growing Sunday school. With so much traffic and commotion, the Warren household was in an almost constant state of upheaval. It was hardly the best living arrangement for a young family, and now Dot was pregnant with their second child.

Many years later, Jimmy would write that "living under the stress" during that time was "probably the major cause" of their losing the baby.

After enduring the tragedy of the stillbirth, the Warrens poured most of their energy into their church work and the San Tomas congregation continued to grow. In 1953, the church voted to participate in a denomination-wide campaign to add one million people to Southern Baptist Sunday school rolls throughout the country by the end of the following year. The enthusiasm quickly caught on at the San Tomas church and the pace of growth began to accelerate, which meant even more of the Warrens' house had to be commandeered for classroom space.

Meanwhile, Dot had become pregnant again, this time with Rick. Early in her pregnancy, her doctor—the same one who had attended the stillbirth three years earlier—insisted that the Warrens move to a quieter location away from the church. So the church bought the Warrens' house next door and Jimmy and Dot purchased a new home a few miles away. They had not yet moved in when Dot went into labor and was rushed to the hospital. After Rick was born, the doctor refused to discharge the mother and child until the family moved out of the old residence. Within a few days everything was ready and Jimmy brought his wife and infant son home to their brand-new house.

No one was happier to see the new baby than six-year-old Jimmy Clyde. It had been a long wait, but finally he had a little brother. He told his parents he wanted the baby to grow up fast so that they could play ball together. Yet as thrilled as he was, he didn't like it that they had named him Richard and not Wayne, the only name he had ever associated with a baby brother. Jimmy and Dot did their best to help their son understand why that would not work. This was a brand-new person, they explained, and he needed a name all his own. So they had named him Richard and would call him Ricky. But they also had given him the middle name Duane, which sounded like Wayne, to honor the memory of the brother who didn't come home. Jimmy Clyde seemed satisfied with that.

At church, baby Ricky quickly became the star attraction. He was the only infant in the congregation at the time and people fussed over him. An elderly couple volunteered to keep the nursery on Sundays during both morning and evening services just so they could hold and coddle the baby while Jimmy and Dot conducted worship. One Sunday after the evening service, Dot went to retrieve her child and found the elderly gentleman standing outside the church visiting with a group of men and holding her infant son in his arms. "This child is going to be famous some day," she overheard him telling his companions. "You just mark my words."

Over the next three years the San Tomas congregation continued to prosper. It outgrew the small church building and the house next door and purchased some property a few blocks away and began construction on a new and larger building. For the first time the congregation was able to pay its pastor a full-time salary, plus a housing and car allowance. To Jimmy and Dot all of this was an unmistakable sign that the Lord was blessing their ministry.

Life was good in the Warren household. Jimmy Clyde was enjoying elementary school and had joined a little league baseball team. Ricky was an energetic toddler and an early talker who kept his mother busy and frequently in stitches with his precocious remarks. "Mommy, I dreamed last night that God came down to earth with his eyes shut," he informed her one morning. Dot chuckled at her son's vivid imagination, but mostly she marveled at the prominent place God already seemed to occupy in his thoughts. At Christmas in 1956, the almost-three-year-old proposed to his family that since it was Jesus' birthday they should throw a birthday party. He would make some Kool-Aid, his mother would bake a cake, and "Jesus will come down from heaven on a ladder and we can sing 'Happy Birthday, Jesus.'" Thus began a Warren family tradition that Rick would carry into his adulthood and to Christmas celebrations at his own Saddleback Church.

The new church building was dedicated on May 19, 1957, and Jimmy and Dot looked forward to growing their ministry in the spacious new facility. Their family also was growing. Dot was pregnant again and her delivery date was just weeks away. Her father had passed away a few years earlier, but her mother was still living nearby in Redwood City, and Dot and Jimmy were enjoying the privilege of raising their children so close to family in an area they both considered home.

But things were about to change. On the morning after the dedication service Jimmy received a telephone call from the executive director of the Baptist General Convention of Oregon–Washington, a denominational organization of Southern Baptist churches in the Pacific Northwest. The man sounded desperate. A congregation in Portland had recently purchased property under a contract requiring that construction of a church building begin by a certain date. The deadline was now just three months away and the project was nowhere close to breaking ground. To make matters worse, the church's pastor had just resigned and left the area. Unless it did something soon the congregation would lose the property. "I believe the Lord has laid you on my heart," the man told Jimmy. "Will you come?" Without hesitating, Jimmy agreed.

That evening Jimmy broke the news to his family. They would put their house up for sale and Jimmy would go to Portland immediately to find a place to live and to get started on the church. He would take Jimmy Clyde and Dot's mother with him so that their son could enroll in his new school and begin to be acclimated to the new surroundings. Dot and Ricky would stay in Campbell with friends until the baby was born. It would not be easy, but Jimmy was convinced that God was calling them to a new place and a new task. Dot felt some reservation about uprooting the family, but she trusted her husband's judgment and shared his desire to follow God's call. The children, after all, would learn to adjust. They all would adjust.

To Ricky it all sounded like an unimaginable adventure. A new baby sister or brother was about to come into his life. And now, on top of that, his family was moving to a new, faraway place. After hearing the news he bounded out into the starlit night and raced around the yard squealing with glee while his amused parents watched from the doorway. Suddenly he stopped in his tracks. For a few silent seconds he stood gazing with wonderment at the glittering celestial display above him. Jimmy and Dot could only imagine what thoughts were racing through his mind. Then, forming a megaphone with his hands, he called out with all the strength and earnestness a three-year-old could muster: "Hey, God! Are you up there?"

ON JUNE 26, DOT GAVE BIRTH to a daughter, Geil Chaundel, at the same San Jose hospital where Rick had been born. She would go by her middle name and would be the last of Jimmy and Dot's children. Six weeks later the Warren family was reunited in Portland.

From the moment he arrived, Jimmy had worked hard to get the new church building under way. Within a few weeks he had completed the construction plans, obtained all necessary permits, and broken ground. By the time Dot and the children arrived in early August, the walls were up and the roof was on—well ahead of the contract deadline. At the same time, as the church's new pastor, he was preaching at three services a week and tending to the needs of a growing congregation. By the end of the year the church began holding services in the new building.

Just as Dot had predicted, the family adjusted well to the new situation. Jimmy Clyde and Ricky made new friends quickly at church and in the neighborhood and seemed to settle into their new surroundings with little difficulty. Both boys doted over their new baby sister. Jimmy Clyde would put her in a wagon and pull her up and down the street to show her off. Ricky, just a little confused, would explain to inquirers that his baby sister's name was Geil Chaundel, "but if she's a boy we're going to call her Russell Nelson."

Ricky continued to amuse his parents with his lively imagination and candid reflections on God and other weighty matters. At Christmas the following year the not-quite-five-year-old surprised Jimmy and Dot by declaring to some house guests, "I know what it means to surrender my life to Christ, and I'm going to do it real soon." A few weeks later he announced that he had asked Jesus to come into his heart, and on the following Easter, March 29, 1959, he climbed into the baptistry at the front of the new church and into his proud dad's waiting arms and was immersed in the warm baptismal waters in the name of the Father, the Son, and the Holy Spirit.

THE WARRENS WOULD STAY in Portland for a little more than two years. During their time at the San Tomas church, part of Jimmy's job at the Golden Gate seminary had involved landscape and construction work at the school's new campus in Marin County, a wealthy suburb just across the San Francisco Bay from the old site in Berkeley. In the fall of 1959, he and Dot were invited back to campus for the dedication of the first completed buildings. While they were there the seminary's business manager took Jimmy aside and asked if he would consider coming back to the school as its building superintendent and oversee the build-out of the rest of the campus. He accepted the position on the spot. A few days later the Warrens packed their belongings in Portland and headed back to California.

After a brief stay in temporary housing in nearby San Rafael, they moved onto the park-like campus on Strawberry Point and into a wing of the girls' dormitory perched on a hill overlooking the bay and the San Francisco skyline. It was an idyllic spot and the accommodations were comfortable if a bit spartan. All three children had rooms of their own, and six-year-old Ricky immediately began filling his with "valuable treasures"—shiny rocks, colorful shells, dead bugs, and other intriguing collectibles that he sorted carefully and put on display.

For twelve-year-old Jimmy Clyde, however, the move from Portland had been difficult. He protested to his parents about having to leave his friends and start over in a new town for the second time in less than three years. He found that the kids at his new school came from families far more affluent than his, and he had trouble fitting in. While he got along well with his little brother, who idolized him, their six-year age difference prevented them from becoming close companions. Jimmy Clyde's adjustment to life in Marin County would take some time.

Not so for Ricky. Both he and Chaundel would find plenty of play-mates among children of married students on campus. Ricky quickly established himself as a ringleader, organizing clubs and games and directing skits and musical shows that he and his friends would perform for their parents or anyone else they could corral as an audience. Young women living in the dormitory were smitten by his blond, freckle-faced charm and lavished him with attention—which he didn't seem to mind in the least. At the birthday party for Jesus that first year at the seminary Ricky found himself surrounded by female admirers. One student asked him how he liked the first grade. "First grade suits me just fine," he responded, doing his best to project an air of grown-up sophistication. "I just might turn out to be the scholar of the family." Another wanted to know who was his favorite person in the world. He answered without hesitating: "My grandma, because she reads to me." Then, glancing around the room, he sensed at once that he had committed a gaffe and hastily offered an amendment. "Oh yes, and my mommy and daddy, and my big brother Jim, and my sister Chaundel, and God, and most everyone I know."

At the age of six, it seemed that Rick Warren had everything working in his favor. He may not have had the material advantages that many of his Marin County schoolmates enjoyed, but he was a happy and obviously bright child secure in the love of his family. He was inquisitive and took great delight in discovering and exploring the natural world around him. He was self-confident, perhaps to a fault, but also demonstrated a surprisingly mature sensitivity toward the feelings of others. Consequently, people liked him. Most of all, he was eager to please his parents and to learn about the God they served. Rick's young life was off to a promising start.

Then, in his seventh year, a malady struck that would shake the Warren household and cast a shadow of uncertainty over his future.

THE FIRST TIME IT HAPPENED, Rick had just gotten off the school bus and was walking alone up the hill toward the family's dormitory apartment just a hundred yards or so from the bus stop. Behind him he could hear two of his schoolmates, second-grade girls who lived nearby in married housing, laughing and skipping along the sidewalk as the bus roared off in the distance. Suddenly they were standing over him, calling his name, their faceless silhouettes black against the sun. "Ricky! Ricky! Are you okay?"

He had been unconscious for just a few seconds. When he came to he was lying on his back in the grass, his lunch box spilled open next to him. From the dent in the box and the dull pain he felt in his hip he guessed he must have fallen on top of it. Feeling embarrassed he jumped to his feet and quickly gathered up his lunch box. Without saying a word he brushed past the girls and ran home.

When he got to the apartment he seemed to feel fine. Mostly he was confused about what had happened. Had he tripped? Had someone knocked him down? Since he wasn't sure, he decided not to mention it to his mother, and he hoped that the two girls had not told their parents. That night he felt more tired than usual and went to bed early.

A few days later it happened again, this time while he was playing in the apartment after supper. And this time there was no hiding it from his parents, who saw him buckle onto the living room floor, just for a moment, and then resume playing as if nothing had happened.

Early the next morning Jimmy and Dot took their son to the family doctor. He conducted a thorough examination but could find nothing wrong. He suggested that the fainting spells could have been a type of seizure, so he sent them to a neurologist. The neurologist ordered a battery of tests—an electroencephalograph (EEG), an electrocardiogram (EKG), blood work—in order to rule out some of the scarier possibilities, such as a brain tumor or heart defects. He said epilepsy was another possibility. The tests showed no sign of tumors or heart problems but otherwise were inconclusive. The neurologist decided to put Rick on an epilepsy drug, at least for a while, to see if it made a difference. He said because Rick was so young maybe he would simply outgrow it.

A week or two passed before he had another fainting spell. As time went on, it seemed that the spells occurred less frequently but they never completely went away. Rick continued to tire easily and Jimmy and Dot continued to worry and to pray. Gradually they all would learn to live with the mysterious condition. It would take many more years and many more tests before they would begin to get to the bottom of it.

# CHAPTER FOUR

# "Huck Finn"

IN 1965, JIMMY WARREN ACCEPTED A CALL from the Home Mission Board of the Southern Baptist Convention to become director of missions for the Yokayo Baptist Association overseeing a handful of new and struggling churches, or home missions, in Lake and Mendocino counties in Northern California. The job involved both pastoral and supervisory duties, providing spiritual and professional guidance to younger, less-experienced ministers. Jimmy welcomed it as a new phase of his ministry and a chance to pass along some of the lessons he had learned over the years as a pastor. So he packed up his family and moved to Redwood Valley, a rural community about eighty miles north of San Francisco and just up the road from Ukiah, the Mendocino County seat. Jimmy Clyde, who was about to turn eighteen and had had enough of moving, stayed behind to finish his senior year of high school and to attend college in the Bay Area.

Mendocino County in the mid-1960s was an economically stressed region blessed with breathtaking natural beauty, a vast expanse of wooded hills and deep emerald valleys that descended westward from the peaks of the Pacific Coast Range to the craggy bluffs and beaches of a largely unspoiled coastline. Along its slopes and rushing streams, stands of giant redwoods, thinned by years of aggressive commercial logging, towered over seemingly endless acres of Douglas fir and other smaller trees. But the lumber industry had fallen on hard times and with it the tiny milltowns that once thrived along the Russian, Eel, Navarro, and Noyo rivers. As lumber and related manufacturing jobs dwindled, so did the county's population: after nearly doubling during the previous two decades it stagnated through the 1960s at just over 51,000. Agriculture remained the only economic bright spot. The region's temperate climate and rich sandstone soil provided a hospitable environment for fruit groves and grape vineyards, and big wineries had begun snapping up the inexpensive land, expanding the northern boundaries of California's wine country. Its remote valleys and hidden meadows also were perfect for growing what rapidly was becoming the county's biggest cash crop: marijuana.

By the mid-1960s Mendocino County had become a popular haven for hippies, burned-out druggies, and assorted return-to-the-land enthusiasts who migrated north from San Francisco's Haight-Ashbury district and other urban precincts to live on isolated communes unmolested by law enforcement. Among the famous and the infamous who would spend time there were psychedelic drug guru Timothy Leary, beat poet Allen Ginsberg, religious cult leader Jim Jones, and at least two of newspaper heiress Patty Hearst's Symbionese Liberation Army kidnappers. Members of the Charles Manson family settled briefly in Navarro, a onetime milltown about forty-five miles southwest of Redwood Valley. Manson himself visited there once and was arrested on July 28, 1967, charged with interfering with police questioning of a suspected runaway. He was given a thirty-day suspended sentence and was placed on three years' probation. Two years and eleven days later he directed the grisly slaughter of actress Sharon Tate and four others in Los Angeles.

It was a tumultuous time, to say the least. Already troubled economically, Mendocino County was becoming a crucible of social experimentation and the epicenter of an emerging counterculture devoted to "sex, drugs, and rock 'n' roll." As such it was also fertile ground for Christian missionaries. The Southern Baptist Convention had targeted California's North Coast region as a "pioneer mission"—an area essentially devoid of Baptist churches—and launched a concentrated effort to plant new congregations there. But its early efforts had not gone well. Seven churches were organized in Mendocino and Lake counties in the early 1960s and already five had lost their pastors. Three had voted to disband. The Home Missions Board sent in Jimmy Warren to turn things around.

ALTHOUGH RICK WAS ELEVEN when the family moved to Redwood Valley he would come to think of that place, more than anywhere else he had lived up to that time, as his boyhood home—"the one that

— 45 —

shaped me most." The house was a modest one-story wood-frame structure surrounded by oak, fir, and redwood trees on ten gently rolling acres that fronted on a paved country road. A small stream meandered across the property and flowed into a one-acre pond about fifty yards behind the house. Beyond the pond were a pasture and an old barn where the Warrens sometimes raised a cow or two for meat. A large vegetable garden and a fruit grove across the stream from the house produced enough bounty to feed the Warren family and to share with neighbors and the families of pastors who were under Jimmy's charge.

The pond quickly became Rick's favorite outdoor adventure spot. In the summertime, he and his friends would spend hours swimming, fishing, gigging frogs, catching tadpoles, rope swinging, or gliding across the water on homemade wooden rafts. "In many ways I enjoyed a Huck Finn childhood centered around that body of water," he would recall later in life. An old army tent pitched on a patch of grass on the backside of the pond served as a clubhouse, and on lazy summer afternoons Rick and his friends would lie there reading comic books and listening to a transistor radio. His winter hangout was a tree fort his dad had built in a nearby giant oak.

The house itself seemed to be a constant work-in-progress. Almost immediately after moving in, Jimmy ripped apart a living room wall on the side of the house facing the pond and installed a wide floor-to-ceiling bay window to afford a panoramic view of the sylvan setting. Next he turned the detached garage into an apartment for Dot's mother, who had moved with them, and later added a two-story addition to the house. In all, his renovations over the years would nearly double the living space, providing plenty of room to accommodate the visiting pastors, missionaries, student interns, and other overnight houseguests who regularly showed up at the Warrens' door.

Rick's room was small but had its own attached half-bathroom and its own door to the outside, which he often left open at night so he could listen to the chirping crickets and croaking bullfrogs through the screen. The room was crammed floor to ceiling with his carefully arranged collections of rocks, shells, stamps, coins, chicken bones, horseshoes, and other treasured items—including forty-two years' worth of *National Geographic* magazines. "I literally was interested in everything," he recalled. "But what interested me most was not so much the collecting but the sorting and categorizing, trying to figure out relationships between things, how they fit together." It was the same process he would apply later in life as a pastor and author. "Only now I do it with ideas. I'm a collector and synthesizer of ideas. It could be medieval literature and it could be modern-day marketing and it could be Christian history, and I go, 'How does that fit together?' I'm able to see the relationships and the order of things. My brain is just wired that way, and it showed up very early in my life."

After his own room, Rick's favorite part of the house was the kitchen. It was a warm and inviting place, "always full of delicious smells and happy sounds. Mom was an extraordinary cook who could whip up literally anything. It didn't matter if it was cooking for a dozen of my friends or a hundred people that Dad had just invited over after a meeting. She loved the challenge." Jimmy once estimated that in one year's time Dot had served over two thousand meals to guests in their home. With people so often staying over, whether visiting clergy or some needy person who turned up in the middle of the night, Rick frequently went to bed not knowing who would be at the breakfast table. "Mom and Dad both just had tremendous gifts of hospitality and of serving others"—two traits that Warren would incorporate into his Purpose-Driven model of ministry. In their later years, Jimmy and Dot would apply those same gifts doing disaster relief all over the world. Jimmy would work with construction crews rebuilding after an earthquake, a hurricane, or a tsunami, and Dot would cook for hundreds of relief workers, sometimes for weeks and months at a time. "My parents modeled giving their life away pretty unselfishly. So I learned those two purposes—fellowship and service, or ministry—from them."

The sound of laughter was common in the Warren household and lighthearted banter was typical mealtime fare. As a preacher Jimmy seldom shied from using a corny joke or a touch of self-deprecating humor to lighten a sermon. "At home he was just a cut-up," Rick's sister, Chaundel, recalls. "He loved to make Mom laugh—he would make us all laugh—and Rick took right after him." One of Jimmy's specialties was the good-natured practical joke, and his were usually at Dot's expense. "Probably the classic one," Chaundel recalls, "happened one

Sunday night after church. My dad was driving a visitor to our house, and Rick and I were in the backseat, and my dad turned to the guy and said, 'I need to tell you about my wife. She is painfully reserved and has had some mental problems. She can be really, really touchy. So please be very careful what you say to her.' So we pulled in and started to walk across the patio, and my mom suddenly flung open the sliding door and squealed out, 'Hi! I've been waiting for you to get here!' And the guy froze. He didn't know what to do. He thought she's flipped her lid. And my dad just started cracking up."

Jimmy's mischievous sense of humor obviously rubbed off on his kids. It didn't take long for Rick and Chaundel to become as adept as their dad at spoofing their house guests. Chaundel tells the story: "We had this family shtick that Rick started. We went to a small church and we'd get summer missionaries, young people who would come to help during Vacation Bible School, and they'd stay at our house. One night at dinner my dad and mom were cutting up and picking at each other and my dad took a kitchen towel and snapped it at my mom. All of a sudden Rick, who was maybe thirteen or fourteen at the time, grabbed me and went, 'Oh, Daddy, don't! Please, don't do that! Oh, please, not in front of company! Don't worry, Chaundel, I'll protect you. It's okay, honey. I'll take care of you.' And of course my mom is just cracking up and the people don't know what to do. They're probably thinking, 'What have I gotten myself into? This guy is a pastor! He's the director of missions!' And of course my dad would never do anything to hurt my mom, and she's just cracking up. And then she'd go, 'Rick, stop it! Just stop it!'—and the visitors don't know if she's just trying to cover up for Dad or what. They're sitting there just horrified. People never knew what to think of us."

Yet life at the Warrens' was not all lightness and laughter. As Christian parents, Jimmy and Dot were serious disciplinarians who tried to raise their children according to biblical standards that reflected a fairly traditional Southern Baptist ethos. They expected obedience, and when the children were young direct defiance generally meant a spanking. But those occasions tended to be rare. "We weren't Pollyanna perfect," Chaundel explains, "but there were no big issues with Rick or me. We could feel guilty and remorseful pretty easily." Rick recalls that neither of his parents was harsh when it came to discipline. "Part of that was that I never went through the typical rebellion. I did go through the stage where you learn to be independent, and so we had minor skirmishes—things like over the length of your hair. But even in that my parents' attitude was, 'If that's the worst thing he ever does, forget it.'"

Older brother Jim was a different story. By the time he was a teenager, Chaundel recalls, "it was pretty clear that Jim wasn't living for the Lord, and that was a real source of heartache for our parents." Once he was in college and on his own he dropped all pretense of abiding by family and Southern Baptist rules against drinking and smoking, although he never flaunted it at home. While Jim had accepted Christ as a child and had never openly recanted his belief, it was apparent to his family that he had strayed. "I remember praying for him earnestly as a little girl and being very sad for his condition," Chaundel recalls. Many years later, Rick would describe his brother's turn away from the Lord as "not rebellion so much as it was materialism. Jim saw my parents living with very meager means, living at a poverty level in many ways, and he thought, 'Well, if God loves them, how come they're not doing better? My parents are genuine, they're great, they're good people. Why aren't they making any money?' And so in college, he decided he wanted to make money. That became his priority."

Nonetheless, Rick grew up idolizing his older brother. Jim was smart, athletic, loved rock music, and seemed to have a sixth sense for what was cool and what was not, and Rick would often try to copy him. "When he bought the first *Meet the Beatles* album, within two days I went out and bought *Meet the Beatles*. When he bought the *Summer's End* Beach Boys album, within two days I went out and bought it. When he got into scuba diving and we were extremely poor and didn't have any money, he bought himself a wet suit and then went out and bought me a pattern and made me a wet suit so I could go diving with him. That was the kind of brother he was."

Later, when Rick and Chaundel were teenagers and wanted to go to school dances—a "worldly amusement" considered taboo by most Southern Baptists—Jim intervened on their behalf. It was the era of "free love" and Woodstock, Jim reminded his apprehensive parents, and while many of their generation were experimenting with sex and drugs, Rick and Chaundel were wholesome, responsible, God-fearing kids who merely wanted to attend an occasional chaperoned dance. It was simply "not a big deal." Jimmy and Dot eventually relented.

It is little wonder that Rick was in awe of his brother or that, when Jim came home to Redwood Valley one weekend during college, Rick was eager to impress him. Rick recently had added chemistry to his growing list of interests and had come across a recipe for making gunpowder out of three readily available ingredients: sulfur, powdered charcoal, and potassium nitrate—a chemical used in fertilizer and for curing meat. So he obtained a small quantity of each of the ingredients and mixed up a batch in a Mason jar. He was looking forward to showing his big brother what it could do.

Late that Saturday morning the two brothers went into Rick's room and closed the door. Rick scooped out a teaspoonful of the gray powder from the nearly full jar on his desk and touched it with a match. It immediately burst into flames, spewing bright sparks and pungent smoke. A piece of the burning material fell into the jar, which ignited with a *whoomp* like a giant roadside flare and sent sparks nearly to the ceiling, shattering the jar, and setting fire to the desktop and its contents. Jim grabbed the first thing he saw, a foam-rubber pillow, and tried to smother the flames, but the pillow caught fire and began filling the room with billowy black smoke. Hearing the commotion, Dot came running and the three of them managed to extinguish the flames.

Meanwhile, the smoke had wafted onto the patio where Jimmy was meeting with a group of pastors. "Oh, Dot, honey," he called out, "I think the biscuits are burning." His frazzled wife threw open the patio door and gave him a withering look. "You had better turn this meeting into a prayer meeting," she suggested sardonically, "and just thank the Lord that your house didn't burn down!"

That was the kind of trouble Rick would get into as a kid, Chaundel recalls—"nothing really naughty or deliberate." The fire had been an accident, no serious damage was done, and there was no real punishment—although Jimmy gave his boys a stern reprimand. "What in the world were you thinking?" he demanded. Rick and Jim were mortified by their nearly disastrous misadventure. Years later they would laugh at the memory as something out of a Laurel and Hardy movie.

———

BOTH RICK AND CHAUNDEL attended public elementary and junior high schools in Redwood Valley. Having come from a more rigorous school system in affluent Marin County, they found themselves academically ahead of most of their classmates, and Chaundel was allowed to skip an early grade. In high school both would become honor students. For Rick especially, the high school years would prove to be dramatically decisive.

By the time he arrived at Ukiah High School in the fall of 1968, his already wide range of childhood interests had grown significantly and he loaded up his schedule with a variety of extracurricular activities—band, the forensics team, the pep club, drama, the chess club, student government. Although he had played basketball in junior high he quickly learned that, unlike his older brother, athletics was not his strong suit and he didn't bother going out for high school sports. Yet that would not stop him from becoming a big man on campus. His gregarious personality and easygoing manner made him instantly popular among many of his peers, and he was elected class president all four years. "People liked Rick because he was a gentleman—always very calm, very thoughtful," recalls Mark Pardini, a Warren classmate and now an appliance store owner in Ukiah. "I never saw him get upset. He would preside over class meetings and he'd have twenty or thirty kids all wanting to talk at once. Rick was a calming influence and always made sure the meetings ran smoothly." Francine Selim, who was a new teacher at Ukiah at the time, remembers Rick as "a very strong, well-rounded student. The teachers respected him because he wasn't one of those show-offy, 'out there' kind of kids."

Yet even then, a ham and a would-be showman lurked just beneath the surface. Like many of his peers growing up in the sixties, one of Rick's earliest ambitions was to become a rock star, and by his freshman year he had begun to look the part—tall and thin with long blond Beatle bangs swept across his forehead, a somewhat avant-garde look for a high school student at the time. His grandmother, Nell, had given him a set of drums. Later he bought himself an electric guitar with an amplifier the size of a small refrigerator and taught himself to play during long practice sessions in his bedroom, where he tried his hand at writing songs. When he and some friends from school decided to form a garage band, Jimmy and Dot diplomatically suggested that they rehearse in the barn several hundred yards away so as not to be disturbed by house noises.

As a growing hippie haven, Mendocino County had become a magnet for not-yet-famous rock groups touring from San Francisco and Los Angeles, and Rick often managed to get close to the action by working as a volunteer stagehand at local venues. On one occasion he conducted a psychedelic light show for an up-and-coming band called Big Brother and the Holding Company, led by a raspy-voiced singer named Janis Joplin, and for a group called the Golliwogs, later to become known as Creedence Clearwater Revival. Yet as much as he loved the music and the excitement of the concerts, Rick never felt entirely comfortable with the Mendocino rock scene. "I never got into drugs," he explained to an interviewer many years later. "I just wasn't interested in them. All my friends did drugs. I was just extremely interested in the music." Consequently, his life's ambitions quickly turned elsewhere.

With the Vietnam War dividing the nation and stirring unrest on college campuses, Rick started to become "pretty tuned in to politics," his sister recalls. He had favored Richard Nixon and Barry Goldwater early on, but now was "kind of antidraft and antiwar, although he wasn't fanatical." He began collecting campaign buttons, bumper stickers, and other political memorabilia and scrawled political graffiti on the walls and ceiling of his room at home, some of it humorous but most of it expressing a stinging social commentary. One of his favorites was a famous quotation from Harvard theologian Harvey Cox: "Not to decide is to decide."

His political awakening soon shifted from his walls to the streets. In the spring of 1969, he and three other student leaders organized a march on the county courthouse in Ukiah to protest voter rejection of a local bond issue that would have provided funds for a new high school building. "The building we were in at the time was built in the 1930s and it was in bad shape," he explained. "It would have crumbled in an earthquake, and it just wasn't safe. Something had to be done." On the day after the vote, Rick and some three hundred of his classmates cut classes and marched double file from the school to the courthouse carrying placards and bearing a coffin containing the effigy of a student. The protest, though peaceful, attracted the attention of local police and the *Ukiah Daily Journal*. The noontime rally lasted little more than fifteen minutes, "and I thought we could get back to the school without my dad and mom knowing about it. But the next morning it was all over the front page of the paper. Man, was I busted!" His parents gave him a good scolding. Two years later Ukiah voters reversed their decision and a new state-of-the-art high school was completed in 1978.

Not long after the courthouse protest, Rick was contacted by student leaders in Berkeley who wanted to recruit him into the radical Students for a Democratic Society. He turned them down, but an idea had been planted. "People kept telling me, 'You're a natural leader. You ought to go into politics.' And all of a sudden I realized that I wanted to make a difference with my life. I think everybody wants to make a difference." The thought of a political career continued to grow on him, and he began to fantasize about someday running for president. Near the end of his sophomore year he took what he hoped would be an important step in that direction and applied to be a page in the United States Senate. The application process was rigorous and highly competitive, with thousands of high-caliber students from all over the country vying for a handful of coveted slots and the opportunity to live and work on Capitol Hill for a semester. To Rick's surprise, and to his parents' chagrin, he was selected for a five-month appointment and was invited to report to Washington, D.C., the following fall. But before he could get there he would discover, as he put it later, that God had other plans for his life.

LIKE MANY EVANGELICAL YOUNG PEOPLE, Rick often spent at least part of his summers when he was growing up attending Christian summer camps—spiritual retreats where the usual recreational fare of swimming, hiking, canoeing, and craft-making is supplemented with heavy doses of Bible instruction and revivalist preaching. For kids, the camp experience was mostly an opportunity for being with friends and having fun. But for evangelical parents, the Christian camp served a much more serious purpose. It was a summer sanctuary against the world's depredations, a place where they could confidently send their kids knowing that everything about the program—the strict rules, the wholesome activities, the music, the biblical teaching—was carefully crafted to motivate young people to make or strengthen their commitments to Christ. And for parents of teenagers, especially, that was of singular importance.

In the summer of 1970, Rick signed on for a ten-week job as a lifeguard and kitchen worker at Cazadero Baptist Camp, a jumble of rustic wooden buildings nestled under the redwoods in coastal Sonoma County about two hours south of Ukiah. The camp had first opened in the 1950s and was operated jointly by several Southern Baptist associations in the area. Jimmy had helped build some of the cabins.

Besides his daytime duties setting tables and washing dishes in the dining hall and watching over swimmers in the creek, in the evenings Rick often was called upon to play guitar and lead singing around the campfire. The evening campfire at Cazadero was a standard, almost obligatory, ritual—just as it was at most Christian camps and youth retreats. It was a time for singing and praying, for gazing into the glowing embers and deep into one's own soul, and then, in the comforting warmth of the crackling fire and the circle of Christian friends, to give a personal accounting of one's walk with the Lord. It may be the closest thing young evangelicals have to a confessional.

Yet for Rick, at the start of the summer at least, the campfires proved to be anything but comforting. Each night he would dutifully play his guitar and sing the choruses and then sit back and listen quietly as one teenager after another spoke passionately about the struggles and successes they faced as they tried to live for the Lord. Some tearfully confessed the difficulties of standing up to temptation and peer pressure at school. Others spoke of wrestling with fear and finally finding the nerve to tell an unsaved friend about Jesus, and of the joy they felt when that person came to Christ. Still others told of a crisis at home, a sick parent, a sibling in trouble. They laughed and cried and prayed together around the campfire, and as Rick listened he sensed a void in his own life. "I knew I was from a good Christian home, and I really did consider myself a believer. But week in and week out I would see a new group of young people and youth leaders come in, and I could see that there was something different in their lives. They had something that I didn't have"—a personal, vital, life-transforming, identity-defining, all-encompassing relationship with Jesus Christ.

One night after the campfire he decided it was time to do something about it. He went alone to his cabin, closed the door, and knelt quietly beside his bed. The prayer he prayed that night would stay with him forever: "Dear God, if you're really real, I want to know you. And I don't understand it all, but as much as I know how, I surrender my life to you. I give it to you. And if you're real, I need you to make yourself real to me. If you can make my life something that you want it to be, well then, I invite you to do that. And I'm yours."

He finished praying and pulled himself up onto his bed. Nothing seemed different. "I don't know if I was expecting thunder and a bolt of lightning, but nothing happened. I didn't feel emotional. It didn't seem significant at the time. It was just a pretty matter-of-fact decision. But as I look back at it now, that was really the turning point." Later he would describe the moment as his "conversion to Christ and to the ministry at the same time," and from that point on he knew, at least in broad strokes, what he would do with his life. "I was determined to go all out for God and live for Him."

As a result of his decision, he began to lose interest in politics. "I realized that you can't legislate a change of heart. You can't change society through laws if people want to break them. To really make a difference in the world you need to change people's hearts, and only Christ can do that. So that is what I began to care about." He decided to turn down the Senate page appointment, along with his dreams of the White House, and take up the mantle of Christian ministry.

# CHAPTER FIVE

# Boy Preacher

A FEW DAYS AFTER HIS CAMP CONVERSION, Rick went home for a weekend visit and shared the news with his family. Jimmy and Dot were elated. "My parents and I were very excited at the ways God was working in Rick's life," Chaundel recalls. "It wasn't as if he was a terror before. He had made a childhood decision for Christ and had shown every evidence of being a Christian. But this was his total sell-out to Christ and it really changed everything in his life—his values, the way he spent his time and money, the songs he wrote, and the whole direction of his life." She also remembers that he was "definitely nicer to me after that, and more engaged with the family both in conversation and in helping around the house."

Having said "yes" to God, Rick almost immediately began to find opportunities for ministry. Back at Cazadero, he suddenly was emboldened to speak up at the campfires and tell the story of his coming to faith and surrendering to the Lord. He told the story so often and with such enthusiasm that by the end of the summer he had received several invitations to speak at church youth rallies and teen revival meetings.

While he didn't fancy himself a preacher or even sense yet that God was calling him to be one, he already had demonstrated his skill as a public speaker at school and he welcomed the opportunity to use that talent for the Lord. That fall he crafted a basic salvation message based on the familiar New Testament passage John 3:16: "For God so loved the world that He gave His only begotten Son that whosoever believeth on Him should not perish but have everlasting life." He carefully rehearsed his message in front of a mirror, doing his best to mimic the famous finger-jabbing, machine-gun-delivery style of Billy Graham: "We've all disobeyed our heavenly father . . . and sin demands a punishment . . . but Jesus took our punishment for us . . . God cared enough to send the very best—His only Son!" He used the message over and over at area youth events with only slight variations and ended each time by inviting his young listeners to come forward and accept Christ. "Jesus walked to Calvary for you," he reminded them. "The least you can do is walk to the front of the church for Him!" Generally he would get at least a few takers at every event.

Considering the positive response both in numbers of decisions for Christ and in the encouraging comments he received from youth leaders, Rick had every reason to judge his early preaching efforts a success and a promise of things to come. Yet he was not at all satisfied that he had found his calling. "It wasn't that I thought I was a bad speaker or that I wasn't outgoing enough. I just didn't feel that preaching was my gift." He felt far more at home in the role of worship leader—playing the guitar, leading the singing, giving an enthusiastic word of testimony, and generally revving up a crowd prior to the message. That, he believed, was his true talent. Influencing his thinking along those lines was the rising popularity of Christian rock, a new musical genre spawned by the Jesus Movement, a counterculture of born-again young people that had grown out of Christian evangelizing among California hippies in the late sixties. The music was a catchy blend of Gospel lyrics set to a rock 'n' roll sound, and Rick embraced it enthusiastically. Being a worship leader would allow him to harness his previous passion for rock music and put it to sacred use. It seemed to him the best of both worlds.

Still, he was not ready to give up on preaching. He continued to accept speaking invitations at youth events and sometimes combined his singing and guitar playing with an abbreviated message and an invitation. But the more he spoke the more he began to notice a recurring and worrisome problem. Often when he got up to speak his head suddenly would begin throbbing and his vision would blur as though he were looking through cheesecloth. Sometimes he felt panicky and started to perspire. "It was almost like an anxiety attack," he recalls. "But it wasn't stage fright. I wasn't afraid of being in front of a crowd." Whatever was causing the distress, after a few minutes the symptoms generally would subside and he would carry on without his audience ever suspecting anything was amiss. Only later as he began to discern a pattern would he associate the headaches and blurred vision with the mysterious fainting spells that had plagued him as a child. That correlation would lead to more trips to the doctor and more hospital tests, all of which seemed to bring him no closer to a diagnosis.

WHEN RICK RETURNED to Ukiah High School in the fall of 1970, he compared notes with several of his Christian friends and discovered that a number of them had undergone an experience similar to his over the summer and had become, as he described it at the time, "turned on to Jesus and the abundant life that He gives." In the afterglow of their spiritual awakening, they decided to organize a Christian club at school that would serve both as a means of building up one another in the faith and as an outreach to unsaved students. They would call it Fishers of Men.

Getting the club started, however, would take some doing. The school's principal refused to recognize the club or grant it permission to meet on school property on grounds that it would violate the separation of church and state. Undeterred, Rick and his friends circulated a petition, collecting seventy-two signatures from Ukiah students who supported the organization, and presented it to the principal. After a series of contentious meetings spread over several weeks, the principal finally admitted that the decision was not his to make. To become a recognized club they would need a charter from the board of education, and to be chartered they would need a constitution. So the students drafted a constitution laying out the purpose and structure of their club. When the principal read it he assured them it would never pass muster with the school board because it identified Fishers of Men as a Christian organization with religious purposes, and that, in his view, clearly was illegal. He suggested that they rewrite the document to expunge the exclusively Christian terminology and add some references to other faiths.

But the students were not about to turn their Christian club into a comparative religion study group. Instead they asked the Mendocino County district attorney for a legal opinion. The district attorney reviewed their proposal and told them he thought the principal was mistaken, that there was nothing unlawful about having the kind of club they envisioned at a public school. But just to be sure, he would forward the matter to the California attorney general. A few weeks later, the attorney general responded in a letter that as long as the school did not give the club preferential treatment, it did not meet during class time, and membership and participation in all of its activities were open to everyone, the club they were proposing was perfectly legal.

Three months after they began, Rick and his friends took their proposal and the attorney general's letter to the school board and Fishers of Men was granted a charter. It started out with eighty-nine members and quickly became the largest club on campus. Rick was elected its founding president. His mother, as an assistant librarian, became a faculty adviser.

Under Rick's leadership the club adopted a high profile and a frenetic schedule of activities—weekly after-school rallies in the school auditorium, daily prayer meetings before school in a classroom, evening Bible studies once a week in private homes. Its members distributed Bibles and religious tracts on campus and later that spring performed a Christian musical in place of the annual senior play. "Fishers of Men was life-changing as far as the school was concerned," recalls Mark Pardini, a Warren classmate and a member of the club. "It wasn't so much proselytizing as it was (saying), 'Here is a bunch of good kids who are just trying to live a wholesome Christian lifestyle.' That sent a strong positive message to the rest of the school."

A few months after the club's launch, Rick wrote an article for the *Hollywood Free Paper*, an underground newspaper published by the Jesus Movement in Southern California, describing the drawn-out battle to establish Fishers of Men and the considerable influence he believed the club was having at school. "Because of the Holy Spirit's work through the club, the number of Christians at the high school has greatly increased," he reported. "The Christians now hold a majority in the executive council of the student government. The president of Fishers of Men was also recently elected student body president . . . God is continuing to work through Fishers of Men and the impact that it is having in our community has just begun." He concluded by inviting readers to contact him for more information. Within weeks he was deluged with mail, most of it from California high school students who wanted to start Christian clubs of their own. So he printed up instructions—"How to Start a Christian Club"—and distributed them along with copies of the attorney general's letter. Later he would learn that hundreds of clubs had been organized around the country with little or no opposition from school administrators because of the experience at Ukiah.

AT THE SAME TIME THAT THE WARRENS were moving to Mendocino County early in the summer of 1965, a group of religious pilgrims and their charismatic leader set out from Indianapolis, Indiana, in a caravan of cars, pickup trucks, and moving vans and headed west toward the promised land of Northern California. They settled in Redwood Valley on an isolated plot less than two miles from the Warrens. There, behind heavily guarded gates and a darkening veil of paranoia, the Reverend Jim Jones and his disciples began to build a utopian society they called the People's Temple. Thirteen years later their utopian dream would die in a South American jungle along with Jones and more than nine hundred of his followers in one of the worst mass murder-suicides in history.

Jones reportedly had chosen to relocate his congregation to Redwood Valley after reading an *Esquire* magazine article in 1962 on "Nine Places in the World to Hide" in the event of a nuclear war. Jones had become obsessed with the imminent threat of nuclear holocaust and preached about it often. He was determined to find a place where he and his flock could survive the devastation, and Northern California between Ukiah and Eureka, according to the magazine article, was one of only three "safe" locations in the northern hemisphere—"west of the Sierras and upwind from every target in the United States."

From the moment they arrived, Jones and his 140-member interracial flock made their presence known. The *Ukiah Daily Journal* carried an admiring story, written by the wife of the newspaper's editor, with the headline "Ukiah Welcomes New Citizens to Community." The transplanted congregation quickly set up programs to feed the poor and care for the elderly, pursuing the same social-improvement mission it had followed in Indianapolis, although on a smaller scale until the congregation grew and its members found gainful employment. They took whatever jobs were available—picking grapes or pears—but work was hard to find. Eventually, Jones's wife, Marceline, was hired as a social worker at Mendocino State Hospital and helped other People's Temple members land jobs there. Jones, with an education degree from Butler University, took substitute teaching jobs in Redwood Valley and nearby Potter Valley and later taught sixth graders in Boonville, about forty-five minutes away. In the fall of 1966 he began teaching a night civics class at Ukiah High School, which provided him a new platform and higher visibility in the community. Later he was appointed foreman of the Mendocino County grand jury and began nurturing relationships with politicians and the local news media. Within a few years he would forge strong ties to San Francisco mayor George Moscone, California assemblyman Willie Brown, and other powerful figures who would laud him as an altruistic visionary and champion of the poor.

It was an opinion that ordinary folks in Ukiah during those early years tended not to share. Some locals simply resented the fact that Jones had brought so many African Americans into their mostly white rural community and that they were snatching up jobs at a time when jobs were becoming scarce. Christians in town were much more appalled at Jones's religious teachings, which they felt bore little resemblance to biblical Christianity. Indeed, although Jones was an ordained Disciples of Christ minister, he was known to give little credence to the Bible or to traditional religion, advocating instead a form of Christian communalism—he called it "apostolic socialism"—which was based more on the teachings of Marx and Lenin than of Jesus and the apostles. There were reports of fake healings and resurrections, of loyalty tests and intimidation, of all-night services during which Jones vaunted himself as God incarnate and ranted against the U.S. government and enemies in the community who he insisted were out to destroy him.

The fact that the church was a fenced compound with armed guards also naturally raised suspicion. "You couldn't get in and it was very secretive," Chaundel remembers. "That felt wrong to us. I mean, we were *trying* to get people to come to our church. And they had big crowds, but they bused them up from San Francisco." At its height, seventeen or eighteen busloads would make the weekly two-hour trek, and the church continued to grow. "And so all the Christians were saying, 'Something's wrong with this guy,' and the non-Christian people in town were saying, 'Well, you're just jealous because he is drawing a big crowd and he is doing a lot of good.'"

Like many people in the community, the Warrens were keenly aware of the People's Temple's presence. Although they had no direct contact with Jones himself, their next-door neighbors were People's Temple members, an African American couple who had moved from Indianapolis. "They were the sweetest, kindest people," Warren recalls. "At Christmastime they made candy and delivered it to all the neighbors." The husband drove the school bus that Rick and Chaundel took to school. "But we would hear these weird stories of fake healings and really long services and stuff like that, and we knew it was a goofy cult." On a few occasions the Warrens mistakenly received mail intended for Jones. The mix-up was understandable: the Rev. James R. Warren lived on West Road in Redwood Valley and the Rev. James Warren Jones lived on East Road.

People's Temple families sent their children to public schools in Redwood Valley, Ukiah, Potter Valley, and other nearby communities. At Ukiah High, former student Mark Pardini remembers that the People's Temple kids "tended to keep to themselves. They were always tired, and it seemed like they could never do anything after school—clubs and sports and such. They had to go home or to jobs. We knew something was going on." Dot Warren became acquainted with four or five of the young people, who sometimes helped her in the library during school hours. On a few occasions, Chaundel recalls, Dot witnessed to them about salvation and faith in Christ but apparently to no avail.

Rick's most direct contact with his People's Temple schoolmates came unexpectedly during a weekend youth revival in the fall of 1970. A small Pentecostal church in Ukiah had organized the event and invited Rick to be the speaker. It also had contacted all the area churches and invited them to send their young people. About thirty teenagers from the People's Temple showed up and volunteered to sing in the choir.

Sitting on the platform as the service was about to begin, Rick looked behind him and then turned to the person next to him who had organized the event. "I whispered to him, 'You invited the People's Temple?' He said, 'Well, yes. They're the People's Temple Christian Church.'

I said, 'Do you know anything about them?' 'Well, no.' I said, 'They're a cult.' There were maybe seventy-five kids out in the audience and thirty were sitting behind me in the choir, and I thought, 'These people need it more than those people,' and so I turned around and preached to the choir."

His message was taken from Joshua 1:8: "This book of the law shall not depart out of your mouth, but you shall meditate on it day and night . . . for then you shall make your way prosperous, and then you shall have good success." He preached for about twenty-five minutes, declaring that "success in life comes only from abiding by God's plan, by sticking to the word of God"—not the plans of men. At the end he gave an invitation to accept Christ, but no one from the choir stepped forward. Afterward, Chaundel recalls that one or two of the People's Temple kids talked with Rick briefly. "They were afraid—not that they wanted to leave their church. They just wanted to understand what Rick was saying." It was far different from anything they had heard from Jones.

Seven years later, in the summer of 1977, Jones led nearly a thousand of his followers to a 3,800-acre patch of jungle in northwestern Guyana where they established the "People's Temple Agricultural Project" as a socialist commune. On November 18, 1978, after directing the murder of California congressman Leo Ryan and four others who had come to investigate reports of abuse, Jones ordered his flock to drink a cyanide potion. In all, 913 lives were snuffed out—276 of them children.

When Rick and Chaundel saw news reports listing the names of the dead, they recognized several as having been their schoolmates. "I remember sitting and watching the TV coverage and just going, 'Oh, I knew that person. I knew that person,'" Chaundel recalls. "We were all crushed and so sad but not entirely surprised. We knew that Jim Jones was a false prophet and that he was leading people down a weird path. But we never expected this."

IN SPITE OF HIS PREVIOUS MISGIVINGS and the occasional physical discomfort he felt in the pulpit, by the winter of 1971, at the age of seventeen, Rick began to sense that God was calling him to be a preacher, or, in Southern Baptist parlance, to "the full-time Gospel ministry." That spring he applied for a preaching license at the Trinity Baptist Church in Ukiah, where he and his family were members.

Becoming a licensed preacher in those days was often a step toward ordination, a higher recognition generally reserved for preachers with more extensive preparation and experience and who are called to be pastors. It meant that an aspiring minister's home church was willing to vouch for his preaching ability, the soundness of his doctrine and lifestyle, and the legitimacy of his call so that other congregations could confidently permit him to preach from their pulpits. The purpose of the license was to give a man—and in the Southern Baptist church it was *always* a man—the time and opportunity to prove himself worthy of ordination.

But Rick's application ran into an unexpected snag. In May he appeared before a licensing committee consisting of the pastor and deacons of his church. They quizzed him about his salvation experience, his doctrinal beliefs, his call to preach, his plans for future study—all standard questions in the licensing process. Rick gave thorough and seemingly satisfactory answers and everything appeared to be in order.

Then his pastor spoke up. He had a problem with Rick's appearance. Rick had allowed his wavy blond hair to grow so that it covered his ears and forehead and spilled over the top of his collar. He also wore wire-rimmed glasses. It was a look the pastor associated with rock musicians and antiwar protesters, not Baptist preachers, and he told Rick that unless he cut his hair he would not approve the license. No churches would allow him in their pulpits looking the way he did. Rick demurred, explaining that his appearance was not a political statement and certainly was nothing extreme. In fact, it helped him to establish rapport with young people, who were the primary target of his preaching. He didn't think he should have to cut his hair. The pastor was adamant, but the deacons on the committee took Rick's side and approved the license over the pastor's objections. "Grow it while you've got it, son," his dad, who was balding, told him later.

At Wednesday night prayer meeting the following week the pastor came into the sanctuary and pitched Rick's certificate across several pews. "Here is your license," he hissed, and turned and walked away.

A visiting pastor from a nearby church leaned over and put his hand on Rick's shoulder. "You can preach at my church any time you want," he said.

DURING THAT SAME SPRING the California Southern Baptist Convention launched an ambitious and, for its time, innovative campaign to reach unsaved young people with the Gospel and to train and motivate young Southern Baptists to do street evangelism. It was the height of the Jesus Movement, and shaggy-haired denizens of California's counterculture were being targeted for conversion by every manner of street preacher and one-on-one evangelist—many of them sponsored by parachurch organizations like Campus Crusade for Christ or by independent churches like the street-savvy Calvary Chapel in Costa Mesa. Southern Baptists, by and large, had stayed on the sidelines. "These kids who were becoming Christians were not being welcomed into our churches, what with their long hair and all," recalls Harry Williams, director of evangelism for the state convention at the time, "and churches were afraid to let their young people witness on the streets. That bothered me, and I wanted to do something about it." So he decided to organize summer evangelism teams made up of college and seminary students to hold youth revivals throughout the state and to train and dispatch Christian young people to witness to their peers.

Even though Rick was still in high school and, therefore, technically ineligible to join a team, Williams knew of his ministry experience and was well acquainted with his father. He invited Rick to apply and accepted him into the program along with his own son, Steve, who also was still in high school. Four teams were organized that first summer, each consisting of a preacher, a music leader, a fellowship director, and a pianist. Rick was selected as a music leader and was assigned to a team led by Steve Williams as preacher.

"I was in for a surprise the first time I met Rick," Harry Williams recalls. "He was six feet tall and skinny as a rail and had yellow hair about four inches below his shoulders. Knowing that long hair would not be acceptable in our churches, I required that our team members wear their hair above their collar. Rick was very resistant to our rule, but finally had his hair cut just short enough to meet the requirement. But hair grows. By the end of the summer his hair was on his shoulders."

After a week of training the teams were sent out to work at two churches per week, twenty churches total in the course of the summer. They kept to a busy schedule, holding evangelistic services in the evening followed by a fellowship time with snacks, games, and a brief devotional. In the morning they trained church kids in one-on-one witnessing and in the afternoon took them to a park or street corner to try out their skills. In the evening it was back to church for another service and fellowship time, and the cycle repeated—Friday through Sunday morning at one church, Sunday evening through Wednesday at the next. Thursday was their only day off. At each stop they stayed in church members' homes or slept in the church. Offerings were divided among team members to cover travel expenses and to save toward school in the fall.

All the hard work seemed to pay off. By the end of the summer Rick's team alone had registered more than two hundred decisions for Christ. Fifty of them came during one particularly productive weekend in Barstow, a tired and dusty military town on the edge of the Mojave Desert. After two long but fruitful days of preaching and teaching at the First Baptist Church in the center of town, Rick and Steve were exhilarated. When the Saturday night revival meeting and fellowship time ended they went back to the streets and waited for the bars to close so they could witness to the inebriated patrons who stumbled out into the night. Standing under a street lamp at two in the morning they explained to a besotted marine sergeant from the nearby base that Jesus loved him and died for him. The man bowed his head and they led him in the "sinner's prayer." Later that morning he showed up for church and brought along a dozen of his men. Several accepted Christ.

"Rick and I were really on fire for the Lord that summer," Steve Williams recalls. "He was fearless in witnessing, and in the services he would give his testimony, telling how he had committed himself totally to Christ. He was a powerful speaker and people really responded to him. One time I had strep throat and I asked him to fill in preaching for me. He did a great job but he hated doing it. It wasn't until years later that I would learn about his problem." He also remembers that Rick did lots of reading on his days off. "He must have read four or five books that summer. I'd be goofing off and he'd be in the pastor's library making a list of books that he wanted to read. He was a gatherer of information even then."

Steve and Rick became fast friends that summer. Both came back to the program the following year but were assigned to different teams, Rick again as a music leader and Steve as a preacher. During the third summer, both preached and led their own teams, and for several years after that they came back just for the training week to help new recruits prepare for their summer of service. Over its fifteen-year run more than three hundred young people would serve on the evangelism teams. Among them were Rick's future wife, his sister and future brother-in-law, and about ten future members of his Saddleback staff. Looking back many years later, Rick would describe those summers on the team as crucial in shaping the direction of his ministry. "That is where I really learned how to do evangelism. Next to my own dad, Harry Williams was my mentor on evangelism."

IN THE FALL OF 1971, Rick began his senior year of high school, and because he had been taking heavy course loads he was on track to graduate a semester early so that he could spend more time on ministry teams before heading off to college. He also kept up a hectic schedule speaking on weekends at area youth revivals. His "sell-out" to Christ and his conversion to the ministry at camp a year earlier had, indeed, changed the course of his life. He was going all out for God. But, as he later observed, he was about to discover that "God wasn't finished working on me."

One weekend that fall Rick read a brief book entitled *The Key to Triumphant Living* written by Jack R. Taylor, a Baptist pastor and conference speaker from Texas. The book was essentially an extended sermon, filled with folksy alliterations and exuberant personal testimony, on being "filled with the Holy Spirit" and "submitted to the total reign of Christ" as the only sure way to an effective and fruitful Christian life. "It is by the Holy Spirit," Taylor wrote, "that Christ *comes to live* in the human spirit, *abides to master* the human spirit, and *continues to minister* through the human spirit to a world in desperate need." But he warned that God "will not, he cannot, take control of any thing or person in which resides the slightest sin. Therefore, our sins must be confessed up to date." He exhorted his readers to write out a list of sins—"everything in the heart and life that is unholy should be included"—and confess them to God. Any sins that were against other people would require restitution. Only then would a Christian be "ready to do business with Holy God regarding the Holy Spirit's fullness."

Sitting in his room one Friday night Rick began writing out his list. He searched his conscience and asked God to show him "the junk in my life that I need to confess and get rid of"—a feeling of jealousy, a lustful thought, a moment of anger, an unkind spoken word—and he wrote it down on a yellow pad. He kept writing until about midnight when, finally, he could think of nothing more to write. By then his "sin list" filled nearly four pages. Across the top he wrote in block letters "I John 1:9"—a New Testament verse that reads: "If we confess our sins, He is faithful and just to forgive us our sins, and to cleanse us from all unrighteousness."

Having made his confession, he crossed out all of the sins that were between him and God and left the ones that were against other people and that would require restitution. As he recalls it, there were three. "When I was a little kid I used to regularly rip off my sister's piggy bank. I figured out how to take two pencils and shake it upside down and get money out of it, and then I'd go buy comic books. I never told her about it. And so God said, 'You need to go pay her back for that and you need to admit it to her.' The second thing was, I really didn't like the pastor of my church in Ukiah. He didn't like me and I felt offended. I had long hair and he hated long hair, and so I felt ostracized. And God said, 'I don't care if it's one hundred percent his fault. You need to go and confess your bad attitude toward him and ask his forgiveness.' And the third thing was, my senior year I was a photographer on the yearbook staff, and two friends of mine were also on the yearbook staff and we had gone to a drug store to buy some film. As we were backing out in the parking lot I accidentally backed into another car and dented the bumper. Now, I'm a kid, and we got scared to death and I just took off. I didn't leave a note. We just split. And the Lord said, 'Okay, I want you to go to the police and report that and see if they can find the car, and you go and make that right. You pay for that bumper.'"

But when he climbed into bed that night the issue was far from settled. "I just told the Lord, 'No, I'm not going to do it.' And I'm wrestling with it, really spiritually struggling with it. In my mind I felt like the Lord was saying, 'Rick, I want to use you, but you've got to be serious about this, and if you want my blessing in your life you've got to be clean. This is a test of your obedience. Will you obey me even in the little details?' And I said, 'But Lord, it's not a big deal.' 'Yeah, but a sin is a sin, and this is a test. Will you follow me?' And so I'm wrestling back and forth, and finally about four o'clock in the morning I just go, 'O-K!' I really said it just so I could go to sleep."

The next morning he got up and busied himself to avoid thinking about what he knew he needed to do. He washed the family car. He cleaned the patio. He did the laundry. He did his homework. That evening he drove forty-five miles through the mountains to Fort Bragg, a little town on the coast where he was to lead a youth rally for a group of small churches. "When I got up to speak I just felt like a total hypocrite. Inside I was going, 'What are you talking about here? You're not even willing to get this thing right.' And I *knew* that this was a test. God was saying, 'I want to bless your life, but if you're not real with me I won't be real with you, and if you're not honest in these little things you can't expect my blessing in your life.'" There was no response to his message, no decisions for Christ. The service seemed dead. He drove home and got into bed and was miserable.

His dad had asked him to preach the next day at a little church in Laytonville, a logging town about an hour north of Redwood Valley that didn't have a pastor. So he drove up and delivered the Sunday morning message. Once again he felt spiritually drained and once again no one responded to his invitation. He spoke at the evening service and it was more of the same. "I just knew that my heart wasn't right and that I couldn't expect anything to happen." He got into the car and on the way home that night he finally broke. "I said, 'Okay, Lord. I don't care how embarrassing it is. I don't care what happens. I'm going to do those three things.'"

When he got home his parents were in the living room watching *Bonanza*. He walked over and switched off the television and called Chaundel into the room. "I said, 'I just need to confess these three things, and I need you to pray that I'll have the courage now to go to the police, to go to the pastor, and, sister, I'm sorry.'" He got down on his knees, and as his parents began to pray he felt a release. "I felt God's power come over me like I had never felt it before. I felt a recharging, a renewal. I felt an anointing." He followed through on his confessions to the pastor and to the police, although not much came of either. But almost immediately his ministry seemed to take off. "All of a sudden I'd go out and speak and twenty, thirty kids would give their lives to Christ. There was something different. It was like God was saying, 'Okay, Rick, now I know you're serious about this.'"

At his conversion at the Cazadero camp, he would come to understand, Christ had established a beachhead in his life. "But he didn't really get all of me then because I didn't know what that meant. I gave as much as I could." Now he understood that the rest of his days would require a constant surrendering of his will to God's and an unwavering vigilance against the encroachments of sin which, if left unattended, would quench God's spirit in his life. He would continue to keep his sin lists and make his confessions regularly "in order to keep short accounts with God."

Warren was coming to the end of his high school years with a maturing faith and a rekindled zeal for evangelism. With a Baptist preacher's license in his pocket, he was ready to head off to college, where he would find a life's mate and refine his life's calling.

# CHAPTER SIX

# *Kay*

IN THE FALL OF 1972, RICK ENROLLED at California Baptist College in Riverside, a fully accredited liberal arts school affiliated with the California Southern Baptist Convention. There he would declare a philosophy major and a minor in biblical literature. He also planned to spend weekends ministering at area churches, just as he had during high school. Choosing Cal Baptist, as students called their school, had been an easy decision. The tidy 103-acre campus, with its lush tropical landscaping and Mission Revival–style architecture, was the only Southern Baptist college on the West Coast. Rick's decision to go there was based in no small part on financial considerations, which were important to the Warren household. The school had offered him two scholarships, and its proximity to a sizeable concentration of Baptist churches in the Los Angeles area increased the likelihood that he would find steady weekend work.

Rick was already quite familiar with the Riverside campus, having spent a week there for summer evangelism training a year earlier. Also in that group of summer trainees was a petite young brunette named Elizabeth Kay Lewis, a pastor's daughter from Fresno who had signed on as a team pianist. Although musically talented, Kay, as her friends called her, was a bit of an introvert who, unlike Rick, tended to avoid the limelight and seemed to care little about making flashy first impressions. While Rick retained only a vague recollection of her from that summer, she remembered him vividly. "There was a talent contest one night and Rick was imitating Billy Graham. He was way too brash, way too loud, way too everything I wasn't interested in." Other than their Baptist faith and their commitment to evangelism, Rick and Kay seemed to have little in common; their tastes and personalities were so starkly different. Yet they had traveled similar paths.

Kay was born on February 9, 1954, in San Diego, the second child of Bert and Bobbie Lewis. Like Rick's parents, the Lewises were assigned to "pioneer mission" work in California by the Southern Baptist Home Mission Board. They pastored several small churches in the San Diego area during the 1950s and early 1960s and then moved to Fresno in 1969 in the middle of Kay's first year of high school.

Her parents had met at Hardin-Simmons University, a Southern Baptist school in Abilene, Texas, where Bert went to begin preparing for the ministry. Bobbie grew up in a non-Christian home in nearby Stamford, Texas. She was saved as a teenager and had to pay her own way at Hardin-Simmons because her parents refused to support her at a Christian college. They met on Bert's first day on campus in the fall of 1945, quickly became an item, and were married on June 1, 1946. Not long after that, Bert, who was raised in rural Arizona in a staunch Baptist family, began witnessing to Bobbie's parents and eventually won them to the Lord. After they graduated in 1949, they moved to California and Bert enrolled at Golden Gate Baptist Theological Seminary and pastored a small church not far from the Berkeley campus. He dropped out after a year in order to be a full-time pastor. They moved to San Diego in 1953 to pastor the First Baptist Church of Bay Park. A year later, Kay was born.

Growing up in parsonages in San Diego and Fresno, Kay led what by all appearances was a sheltered life focused on the church and on avoiding the snares of worldly temptation. She attended public schools, where she considered herself "just an average student" and seldom participated in extracurricular activities. Her social life as a teenager centered mainly on her youth group at church. As in most Baptist families, she was taught to abide by strict rules of conduct, which meant no dancing and no movies or risqué television shows.

Like Rick, Kay had accepted Christ as a child and her Christian faith was central in her life. She dreamed of becoming a missionary or a pastor's wife, although she sometimes chafed under the expectations that people at church placed on her. "Because I was a pastor's daughter, everyone expected I would learn how to play the piano, so I took lessons," she recalled years later. Even though she played often and proficiently at church services and at youth activities, she counted her own musical skills as nothing more than average.

Her rather critical self-assessment extended to other areas, including her appearance. By her teen years she had given up on her childhood fantasy of becoming like Cinderella and blossoming into a beauty queen. "While no one has told me I'm ugly, I've never walked into a room and heard audible gasps from those present who are stunned by my beauty. I'm just average." By the end of high school an air of resignation seemed to have settled over her like a comfortable blanket. Hers would be an ordinary existence—productive, reasonably content, serving God to the best of her average capabilities. She headed off to California Baptist College to train to become a schoolteacher and to find "some average Joe" who would marry her. There her path and Rick's would cross again.

AT THE START OF HIS FIRST SEMESTER in college, Rick picked up almost exactly where he had left off in high school. With his outgoing personality and bold, upbeat manner in talking about matters of faith he became instantly popular on the Baptist campus and was elected president of his freshman class. He also became engrossed in his course work and delved hungrily into the advanced Scripture studies and the expository readings on church doctrine and history. Nearly every weekend was booked with speaking engagements at area youth events, where he continued to sharpen his preaching skills while earning extra cash from the honorariums. All of that left little time for dating, which didn't seem to bother him in the least. He and some like-minded friends jocularly proclaimed themselves "Bachelors to the Rapture" and boasted that they would be pleased to remain single until the Second Coming.

Kay, meanwhile, quickly met and fell in love with a young man who also happened to be a close friend of Rick's, and they began dating steadily. One day she asked her boyfriend about Rick and why he did not date. She saw that he was popular on campus and that girls seemed to like him, but he never asked any of them out. Her boyfriend explained about Rick's busy schedule and also the fact that he was very,

very frugal. "Rick just figures, 'Why spend money on a girl you're not going to marry?'" he explained. "He believes that when the right one comes along, God will point her out and that will be that." Kay found that to be an interesting perspective on dating. She promptly filed the information away and thought nothing further of it.

During the following summer, Rick stepped up his speaking schedule and preached at youth revivals all over the state. While he had no way of knowing it, his commitment to bachelorhood was about to be challenged. One weekend he accepted an invitation to speak at the First Baptist Church of Fresno. The church's pastor was Kay's father, and Kay played piano for the service. In a radio interview many years later Rick would recall what happened: "I looked over at her right before I got up to speak, and God said just as clearly as I'm talking to you, 'You're going to marry that girl.' Now, I immediately doubted it for two or three reasons—first, I didn't love her; second, God had never before or ever since talked to me that clearly in my life, ever; and, number three, she was madly in love with my best friend." He decided to keep the revelation to himself.

Soon after they returned to school in the fall, Kay's boyfriend broke up with her. It came as a complete surprise to Kay and she was crushed and certain that she would never love again. Then, as she recalls, "All of a sudden this Rick Warren guy started hanging around me, sitting down next to me in the cafeteria, standing beneath my dorm room and tossing rocks at my window to get my attention—you know, very subtle things," she deadpanned. "And it scared the daylights out of me because I remembered what his friend had said, and I'd never seen him so interested in anybody. And I had this panicky feeling: what does he know that I don't know?"

Rick asked her out and she accepted. On their first date, they went to a nearby Farrell's Ice Cream Parlour, a favorite date spot for Cal Baptist students, and shared the house specialty: a "pig's trough" filled with ice cream and all the fixings. Rick paid the tab. They laughed and talked and, while both were a little nervous, they seemed to enjoy the lighthearted conversation and one another's company. Eight days later they went out again, this time to a youth revival meeting at a nearby church where Kay had been invited to play the piano. Rick went along and sat in a pew while she played. After the service they walked back to the campus and went into a prayer room to pray together; the tone of the evening had been far different from that of the first date. As they finished praying, Rick looked up at her and blurted out, "Will you marry me?"

The proposal, as sudden as it was, did not come as a complete surprise to Kay. The mere fact that he had asked her out signaled that he had serious intentions. Still, she was not prepared for it, not that soon, and her mind raced to come up with an answer. "I instantly said to God, 'Okay, God, I don't love him. I'm in love with his best friend. What in the world do I say to this guy who has asked me to marry him?' And God clearly said to me, 'Say yes, and I'll bring the feelings.' So I said yes." They kissed for the first time.

THROUGHOUT THEIR LIVES, both Rick and Kay would speak often about receiving divine guidance, or, in more dramatic-sounding but relatively common evangelical parlance, of "hearing from God." Asked about it in an interview in 2007, Warren attempted to explain exactly what he experiences when he perceives a communication from God.

"The way I explain it is, God has a will for our lives. I also believe there is a real Satan, and I believe he has a will for our lives. I believe I have my own will, and I'm always choosing. You know, I don't have to accept God's will. I'm making choices all the time. And when Satan gives you a bad idea, we call that temptation. When God gives you a good idea, we call that inspiration. And so, when I say God said something to me, that's inspiration. It's thought.

"Now, I don't know how a cell phone works, but if another person can talk to me through the air, God can certainly put a thought in my mind without him having to say it aloud. I have never heard God say something aloud, ever. Many times I have gotten an idea and I've thought, 'I don't know where that came from.' And I wasn't sure if it was me or God or something else. But I've been a friend with God now for forty years, and I talk to him all the time just like I'm talking to you. I would say that early in my Christian life I had a hard time distinguishing between my thoughts, God's thoughts, and thoughts that came to me from somewhere else—television, something I had read, a billboard advertisement, whatever. But now that I've been a believer for forty years, I've become more comfortable with it. The longer I walk with the Lord the more I just know his voice."

WITH HIS CHOICE OF A LIFE'S MATE seemingly settled, Rick was about to face another life-altering event. Over the years he would speak and write of it often as the clarifying moment when his general call to the "full-time Gospel ministry" suddenly became a distinct call to the pastorate.

The annual meeting of the California Southern Baptist Convention was held that November at the Jack Tar Hotel on the edge of the seedy Tenderloin District in San Francisco. While the meeting itself was not expected to go beyond the usual fare of routine reports and resolutions, excitement had been building for weeks in anticipation of the keynote address that was to be delivered by a denominational superstar, W. A. Criswell, a former Southern Baptist president and pastor of the largest Southern Baptist church in the country at the time, the First Baptist Church of Dallas, Texas. Criswell was a fiery preacher with white wavy hair, a penchant for white suits, and a demonstrated passion for winning souls. Through radio broadcasts of his services he was known nation-wide as a combative defender of the Bible as God's inerrant word but also as a tenderhearted pastor who had built his Dallas flock to over 15,000 members. (It would reach 25,000 by the time he retired in 1994.) Among his fellow pastors he was considered a "preacher's preacher" and in Rick's estimation was the closest there was to a Baptist pope. Rick and a friend, Danny Daniels, cut classes and drove 350 miles to San Francisco for the rare opportunity to hear Criswell speak in person.

On the day of the speech, the hotel ballroom was packed with convention delegates, called messengers, and hundreds of visitors who had come out to hear the famous preacher. True to form, Criswell's sermon that day was "a roller coaster of whispers, bellows and shouts, tempered by the occasional joke" as he exhorted his audience, most of whom were pastors, to "fight the good fight . . . and finish the race" by dedicating themselves to a lifelong commitment to their congregations.

(By the time Criswell retired in 1994, he would have served his Dallas church for more than fifty years.)

Rick sat spellbound, hanging on the master preacher's every word and inflection, and as he listened he experienced what he later would describe as an epiphany. "God spoke personally to me and made it very clear that he was calling me to be a pastor." He had felt for some time that he was called to preach, but up until then his preaching mostly had involved salvation messages delivered at youth revival meetings. He had begun to envision a future as a crusade evangelist; perhaps he would follow in the footsteps of Billy Graham. Now he perceived that God was telling him otherwise. Sitting in that hotel ballroom, he recalled, "I promised God I'd give my entire life to pastoring a single church if that was his will for me."

Afterward Rick and Danny squeezed into a long receiving line and waited for the chance to shake Criswell's hand. When their turn finally arrived Rick extended his hand and he began to tell the preacher how much the message had meant to him. But as Rick tells it, "something unexpected happened. Criswell looked at me with kind, loving eyes and said, quite emphatically, 'Young man, I feel led to lay hands on you and pray for you!' He placed his hands on my head and prayed: 'Father, I ask that you give this young preacher a double portion of your Spirit. May the church he pastors grow to twice the size of the Dallas church. Bless him greatly, O Lord.'"

As they walked away, Rick was almost in shock. "Did he pray what I think he prayed?" he asked his friend. "He sure did," Danny answered. Later he would recall thinking that he could never imagine God using him in the way that Criswell had prayed. Nevertheless, "that holy experience confirmed in my heart that God had called me to pastor a local church."

THE REST OF THE SCHOOL YEAR did not go well for the newly engaged couple. Rick was in love and Kay was not, which led to plenty of bruised feelings and tense, awkward moments as they began to spend more time together and tried to envision their future. "It was just a really confusing, difficult time for both of us," Kay recalls. "We both felt like we had gotten this instruction from God that we were supposed to marry, but it just didn't happen the way it does in the movies with violins playing and bells ringing. It was just very different." At the end of the spring semester they parted company. Both had accepted summer missionary internships: Kay in the inner city of Birmingham, Alabama, and Rick in Nagasaki, Japan. They would remain apart for most of the next year.

RICK ARRIVED IN JAPAN in early June for a ten-week assignment working with a missionary couple from Alabama, Pratt and Rita Dean, at the Nagasaki Baptist Church. The tiny church was located in the coastal city's densely populated central section, roughly three miles from a black stone obelisk that marks the spot where the second American atomic bomb detonated on August 9, 1945. Intervening hills between that older section of town and ground zero had shielded the area from the 21-kiloton blast and most of the resulting fires. The neighborhood of the church was a mixture of small prewar houses and shops and modern apartment buildings built after the war.

During most of that summer Rick taught English and led youth services at the Baptist Youth Center, which was housed in a basement adjacent to the church. He also would occasionally accompany Dean and other Baptist pastors on evangelizing forays into nearby towns and villages. His energy and enthusiasm for soul-winning impressed his American hosts from the start. In a June newsletter to supporters back home, Dean wrote:

> Rick Warren, our "Praise-the-Lord!" summer missionary, is here . . . He is really a Spirit-filled young man and leaves a quiet wake of witnessing wherever he goes. He plays the guitar real well, too, and is quite popular with the young folks. That and his winsome smile and spirit of adventure makes him a valuable instrument for the Lord. He is challenging us and bringing refreshing blessings . . . He uses some picturesque words like "God busted him" (God brought him low or humbled him, and he got right), etc. Anyway, it looks like God has a young man he can use in a wonderful way here in the next two months. Pray that God can use him to the maximum among

us and rebuke Satan and his obstructions in the mighty name of Jesus. Rick signed one of his letters to us, "I hope the devil hates you!" We hope he hates you all, too.

Although Rick did most of his ministering that summer in English, he learned to recite John 3:16 in Japanese, which he would sometimes do over a loudspeaker while riding around town with a Japanese pastor to advertise the church's services. He played his guitar often and enjoyed teaching the Japanese young people some of the popular new praise songs he had learned back home. "One of his favorites," Dean recalls, "was, 'I Get So Happy in Jesus, I Have to Backslide to Go to Sleep.' The young people really loved that one."

Later in the summer, Rick directed youth activities during a missionary conference at a camp near Mount Fuji and preached occasionally during vesper services at the Nagasaki church. During those preaching events, he noticed that the headaches and vision trouble he had experienced earlier seemed to have worsened, and he began to discern a pattern. "I noticed that when I would start to seriously think about something, my mind, in lay terms, would overheat because I would be thinking of five or ten things at once, and when I'm speaking I will often do that." Then his vision would begin to blur, making it difficult to read his notes or the pages of the Bible in front of him. "And if I was really intense, the people in the audience would become blurry, and the headaches would come." Not wanting to worry the Deans, he kept this to himself but made plans to follow up with his doctor when he returned home.

The Deans' home, where Rick stayed, was a white one-story ranch-style house about two miles from the church. Rick's room was at the front of the house across a hallway from a wood-paneled library where he spent much of his free time reading books on prayer by Edward McKendree Bounds, a famous Civil War–era evangelist. Rummaging through the library one day he found an old copy of *HIS*, a magazine published by Inter-Varsity Christian Fellowship, that contained a profile of Donald McGavran, an American missionary to India who had spent his career studying what makes churches grow. Working in India, McGavran had found that the caste system posed an obstacle to the spread of Christianity, and he spent much of his life trying to overcome economic and social barriers to Christian conversion. Church growth was important, in McGavran's view, because it meant more souls being won to Christ. McGavran's ideas resonated with Rick. As he read the article, he would write later, "I felt God directing me to invest the rest of my life discovering the principles—biblical, cultural, and leadership principles—that produce healthy, growing churches. It was the beginning of a lifelong study."

By the end of the summer, Rick had become totally enamored with missions and with Japan in particular, and the thought occurred to him that his call to the pastorate, which had come so powerfully in San Francisco the previous fall, might just as easily involve starting a church in a foreign land. He had felt no clear direction on a location, so he began to pray about it, secretly hoping that God would see fit to send him to Asia as a missionary pastor.

When his time in Japan was up in mid-August, Rick bid farewell to the Deans and flew to Seoul, South Korea, to attend a massive weeklong evangelistic gathering called Explo 74. The event was sponsored by Campus Crusade for Christ, a California-based organization that started out in the early 1950s as an outreach ministry to American college students before expanding into international evangelism. In a letter to the Deans, Rick reported that more than 1.3 million people from 110 countries turned out the first night for a preaching service at downtown Seoul's Yoido Plaza. "I got some fantastic shots by climbing a 200-foot lighting tower and taking pictures from the top. You just can't imagine the number of people that is—a solid mass of humanity (no chairs) a mile long and a mile wide!" Tens of thousands made decisions for Christ.

The following day Rick sat in on a training seminar, Church Management and Leadership for Pastors, and pronounced it "fantastic!" Later the conferees were divided into teams of two and walked around the city streets witnessing to strangers. "My partner for witnessing was a little four-foot Catholic nun from the Philippines," Rick wrote. "With me being a 6-foot-2 long-haired American, you can imagine what a crazy looking pair we made!" Neither of them could speak Korean, so they carried around a bilingual copy of "The Four Spiritual Laws"—a

Campus Crusade tract explaining how to become born again. "I'd hold it open to a page and let the person read it and then I'd turn it to the next page. One girl prayed the prayer and signed the follow-up card asking for Bible studies for new Christians. I led her to the Lord without ever even saying a single word to her!!" It marked a memorable end to an eventful summer.

FINALLY HOME IN REDWOOD VALLEY, Rick had little time to relax before returning to school. Kay and her parents came to visit for a few days. Their separation over the summer had not made the strained engagement any stronger. Efforts to stay in touch had not gone well. "Our letters were just always off," Kay recalled. "He'd get a letter from me and it was two letters behind his. And then I'd get a letter from him, and it was just a very frustrating way to communicate."

Once they were together and had an opportunity to share the details of their summer experiences, Rick and Kay realized that they both had felt a pull toward foreign missions. Kay decided she would change her major from education to home economics so that she could learn to teach homemaking skills to women in other countries. Since Cal Baptist did not offer the program, she would go home to Fresno and enroll at California State University. She and Rick would be separated again.

Back at college in Riverside, Rick resumed a hectic schedule juggling course work with weekend ministry assignments. Late that fall he was hired as youth pastor at First Baptist Church of Norwalk, a medium-sized congregation about forty miles from the college. No longer just a youth-revival preacher or worship leader, Rick, for the first time, assumed the broad responsibility of ministering to the diverse needs of a growing flock. As youth pastor he taught, trained, counseled, and mentored the church's junior and senior high young people in Christian discipleship, instructing them in the basics of the faith and then pointing them toward a more mature walk that included witnessing and making disciples of others. After a few months on the job he saw the youth group more than triple in size.

On May 27, 1975, Rick was ordained at the Norwalk church.

Standing at the altar, surrounded by pastors from around the state with whom he had worked over the years, he repeated the ordination vows and, at the age of twenty-one, officially assumed the title of a Southern Baptist pastor. Less than a month later, on June 21, he would return to the same Norwalk altar—this time to marry Kay.

IT NEVER WOULD HAVE OCCURRED to the proud family and supportive friends who packed the church sanctuary on that sunny June afternoon that the nervous young couple standing before them were virtual strangers who were about to descend into marital hell. "I remember standing in the back of the church," Kay recalls, "waiting to walk down the aisle, going, 'Okay, God, those feelings that you said you'd bring? It would sure be nice if you'd bring those feelings sometime soon.'" Theirs had been an unusual courtship, to say the least. What they had managed to learn about each other during the many months they were apart only seemed to underscore their differences. The bonds of affection that should have grown stronger had barely taken hold. Despite their misgivings, they both still believed that God had brought them together, and so they went ahead with the wedding.

The honeymoon was a disaster. "He was so loving and so tender, and I loved him, but I wasn't in love with him," Kay recalls. "I was scared to death." She had every reason to be. Shortly before the wedding Kay revealed to Rick a secret from her past that she had never shared with anyone up to that time. At the age of three, Kay was sexually molested in the basement of her father's church by the teenage son of a church employee. The young man eventually was caught molesting other children in the neighborhood and was sent to juvenile detention for several years. Kay had never told her parents.

She told Rick the story simply and without emotion, suggesting that it was "no big deal" when in fact, as she would later admit, it was a huge deal; the psychological trauma haunted her into adulthood. "I did my best to block it out of my mind," she would write many years later, "but the effects of the trauma began to affect my developing sexuality."

As a teenager she became "alternately fascinated and repelled by any-thing sexual." She would sneak into her father's study to pore over the Masters and Johnson book *Human Sexual Response*, which was part of his marital-counseling collection. While babysitting for neighbors she found a stash of pornography and quickly became addicted to it. She began experimenting sexually with older friends. "All the while, the 'good girl' part of me loved God passionately and wanted my life to count for something. The 'bad girl' part of me didn't know how to break the cycle." So she learned to compartmentalize. "By the time Rick and I got engaged, I was totally messed up." On their wedding night Rick was unaware of the inner turmoil that had skewed Kay's self-image for so many years and had confused the sexual attitudes that she had carried into their marriage.

They returned from the honeymoon feeling frustrated and angry. "People would say, as they normally do, 'So—did you guys have fun?'" Kay recalls. "And we're like, 'Sure, great.' But inside we were dying. We were just dying." In the following months their relation-ship spiraled downward. They argued and fought over money, sex, in-laws, children—all of the usual marital flashpoints—and felt themselves sinking deeper and deeper into a dark pit. They also felt embarrassed. Rick was a youth pastor and they were concerned about how it would look if people knew that their marriage was a shambles. They felt trapped and alone. There was nowhere to turn, and divorce was not an option. Their Baptist faith had taught them that marriage was a lifetime commitment, a sacred vow that could not be broken. "I wasn't going to go back on the commitment," Kay explains. "But I just saw no hope. What I saw was that I had just consigned myself to a lifetime of misery. And so I wished that divorce was an option. I knew it wasn't for me, but I wished it was because I was so miserable."

Within a few months, the stress of the marriage and an exhausting workload put Rick in the hospital. "I was so sick from the stress. I was angry. It was like, 'Wait a minute. I saved myself for this?' I was just flat-out angry at God and felt cheated, and Kay thought she was going crazy. And that's where we had to say, 'Okay, we're going to get help.'"

They began seeing a Christian marriage counselor and it immediately became clear that there would be no quick fix. The counselor charged $100 a week, about half of the young couple's income. It was far more than they could afford, so they charged it to a credit card and eventually racked up a $1,500 bill. (Years later Rick would joke that he could make a commercial: "MasterCard saved my marriage!") Slowly the counseling began to pay off. "It was the beginning of teaching us how to communicate with each other," Kay recalls. "Rick and I are so different and we didn't know how to deal with that. Neither of us really knew how to handle conflict very well. So it at least opened the door to begin talking about the problems and the struggles and our differences."

They would continue to seek counseling unashamedly over the years, even after the success of Saddleback and of Warren's books. "There are times now when we'll say, 'You know, we could really use a tune-up,' and we'll go for a while and it helps us through a rough spot. Rick and I are big believers in really good counseling."

AFTER RICK'S HOSPITALIZATION, his doctor advised him to slow down; the mysterious spells of blurred vision and headaches continued to be a problem. So Rick dropped out of school a year short of graduation and worked full time at the church. During that year he wrote an instruction guide for his young charges on how to study the Bible, which he later refined and self-published as his first book, *Personal Bible Study Methods*. He also sketched a plan for helping young people grow in distinct steps from spiritual infants to committed lay ministers who reach out to the community around them. With only slight revision, that plan—which he illustrated with a series of concentric circles representing the church and with a baseball diamond representing the stages of individual growth—later became the foundation of the Purpose-Driven movement and the organizational backbone of Saddleback Church.

In the fall of 1976, Rick went back for his last year of college and was invited to teach a course on discipleship. By the time he graduated the following May he had built the Norwalk youth group into a strong and vibrant fellowship with more than ten thousand students on its mailing list. He had also established a growing reputation in Baptist circles as a talented young evangelist and a budding expert on discipleship. As he headed off to seminary in Fort Worth, Texas, the vague outlines of his life's calling were beginning to come into sharper focus.

# CHAPTER SEVEN

# The Texas Years

IN HIS LIFE BEFORE MARRIAGE, success seemed to come easily for Rick Warren. Since his early childhood, his God-given talents and intelligence and the sheer power of his personality had always proved more than adequate for whatever the task at hand. Whether it was schoolwork, social relationships, running for class office, or the demands of Christian ministry, he seemed to glide through life's challenges with a modicum of effort. It all just seemed to come naturally. With his marriage to Kay, he suddenly faced a challenge that was beyond his natural ability. Building a successful marriage would require outside help and plenty of hard work and patience from both of them.

The seminary years marked a turning point for the young couple. Applying some of the skills they had learned in counseling, Rick and Kay slowly began to make progress and they drew closer in what was becoming a more loving, trusting relationship built on mutual respect and a shared desire to be in the center of God's will. The strengthening of their fledgling marriage was undoubtedly helped along by their move away from the comfortable circle of family and friends in their native California to the alien environs of north Texas, where they would have only each other to rely on.

Unlike California, where Southern Baptist churches tended to be small and still something of a novelty, the Dallas–Fort Worth area was a Baptist stronghold and a veritable breeding ground of big churches that were steeped in traditional Southern Baptist culture and in denominational politics. Warren had chosen Southwestern Baptist Theological Seminary in Fort Worth over the much smaller Golden Gate seminary, where he had lived as a child, in part precisely because of its proximity to so many oversized congregations. Just a few miles east of the seminary campus was W. A. Criswell's 15,000-member downtown megachurch, the venerable First Baptist Church of Dallas. Several other churches in the Dallas–Fort Worth area had congregations of 5,000 or more. Among them was the First Baptist Church of nearby Euless, whose pastor, James T. Draper Jr., was a rising star and future president of the denomination. Two hundred miles to the south, Houston's First Baptist Church, led by a young evangelist-turned-pastor named John Bisagno, was one of the fastest-growing Baptist congregations in the country at the time, having grown from 3,500 to more than 10,000 members in just a few years. By observing such churches up close during his time at seminary, Warren hoped to discover the secrets of their success.

But his years at the Texas seminary also would mark the beginning of a period of turmoil for Southern Baptists. Before he would complete his studies, seething antagonism between theological conservatives and moderates that had been simmering for years in Baptist leadership ranks would erupt in a rancorous decade-long battle for control of the nation's largest Protestant denomination.

THE SEEDS OF WHAT WOULD BECOME KNOWN euphemistically in Baptist circles as "the controversy" were sown in the early twentieth century in the fundamentalist-modernist conflict that divided much of Protestantism over the nature and stature of Scripture. In Presbyterian, Methodist, Lutheran, and other major denominations, intense disputes over the divine inspiration and historical accuracy of the Bible— especially in regards to the Genesis creation story—proved so polarizing that some conservative congregations, many of them self-described fundamentalists, broke away and formed their own denominations as bastions of biblical orthodoxy. Baptists were not immune from the denominational infighting. In 1932, hundreds of fundamentalist congregations in the Northern Baptist Convention split off to form the General Association of Regular Baptist Churches and a handful of smaller groups. Their departure left the Northern Convention dominated by theological moderates and liberals. The denomination changed its name in 1950 to the American Baptist Convention and to the American Baptist Churches USA in 1972.

The Southern Baptist Convention, meanwhile, managed to hold together organizationally. Modernism had not established a strong presence in its churches and educational institutions in the early decades of the twentieth century, and so was not perceived as a serious threat by the dominant conservatives. But as the century wore on, as one conservative commentator put it, "it was inevitable that the liberal assumptions concerning the errancy of Scripture would filter into [Southern Baptist] institutions." Professors at some Baptist universities and seminaries began to "adopt the methodology of 'higher criticism' and attempt to reconcile the theory of evolution with the creation account of Genesis. That could only be done by mythologizing parts of the biblical record . . . They began presenting their new beliefs in the classroom and, inevitably, this became known."

The result was a series of protests and skirmishes beginning in 1920 in Texas, where conservatives objected to the use of a pro-evolution textbook at Baptist-run Baylor University in Waco. Leading the Texas uprising was John Franklyn Norris, the fiery fundamentalist pastor of First Baptist Church, Fort Worth, who publicly accused Baylor's president and leaders of the state convention of condoning heretical teaching. The offending Baylor professors eventually resigned under pressure, but Norris's intemperate accusations had so riled Texas Baptist leaders that they soon expelled Norris and his church from the state convention.

The battle over the Bible and evolution at Baylor set a pattern of conflict in the Southern Baptist Convention that would continue over the next half century. On one side were denominational leaders—heads of state conventions, mission agencies, publishing enterprises, seminaries and universities—who considered themselves moderates and who sought to reassure people in the pews by declaring their fidelity to the Bible as "authentic, authoritative, and infallible." They regarded their conservative critics as fundamentalist troublemakers who were out to impose a rigid doctrinal uniformity on a denomination that valued freedom of conscience and congregational autonomy. On the other side were conservatives, many of them pastors of big churches, who saw their denomination barreling down the road to modernism—its agencies and institutions controlled by theological liberals who failed to adequately embrace and enforce an unequivocal standard of biblical inerrancy—and were determined to stop it. Like the early twentieth-century fundamentalists, "these believers insisted on an unwavering faith in the Bible. A literal creation, a literal fish to swallow Jonah, literal miracles, and a literal virgin birth became their tests of true orthodoxy. And like their northern predecessors, they were willing to 'do battle royal' for the beliefs they saw threatened by the changes around them."

Yet by the 1960s the conservatives had made little headway, their efforts at reform stymied year after year by the moderates' firm hold on the seminaries and denominational machinery. By the end of that decade it became clear to many conservative churchmen that changing the denomination's direction would require a change of leadership from the top down, a daunting task that few Baptists on either side of the conflict thought possible.

Most Baptist chroniclers trace the start of the conservative uprising to an alliance formed in 1967 between two outspoken critics of the Baptist establishment: Paige Patterson, a student at New Orleans Baptist Theological Seminary and son of the executive director of the Texas Baptist convention, and Paul Pressler, a conservative Baptist layman and lawyer—soon to be a judge—from Houston. Both were appalled by the liberal drift in their denomination and believed the time had come to return it to its conservative roots. Over coffee and beignets in a French Quarter café in March of that year, the two began to plot the broad outlines of an insurgency.

It would more resemble a war of attrition. Under Southern Baptist polity, agency heads could be replaced only when they resigned or retired; their successors then were appointed by each institution's trustees. Those trustees, in turn, were elected by the convention from nominees picked by a nominating committee, whose members were selected by a committee on committees, whose members were appointed by the convention president. Since terms of membership on all of those committees were staggered, and because the president was restricted to two one-year terms, it would take a succession of conservative presidents and a carefully orchestrated ten-year campaign to recast the denomination's leadership.

Pressler and Patterson were anxious to begin, but first the groundwork would have to be carefully prepared. They set about rallying conservatives throughout the church, a process that itself would take more than ten years to complete. In 1973, they organized the Baptist Faith and Message Fellowship and began publishing a newspaper to expose and denounce "liberal" professors and to challenge Baptist leaders to publicly affirm conservative positions. Gradually their ranks began to grow. As one observer noted, "Pressler and Patterson were the activists, strategists, and tacticians, but the backbone of the movement was a strong cadre of pastors in large, aggressive, high-growth churches in metropolitan areas, who believed that only an inerrancy approach to Scripture would ensure Southern Baptists' integrity."

By 1979 the insurgents were ready to make their move. The convention that year was to be held in Houston, and Patterson and Pressler spent months preceding it traveling around the country to speak at rallies, compiling computerized mailing lists of supporters, and organizing a campaign for the election of a convention president. The conservatives' chosen candidate was Memphis pastor Adrian Rogers, a former classmate of Patterson's at New Orleans with impeccable conservative credentials. With thousands of messengers gathered in the Astrodome, and with Patterson and Pressler working from the skyboxes directing logistics on the convention floor, Rogers was elected on the first ballot over five other candidates. The conservative resurgence was under way.

The successful launch came just as Warren was about to begin his final semester in seminary. It would play out over the next ten years as conservatives maintained their grip on the Southern Baptist presidency and as each successive president repeated the process of appointment and purge until the entire Baptist bureaucracy was under their control. Among the casualties would be Southwestern Seminary president Russell Dilday, an outspoken partisan who had opposed what moderates had begun referring to as a fundamentalist takeover. Appointed to head the seminary in 1978, he was forced out of his job by a newly installed conservative board in 1994.

As conservatives continued to consolidate their hold, a mood of acrimony swept over the denomination and many liberal and moderate congregations eventually left to form their own organizations. Warren managed to ride out the controversy unscathed. In his native California, Southern Baptists, generally speaking, had stayed on the sidelines during most of the conflict. Although many, like Warren, were theological conservatives, they saw themselves as having no direct stake in the national fight and, for the most part, were left alone by belligerents on both sides—shielded and isolated, as it were, from the political upheaval by the Sierra Nevada mountains.

Early in the uprising Jimmy Warren had counseled his seminarian son to stay out of the fray and stay focused on ministry. "You know, son, when you're not reaching people, little things become really important," he said. "But when you're out there, and lives are being changed, you're helping people, you're putting marriages back together, kids are getting off drugs, you're building churches—you don't really have time to nitpick on a lot of other issues." Warren took his father's advice to heart. Although the historic 1979 convention unfolded just four hours away from the Fort Worth seminary, Warren chose not to attend. "I just wasn't interested in denominational politics, then or now," he explained years later. "I was more interested in the work I was doing, preparing for the ministry and, later, building a church. All of that denominational stuff, it meant nothing to me." The young political idealist he had once been now had other things on his mind.

Indeed, his years at seminary would be a time of intense academic preparation and, as had been true of his college and high school years, of weekends filled with church work. There would be little time for denominational distractions. Warren went to the Fort Worth seminary looking to add to his ministry experience and to sharpen the direction of what he sensed was his divine call. He would succeed in finding both.

SHORTLY BEFORE HE GRADUATED from California Baptist College in 1977, Warren was recruited for an internship with the International Evangelism Association, a Forth Worth–based ministry led by a young evangelist and Southwestern Baptist seminary graduate by the name of Billie Hanks Jr. A former preaching associate with the Billy Graham Evangelistic Association, Hanks had developed a ministry approach that emphasized one-on-one "disciple-making" over traditional evangelism, which, in Hanks's view, too often left new converts to fend for themselves with little personal instruction or support. A more biblical model of making disciples, Hanks believed, involved winning new converts through personal witnessing and then mentoring them in the faith and equipping them, in turn, to evangelize and mentor others. It was an approach pioneered by the Navigators, a ministry that began in Southern California in the 1930s as an outreach to sailors and grew into a worldwide network of missionaries who spread the Gospel through one-on-one contact and small-group Bible studies. Hanks provided training and encouragement in disciple-making through a program called Operation Multiplication, which it offered to churches, Christian colleges, and seminaries. Each year it hired a handful of young interns to learn the process and to help in the training.

Hanks and Warren had met two years earlier when the First Baptist Church of Norwalk, where Warren was serving as youth pastor, hosted one of Hanks's seminars. There Hanks learned that Warren had built a thriving youth ministry around a process of progressive discipleship—illustrated by Warren's concentric-circle and baseball-diamond diagrams—that was similar in some ways to his own approach. Warren, too, had been inspired by the Navigators and its founder, Dawson Trotman. The following year Hanks's organization provided funding for a new chair in discipleship at California Baptist College and Hanks recommended that the school hire Warren as a teaching assistant to the new discipleship professor. The college offered Warren the job in December of 1976 and he quickly accepted even though he had just been offered a new position as youth pastor at a Baptist church in Phoenix, Arizona, close to where Kay's parents recently had moved. Warren declined the Phoenix offer and he and Kay moved back to the Cal Baptist campus, where he would teach and complete his last semester of college.

When they arrived at seminary in the fall of 1977, they moved into a tiny two-bedroom house two blocks from the Fort Worth campus that was owned by Hanks's organization. Hanks hired Warren as an intern for $250 a month and charged him $60 a month rent. Kay went to work briefly as Hanks's secretary but left for a better-paying job in the offices of a local cowboy boot manufacturer. Rick conducted a few training sessions at the ministry's West Texas Ranch for Christ near Sweetwater, but soon found that most of his duties as an intern were to involve writing and polishing teaching materials for Hanks's seminars. He was itching to do more hands-on teaching and preaching of his own, so he began seeking out ministry opportunities through the Baptist Student Union and the evangelism department of the Dallas-based Baptist General Convention of Texas. The opportunities came quickly and in abundance. Throughout his time at seminary he kept up a fast-paced weekend schedule teaching leadership workshops for the Baptist General Convention, preaching at area churches and weekend retreats, and teaching his Bible study methods at Baptist Student Union chapters at state universities in Kansas, Iowa, Oklahoma, and New Mexico.

All of that was on top of his schoolwork. At the seminary, Warren carried a heavy course load and worked as a grader and teaching assistant for an evangelism professor, Roy Fish, one of the foremost academic authorities on evangelism among Southern Baptists at the time. Having the opportunity to study under Fish had been another reason Warren chose to attend Southwestern Seminary. He had met Fish one summer during his youth evangelism days and the professor had urged him to come to the Fort Worth school. Warren told him he would go to Southwestern if Fish would agree to become his mentor. "This man was passionate," Warren explained. "He understood the Great Commission and he understood people and the Gospel. I just really had great respect for him." The professor agreed to mentor Warren. Many years later Warren would name Fish one of the great early influences on the eventual direction of his ministry.

Fish was equally impressed by his new charge. "Rick turned out to be a superlative student," Fish recalled. "He received all A's in seminary except for one B, and I think he deserved better than that B. He probably knew more about church growth than any of the professors. He was really tuned in to the practical side of ministry." Working alongside Fish, Warren designed and helped teach a seminary course in discipleship built around the program he had developed as a youth pastor in California. "He had many more ideas on the subject than I did," Fish recalled. "It was the first course ever taught at Southwestern that had the word 'discipleship' in it. The syllabus he wrote is still in use today."

There were other important influences in those years. In the summer of 1978, after completing his first year of seminary, Rick and Kay drove to Fresno, California, to attend the wedding of Rick's friend and former youth evangelism team partner, Steve Williams. The two had stayed in close touch over the years. Steve had been in Rick and Kay's wedding and now Steve had invited Rick to be his best man.

While in California, Rick attended a church growth conference in Orange County conducted by Robert Schuller, the famous founding pastor of a fast-growing congregation in Garden Grove and host of a popular nationally televised broadcast called *The Hour of Power*. Then in his early fifties, Schuller was widely known in the church world as an innovator who defied tradition and conventional methods in order to attract nonchurchgoers, his primary target in building his Southern California flock. Hoping to make it easy for people to attend, Schuller launched his church in 1955 at a rented drive-in theater and conducted Sunday services from the roof of the concession stand while worshipers sat in their cars and listened over the window-mounted speakers. Though ordained and sponsored by the Reformed Church in America, a small denomination of predominantly Dutch heritage, Schuller decided against using the denominational title in his new church's name— "I didn't think the name 'Reformed' would bring the unchurched people rushing in!" he recalled—and instead named it simply the Garden Grove Community Church. By 1977 his congregation had grown to ten thousand and they began phased construction of a $16 million towering edifice of mirrored glass and steel that, when completed in 1980, would become known as the Crystal Cathedral. In keeping with the church's drive-in-theater origins, the three-thousand-seat cathedral's exterior walls were made so that they could be partially opened to allow congregants to view the services from their cars.

Schuller's approach to church growth was somewhat controversial at the time because it drew as much upon modern marketing concepts as on traditional biblical theology. He explained his approach in a 1974 book entitled *Your Church Has Real Possibilities*, a how-to guide for pastors, in which he compared the process of growing a large and vibrant congregation to that of building a successful retail business. Just as in retailing, Schuller wrote, factors such as good location, high visibility, adequate inventory, convenient parking, strong customer service, and sound cash flow were important ingredients for a church's success. "I have sometimes described [my church] as 'a 20-acre shopping center for Jesus Christ,'" he wrote at the time. Schuller insisted that following smart business practices and maintaining a positive faith-oriented mindset—which he called "possibility thinking"—were essential to effective church leadership. Warren had read the book and it piqued his curiosity, so he decided to attend Schuller's conference to learn more.

Kay, many years later, recalled the four-hour drive from Fresno to the Orange County conference as "a very stony ride." While Rick was looking forward to getting an inside look at Schuller's innovative methods, Kay was frightened by the notion of straying from the traditional Southern Baptist ways of doing church—three hymns, a sermon, and an offering—and she was not much interested in hearing what Schuller had to say. But she was about to change her mind.

Sitting in the audience during the three-day conference, Rick and Kay listened attentively as Schuller and his staff described some of the strategies they had followed, such as building a prospect list by canvassing neighborhoods to identify nonchurchgoers; avoiding religious jargon in sermons or preaching on controversial subjects, both of which tended to be off-putting to nonbelievers; and setting goals for growth five, ten, and twenty years out and establishing benchmarks to meet those goals. Those seemed like practical and doable steps and, from an organizational standpoint, they made sense to the Warrens. By the end of the conference Schuller had won them over. "He had a profound influence on Rick," Kay later recalled. "We were captivated by his positive appeal to nonbelievers. I never looked back."

Warren had been especially taken by Schuller's emphasis on growing a church through new conversions rather than by attracting people from other congregations or by birth rate. "That was life-changing for Rick," Steve Williams remembered from conversations with Warren after the conference. "It was there for the first time that he caught the vision of doing a church for the unchurched."

HAVING LEARNED SOME VALUABLE LESSONS from Schuller, Warren set about to widen his exploration of church-growth methods. During his final year in seminary, he conducted an independent study of the one hundred largest churches in the country and the strategies, structures, and styles that accounted for their success. He compiled a detailed questionnaire and sent it to pastors of congregations that he and Fish had identified from denominational reports, Christian magazines, and other sources as the nation's largest. Many of them responded by sending back thick packets that included samples of educational materials, worship guides, and other information.

As he pored over the material, Warren found wide differences in the methods the churches had employed—the type of music they used in worship, the preaching style of the pastor, the degree of engagement in community evangelism, and so on. But there were some common denominators as well. Most important in Warren's estimation, the study confirmed what he had learned a few years earlier from observing Criswell's ministry—that large, healthy churches usually were led by pastors who stayed in one place for a long period of time. While pastoral longevity did not guarantee that a church would grow, he concluded, "changing pastors every few years guarantees a church *won't* grow . . . Long pastorates make deep, trusting, and caring relationships possible. Without those kinds of relationships, a pastor won't accomplish much of lasting value." As a result of his study, Warren reaffirmed his commitment to pastor one church for a lifetime. "I don't care where you put me," he recalled praying at the time, "but I'd like to stay wherever it is for the rest of my life."

At that point, he and Kay had no clear sense of the location of their call, although both still harbored hopes of starting a church in Asia. They tacked a map of the world on their living room wall and began to pray daily, asking God to guide them to just the right place. After about six months, Warren recalled, "God impressed upon us that we were not to serve overseas. Instead, we were to plant a new church in a major metropolitan area of the United States." Kay remembers feeling somewhat disappointed at first that they would not realize their dream of becoming full-time missionaries. "But then we began getting excited about the new dream that was taking shape in our hearts, the church-planting idea that we were beginning to talk about, and our excitement just transferred over to that."

They replaced the world map on their wall with a map of the United States and circled every metropolitan area outside of the South. They began praying about starting a church in Detroit, New York, Philadelphia, Chicago, Albuquerque, Phoenix, or Denver—places where they knew most Southern Baptist seminarians would have little interest in going. A short while later they learned that the three most unchurched areas in the country were the states of Washington, Oregon, and California, and so they narrowed their focus to four fast-growing metropolitan areas on the West Coast: Seattle, San Francisco, San Diego, and Orange County, California.

Warren spent much of the summer of 1979 ensconced in a university library studying U.S. Census data and doing other demographic research in hopes of learning all he could about the four areas. Kay at the time was nine months pregnant with their first child and Rick would call her from the library several times each day to see if she had started labor. One afternoon he came across a report identifying Orange County as the fastest-growing county in the United States, and the fastest-growing part of the county was a place called Saddleback Valley. Describing the moment years later, Warren said the discovery "grabbed me by the throat and made my heart start racing. I knew that wherever new communities were being started at such a fast pace there would also be a need for new churches. As I sat there in the dusty, dimly lit basement of that university library, I heard God speak clearly to me: 'That's where I want you to plant a church!' My whole body began to tingle with excitement, and tears welled up in my eyes. I had heard from God."

Warren rushed home and broke the news to Kay. She listened attentively as her husband described his discovery and his passionate belief that it had come from God. While the prospect of moving back to Southern California and establishing a ministry there was certainly appealing, she did not yet share his certainty that it was providential. Kay was a pragmatist. In her estimation, there were too many unanswered questions and potentially derailing details that would have to be confronted before she could confidently consider the matter settled, let alone divinely ordained. Yet she was fully open to the possibility and she supported her husband, who was ready to act on his conviction.

Warren fired off a letter to Herman Wooten, the Southern Baptist director of missions for Orange County and a longtime associate of Rick's father. In his letter, he told of his desire to start a church in the southern part of the county. "I'm not asking for money or support from you," he wrote. "I just want to know what you think about that area. Does it need new churches?" Unbeknownst to Warren, Wooten was writing a letter at the same time. The missionary director knew from talking with Jimmy Warren that Rick was about to graduate from seminary and that he was considering planting a church somewhere in California. Wooten was in the process of mapping out potential locations for new churches in fast-growing residential areas in his district. There were twenty-one Southern Baptist congregations in the county at the time but none in the extreme southern portion. He wrote to Rick asking: "Have you ever considered coming to Saddleback Valley in south Orange County?" Their letters crossed in the mail.

"When I saw his letter," Wooten later recalled, "I thought, 'This must be what God wants. Not only was God speaking to me but he was also speaking to Rick.'"

Rick's reaction was much more intense. "When I opened the mailbox two days later and saw a letter from the same man I'd just written to, I began to cry. Kay and I both knew God was up to something."

Two months later Warren flew out to Orange County for his first look at the area. For more than a week he consulted with realtors, business owners, bankers, county planning officials, residents, and local pastors, hoping to learn all he could about the needs and demographics of the area. At night he studied local maps and directories and began memorizing the names and the layout of major streets and thoroughfares. At the end of the week Kay flew out to join him and they toured the Saddleback Valley together. He was anxious to gauge her reaction. "If Kay had felt any reluctance toward moving," he explained later, "I would have taken that as a warning light from God. Happily, Kay's response was, 'I'm scared to death, but I believe this is God's will, and I believe in you. Let's go for it.'"

Late on that warm autumn afternoon they climbed to the top of a nearby hill and looked out over the sun-drenched valley with its sparkling clusters of new homes and shopping centers and dusty gashes of red earth where new subdivisions were sprouting. Hand in hand they bowed their heads before God and prayerfully committed together to spend the rest of their lives building the Saddleback Valley Community Church.

# CHAPTER EIGHT

# Saddleback

LIFE WAS MOVING FAST FOR THE WARRENS. By taking heavy course loads throughout his seminary years, Rick was able to complete his master of divinity degree a semester early in December 1979. Four months earlier, Kay had given birth to their first child, Amy Rebecca. They marveled at the miracle of childbirth and were adjusting quickly to their new role as parents. To Rick the birth of his daughter was an apt metaphor for the task he was about to undertake: giving birth to a congregation of new believers. His new dream of starting a church from scratch in the burgeoning suburbs of southern Orange County had become his passion during his final months in Texas, and he was anxious to get started. He hoped to conduct the first service on Easter, which fell on the first Sunday of April that year, and there was much to be done in a relatively short amount of time. He would have to work fast.

Knowing that it would take months and perhaps years before his new church would be up and running and producing plate offerings sufficient to sustain itself, Warren's first priority before leaving seminary was to line up financial backing. The Home Mission Board of the Southern Baptist Convention at the time had a funding program called the 5-1-5 Program in which five churches would agree to support one new mission church for five years. It was up to the start-up pastor to recruit his supporting churches, so Warren set out to find five congregations that each would kick in $200 a month, providing a $1,000-a-month support base that he felt would be more than enough to get things started.

Having ministered at so many churches in California and Texas during college and seminary, he was confident of finding five that would be willing to support him. He made his pitch in written queries, phone calls, and visits to churches, where he explained his vision of launching "a church for the unchurched" in the Saddleback Valley. He received plenty of encouragement from pastors and several congregations indicated they would seriously consider his proposal. But when graduation time arrived Warren had no firm commitments. "We're going anyway," he announced to Kay. "Whether we get any support or not, we're moving." Just after Christmas they loaded their hand-me-down furniture and other worldly possessions into a rented U-Haul truck and set out for Southern California.

Bouncing along in the crowded cab, their car in tow, the young family endured a long and uncomfortable road trip that was made even longer by gasoline shortages that gripped the nation that year. The Islamic revolution in Iran had disrupted oil production in the Middle East, spawning long lines and soaring prices at America's gas pumps. Texas and California were among a handful of states that instituted gasoline rationing by restricting purchases to odd and even days based on vehicle license-plate numbers. After driving a full day in the gas-guzzling truck, the Warrens spent the next day idle at a west Texas motel waiting for the opportunity the following day to fill the tank and move on. It took them three days just to get out of Texas.

They arrived in Orange County on Friday, January 4, in the middle of the afternoon rush hour and, as usual, the Los Angeles–area freeways were jammed. Driving on Interstate 5 in the fading afternoon light, they could make out in the distance the hazy purple profile of the Santa Ana Mountains looming to the east and anchored by a towering formation known as Old Saddleback. The conjoined twin peaks of Santiago and Modjeska, at 5,687 feet and 5,496 feet, respectively, were the highest of the Santa Ana range and when viewed from a distance formed the contour of a saddle. Descending from those mountains to the sprawling Los Angeles basin were two shallow coastal valleys that contained most of Orange County's population, the Santa Ana Valley to the north and the Saddleback Valley to the south. With the mountains in sight, the Warrens knew they were closing in on their destination and, though weary from travel, they felt an invigorating burst of emotion. They were home.

It was close to 5 p.m. when they pulled off the crowded freeway. Rick had arranged for his family to spend the first few nights at the home of Herman Wooten, the local Southern Baptist director of missions who had recruited him. But they would need to find a place of their own very quickly and Rick wanted to begin the search at once. He had called ahead and was referred to a realtor in Mission Viejo, a new planned community in the heart of the Saddleback Valley.

They arrived at the real estate office and were introduced to Don Dale, a young man who was just slightly older than Rick and brand new to the real estate business. "They came in and wanted to rent a house," Dale recalls of that meeting. "I asked him, 'Do you have a deposit?'—because renters typically want to have the first and last month's rent and a security deposit—and he said, 'Not really. I might be able to borrow it.' I asked him, 'Do you have a job?' 'Well, not really. I'm a minister.' I said, 'Well, do you have a church?' 'Well, not really. I'm *starting* a church.' So I had a guy with no money, no job, no congregation, no support, and he wanted to rent a house. I said, 'What the heck. Let's see what we can do for you.' "

Dale knew of another agent in the office who owned a condominium in the neighboring community of Laguna Hills and was desperate to find a renter. The condo was listed at $600 a month, ten times what the Warrens had paid to rent the house in Fort Worth. Dale persuaded his coworker to allow the Warrens to move in without paying the usual deposit if they would agree to paint the place and if Dale would forgo his $75 commission. Within two hours of their arrival the Warrens had secured a place to live with no money down.

They also had found their first congregant. On the way to see the property, Warren asked Dale if he attended church. "I said, 'Oh yeah, I go to a little church up the street,' and he said, 'How do you like it?' I said, 'I go but I'm not real enthusiastic,' and he said, 'Well, I'm starting a new church. Would you come to my Bible study?' And I said, 'Sure.' They seemed like nice folks."

Two weeks later the first gathering of what would become the Saddleback Valley Community Church took place amid moving boxes stacked on green shag carpeting in the living room of the Warrens' rented condominium. Seven people—the Warrens, Don Dale and his wife, Jan, and three others—assembled for prayer and Bible study. Rick played his guitar and they sang a few songs and afterward they snacked on cookies and soft drinks. It was a humble beginning, but the work was under way.

The first weeks of Saddleback brought some encouraging developments. The much-needed financial support Warren had attempted to line up ahead of time finally began to fall into place and none too soon. Rick and Kay were nearly out of cash. When they left Fort Worth they had emptied their savings account—which totaled about $1,500—and spent most of it on the move. By the time they arrived in Orange County they had roughly $200 to last them until their support came through.

Within a matter of days after their arrival they heard from the First Baptist Church of Lufkin, Texas, where Warren had preached several times during seminary, and the First Baptist Church of Norwalk, where he had served as youth pastor during college. Both agreed to provide $200 a month for up to five years. The twelve-hundred-member Crescent Baptist Church in nearby Anaheim agreed to become the new congregation's official sponsor and pledged $600 a month plus other assistance to help get the work started. That meant Saddleback would be classified as a mission of the Crescent church and its baptisms and other statistics initially would be counted as part of Crescent's. A few weeks later, Warren heard from the Southern Baptist Home Missions Board in Atlanta. It agreed to contribute $500 a month to help underwrite the project. Having secured a total of $1,500 a month in outside support, Warren finally was able to turn his attention in earnest to the work of building a church.

Over the next three months the Bible study group, which had grown to fifteen, continued to meet weekly in the Warrens' living room for worship and prayer and to make preparations for the first public service on Easter Sunday. Before he left Texas, Warren had identified many of the tasks that would need to be completed before the official launch. At the top of the list was finding a place to hold services. He had decided upon renting a school on Sunday mornings and using its auditorium for worship and its classrooms for Sunday school until they could afford to buy land and build a permanent building. That had become a fairly common practice in starting new churches.

Ideally the school would be located close to the church's eventual home. Warren planned for that to be in Aliso Viejo, an upscale community that was about to be built near the coast between Laguna Beach and Laguna Hills. Since the town was still on the drawing board at the time, Warren figured that his would be one of the first churches to locate there. After visiting schools in the two neighboring towns he settled on Laguna Hills High School as the church's temporary quarters. It had a 250-seat theater with plush velour carpeting and plenty of classrooms with furniture that would comfortably accommodate both adults and children. And it was in the heart of a bustling upper-middle-class community from which Warren expected to draw many of his congregants.

With a worship facility secured, it was time to move on to the next task. But there were so many on his list and Warren was not sure which to turn to next. He knew he needed to set priorities and manage his time wisely if they were to be ready by the launch date, but he needed help getting organized. He found it in one of the volunteers from the Crescent church, Bruce Medley, a former Pentagon planner who had been with him since the first Bible study. Medley and Warren sat down one afternoon and put together a PERT chart (program evaluation and review technique). It was a system used in the defense industry to organize complex projects by analyzing and scheduling the various tasks necessary to complete the project. "We wrote out on little cards every single detail that needed to be done to start the church and we ended up with a stack of cards," Warren explained. "Then we got a big piece of butcher paper and we laid it all out and taped them together. And we said, 'Okay, we've got to do this by this date, and this by this date, and this by this date.' I would never have known how to do that. God brought the right person at the right time."

Warren would credit divine help often during that critical time as other details began falling into place. One weekend, as he would tell the story later, he and Kay went scouting garage sales for used nursery equipment for the first service. At one location they found exactly what they needed: a crib, a changing table, an infant swing, and a few other items. The total came to $37.50. They wrote a check for that amount knowing that the $100 or so that they had in their account at the time would have to last until their support money arrived. "When we got home," he said, "I opened the mailbox and found a check from a woman in Texas who had heard me speak one time and somehow traced us to California. The check was for $37.50. Where God guides, God provides. I could tell you a thousand stories like that."

Next on Warren's to-do list was conducting a community-wide survey to learn what was on the minds of the unchurched Southern Californians that he was setting out to reach. One of the lessons of church growth that Warren had learned from Robert Schuller and from his own seminary study of the nation's largest churches was the importance of knowing the community and designing a ministry to meet its needs. Schuller had accomplished that in the 1950s by canvassing the neighborhoods of Garden Grove prior to the launch of his church in order to identify nonchurchgoers and to learn something about their attitudes about church. From that survey Schuller compiled a "prospect list" of some fourteen thousand households that became the target of his successful outreach efforts. Warren had decided to do likewise. Over a twelve-week period he and a corps of volunteers from his Bible study group and the Crescent church went door-to-door in and around Laguna Hills surveying residents and compiling a prospect list. The questions they asked were an updated and expanded version of Schuller's.

Warren did much of the interviewing himself and followed a carefully honed script. "Hello, my name is Rick Warren and I'm taking a survey," he said at each house. "I'm not here to sell you anything. I'm not here to convert you. I'm just doing a poll." He then asked if the person was "an active attender of any religious house of worship." If they answered yes, he thanked them and moved on to the next house and scratched their address off his prospect list. If they answered no, he said, "Great! You're just the kind of person I want to talk to," and proceeded to ask more questions. "What do you think is the greatest need in this community?" He listened carefully and jotted down the answer. Next he asked, "Why do you think most people don't go to church?" He knew if he were to ask "Why don't *you* go to church?" people might be offended and say it was none of his business. Instead, they usually rattled off a number of reasons and Warren wrote them down. "If you were thinking of going to church, I know you're not, but if you were, what kinds of things would you look for?" He recorded the response. Finally he asked, "What advice would you give to a new pastor starting a church here?"

Each week Warren and his team would analyze the responses and add addresses to a growing database of potential invitees. From the survey responses they identified four common complaints that people had against churches: the sermons were boring and irrelevant; church members weren't friendly to visitors, they were more like a clique; churches were more interested in people's money than in people; and parents worried about the quality of the church's child care. "What we discovered was that what most churches offered was not what most people wanted," Warren explained. "People's hang-ups about church were not theological; they were sociological. They said, 'I don't have anything against God. I just don't see it relating to my life.'" Warren was determined to use those findings to design a church that would meet the "felt needs" of the community and would overcome the barriers that prevented people from attending church.

But ministering to "felt needs" was a controversial strategy in some evangelical circles, and Warren was not the only one seeking to apply it. Schuller had designed his ministry along the same lines and had built a church of twelve thousand members and a successful television ministry. Five years before Saddleback began, Bill Hybels had used a similar approach in launching his rapidly growing Willow Creek Community Church in the northwest suburbs of Chicago. Critics saw those efforts as little more than slick marketing. Churches like the Crystal Cathedral and Willow Creek, some traditionalists argued, offered a feel-good, therapeutic message that softened the "hard truths" of Scripture and of the Christian faith and gave people what they wanted rather than what they needed to hear. "It's a passing fad that will not last," one Southern Baptist seminary dean argued. "You cannot sustain the body of Christ with felt-needs preaching."

Warren rejected that notion out of hand. In an interview with a Baptist magazine two months after the first Saddleback service, he explained his priorities. "The question in my ministry is, 'Who are you trying to impress?' We are not trying to impress other Christians or our denomination, but the unchurched people in the Saddleback Valley who couldn't care less about most things related to the Lord. We want to get their attention long enough to share the Good News with them. Today, instead of the church and the church program being the center of people's lives, television and sports vie for their time and attention. So how do we capture the attention of the normal people who are traveling our streets, roads, and freeways all day long? How do we get their attention in order to tell them about Jesus Christ? Everything we do is determined by what is going to get the attention of the lost person!" Years later he would reflect on it further. "It is not the church's task to give people whatever they want or even need. But the fastest way to build a bridge to the unchurched is to express interest in them and show that you understand the problems they are facing. Felt needs, whether real or imaginary, are a starting point for expressing love to people."

After digesting the survey results, Warren composed an enthusiastic "open letter" to the community that would serve as the public unveiling of the Saddleback church and an invitation to its inaugural service. "Hi neighbor!" he wrote in a colorful leaflet peppered with exclamation points. "At last! A new church designed for those who've given up on traditional church services!" The letter described the new congregation as "a group of friendly, happy people who have discovered the joy of the Christian lifestyle." At Saddleback, the letter promised, worshipers would "meet new friends and get to know your neighbors, enjoy upbeat music and contemporary flavor, hear positive, practical messages which encourage you each week, and trust your children to the care of dedicated nursery workers. Why not get a lift this Sunday? . . . If you don't have a church home, give us a try!"

The Warrens and the Bible study group hand-addressed and stamped fifteen thousand copies and dropped them into the mail ten days before Easter. They had come to realize that mail delivery was the only sure way of penetrating the gated communities in which so many Saddleback Valley residents lived. By making cold calls door-to-door they could hope to reach only a fraction of the area's population. They were hoping for a 1 percent response rate to the mass mailing, which would mean 150 people showing up for the first service—a seemingly modest number, yet one that would exceed the size of any church that Warren's father, Jimmy, had pastored in his entire career.

A week before Easter, Warren announced at the Friday night Bible study that they would conduct a rehearsal service that weekend at the Laguna Hills High School. "We'll practice singing the songs, I'll preach like there's a crowd of 150 people, and we'll work out all the bugs in the order of the service. This will insure that when all the visitors show up the next week it will at least *appear* that we know what we're doing." When Palm Sunday morning arrived they were expecting just their own small group. What they did not know was that some of the fifteen thousand letters they had dropped into the mail a few days before were delivered early and, as a result, sixty people from the community turned out for the dress rehearsal.

The Warrens and their team were somewhat taken aback but managed to pull off the service without a major hitch. The visitors were welcomed as though they had been expected. Kay played the piano and Rick, wearing a three-piece suit and tie (his casual Hawaiian-shirt motif was still years away), led the congregational singing and delivered a message. At the end of the service five people accepted Christ.

At the conclusion of his "practice" sermon that day, Warren spelled out his vision for Saddleback Church. It was an ambitious vision to say the least, but also an amazingly prophetic one:

> It is the dream of a place where the hurting, the depressed, the frustrated, and the confused can find love, acceptance, help, hope, forgiveness, guidance, and encouragement.
>
> It is the dream of sharing the Good News of Jesus Christ with the hundreds of thousands of residents in south Orange County.
>
> It is the dream of welcoming twenty thousand members into the fellowship of our church family—loving, learning, laughing, and living in harmony together.
>
> It is the dream of developing people to spiritual maturity through Bible studies, small groups, seminars, retreats, and a Bible school for our members.

It is the dream of equipping every believer for a significant ministry by helping them discover the gifts and talents God gave them.

It is the dream of sending out hundreds of career missionaries and church workers all around the world, and empowering every member for a personal life mission in the world. It is the dream of sending our members by the thousands on short-term mission projects to every continent. It is the dream of starting at least one new daughter church every year.

It is the dream of at least fifty acres of land, on which will be built a regional church for south Orange County—with beautiful, yet simple, facilities including a worship center seating thousands, a counseling and prayer center, classrooms for Bible studies and training lay ministers, and a recreation area. All of this will be designed to minister to the total person— spiritually, emotionally, physically, and socially—and set in a peaceful, inspiring garden landscape.

I stand before you today and state in confident assurance that these dreams will become reality. Why? Because they are inspired by God!

In the years ahead the vision statement would serve as a roadmap for Warren and his Saddleback co-laborers, and they would refer back to it often even though some would find parts of it—the goal of twenty thousand church members, in particular—to be a bit of a stretch. "From the very beginning Rick had this focus that he was going to create a megachurch," Don Dale recalled. "I didn't always buy into it because *he* had the dream. I didn't have the dream. To me it seemed beyond reality that we could do what he wanted to do. But it's good to have an objective, and that was his."

The following Sunday Warren and a crew of volunteers arrived at the school early to set up for the Easter service. They hauled in sound equipment, nursery furniture, musical instruments, boxes of teaching materials and printed bulletins, an arrangement of Easter lilies for the front of the auditorium, and other items that would make the school building seem a bit more churchlike than it was on other days of the week. By ten-thirty everything was ready. Saddleback Valley Community Church was about to open its doors to the public—officially—for the first time.

Warren made his way to the main entrance to await the first arrivals, and for a fleeting moment he allowed himself to wonder—what if no one came? After all of the work, the months of planning, prayer, and preparation; after all of the research during seminary and the sharing and sharpening of his dream with his family, seminary professors, and other pastors; after weeks of canvassing the neighborhoods of southern Orange County, and of stuffing envelopes, and tending to the morale of the overworked members of his Bible-study team whom he had dutifully counseled to persevere even though there were no guarantees that their efforts would amount to anything—what if it had all been for naught? What would he tell them? What would he tell himself? Was his vision for Saddleback really God-inspired? Or had it all been "just a wild dream of an idealistic twenty-six-year-old?"

He glanced out the glass door toward the parking lot. Down the walkway headed in his direction came a procession of smiling suburbanites: young families, elderly couples, giggling teenagers, all people he had never seen before, dressed in their Sunday best. In the street behind them a dozen or so cars waited in an orderly line to turn into the parking lot. Warren propped the door open and stepped outside to greet his flock.

By the time the service began, the auditorium was three-quarters full. In all, 205 people had turned out—far more than Warren had dared to expect. He would learn later that only five of them professed to be Christians. The rest were exactly the people Warren had hoped to reach: seekers who were interested in God but who had been turned off by traditional church. They had responded to his invitation to come and see what this new way of doing church was all about.

What they saw on that first Sunday was an upbeat and user-friendly service that put no one on the spot, assumed no previous church experience or training, and made no overt demands, yet that in some other ways was not radically different from a traditional service. The service began with the singing of traditional hymns—not "contemporary praise" music or the Christian rock that Warren had embraced as a teenager—and with Kay playing the piano. The lyrics had been modified to eliminate King James English ("thee" and "thou") and unfamiliar religious jargon and were printed in the bulletin so that worshipers would not have to fumble with hymn books. Bible verses related to the morning message also were printed in the bulletin. Essentially everything a person needed to participate in the service was contained in the pamphlets handed to worshipers as they entered the auditorium. While such accommodations would become commonplace at churches later on, Saddleback was breaking new ground in an effort to make unchurched people feel at ease.

Warren's sermon that morning was a low-key evangelistic message entitled "Jesus Sets Us Free" based on John 8:32: "And you shall know the truth, and the truth shall make you free." "What can Jesus set us free from?" Warren asked rhetorically from behind the lectern at the center of the auditorium stage. With practiced skill honed by years of youth revival preaching, he enumerated and expounded upon the answers, carefully framing them in a way he hoped would be grasped easily by nonbelievers. "He sets us free from the pain of yesterday" (the burden of guilt and the poison of bitterness), "from the pressure of today" (personal insecurities and the expectations of others), "and from pessimism about tomorrow" (economic uncertainties and the fear of death). It was a simple salvation message couched more in psychological than theological terms and delivered in a conversational tone, without the pulpit pounding and heavy-handed emotional manipulation that often characterized evangelistic preaching at the time.

Warren spoke for a little more than half an hour and wrapped it up with a personal appeal. "Would you like a fresh start with God? You can have it. How do you do it? Jesus tells us how. 'I stand at the door and knock.' He's talking about coming into your life. 'If anyone hears my voice and opens the door, I will come in and fellowship with him.' . . . Have a relationship with him. Not religion, a relationship! Here's the good news. When Jesus Christ comes into your life, you don't have to clean up your house first. He doesn't say, 'Get your act together and then come to God.' No, he says, 'Let me into your life and I'll help you clean it up. I'll help you get it together.' You need God's power in your life and he says, 'Just let me in.' So what do you have to lose?

The pain of your past, the pressures of today, and pessimism about tomorrow. What do you have to gain if you open up your life to Christ? Everything! My past is forgiven. I get a purpose for living. And I get a home in heaven. What a deal! Why in the world would I walk out on that kind of love? You can have it. You can have it today."

Warren decided against ending the message in the usual Baptist manner, with the standard altar call in which people are exhorted to come down the aisle to accept Christ at the front of the church. Some preachers who used that method were fond of adding a not-so-gentle nudge by reminding their listeners of Jesus' words in the gospel of Matthew: "Whoever acknowledges me before men, I will also acknowledge him before my Father in heaven. But whoever disowns me before men, I will disown him before my Father in heaven." To Warren's way of thinking, that was a browbeating approach that created an unnecessary barrier to conversion—why make people feel uncomfortable? Baptism, after all, was the occasion when new converts made their public profession of faith, not the moment of conversion. He wanted to make it as easy as possible for people to make a commitment to Christ.

Instead of the traditional invitation, he concluded his message by praying a salvation prayer aloud and inviting his listeners to pray along silently. Then he urged them to fill out a "decision card" that had been inserted into each bulletin and indicate "Today I am committing my life to Christ" or "Today I am renewing my commitment" or "I want to join this church" or "I want to be baptized" and drop it into the offering plate. Decision cards were a relatively recent innovation and few churches had yet discovered them, but Warren considered them well suited to his seeker-oriented style of ministry. A count of the cards later revealed that three people had accepted Christ that morning. After just two services, one of them a rehearsal, Saddleback Church had made eight new converts.

Just before the closing hymn, the offering plates were passed. Warren did not make a big pitch for money. He knew that was one of the grievances many people had about churches, so he deliberately avoided saying much about the offering. He could have said plenty. He and members of the Bible study group had gone $6,500 into debt to pay for the mass mailing, newspaper advertisements, rent on the school, and the purchase of equipment for the first service. They had put most of it on their personal credit cards and there was no telling when they would be repaid. The unchurched people in the auditorium that morning had no familiarity with the biblical concept of tithing, giving a tenth of one's income to support the work of the church. Warren felt he would be fortunate if many of them tossed a five- or ten-dollar bill into the offering plate. While every little bit helped, it would not be nearly enough to sustain the church. Eventually he would have to teach them about tithing, but not on the first day.

After the service Warren retreated to the front door to shake hands with the departing visitors. He was delighted with the positive feedback he received. People congratulated him on his message. They thanked him for the warm welcome and friendliness they were shown. The upbeat, informal tone he had hoped to set apparently had resonated, and many of the visitors promised they would come back.

When the last person had left the building Warren headed back to the auditorium to help break down the equipment and load it onto a truck in the parking lot. On the way he was accosted by the church treasurer—a CPA who had been saved at the previous week's rehearsal service—who came hurrying down the hallway with a bag containing the morning offering in one hand and a check in the other. She explained that a man who had been sitting on the front row had dropped the check into the offering plate. It was for $1,000. Warren took the check and stared at it for a moment, then handed it back to the treasurer. "You know," he said quietly, "I think this thing is going to work."

OVER THE NEXT TEN WEEKS, fifty people made commitments to Christ at Sunday services in the Laguna Hills High School auditorium. Worship attendance, after falling by about one hundred the week after Easter, as had been expected, climbed steadily until it passed the 130 mark. Saddleback Valley Community Church was on its way. In a little over two months, it had grown larger than nearly half of the Southern Baptist churches in all of California at the time—an amazing feat that caught the attention of denominational leaders in the state.

Late in May, a writer for the *California Southern Baptist*, the official publication of the state convention, visited Saddleback and wrote a feature article that appeared in the June 5 issue with a picture of the Warren family on the cover. The article recounted the story of Warren's call, his arrival in Orange County, and the early steps and new methods he and his coworkers employed in launching the new congregation. It quoted him at length describing the hand of Providence at work—from the exchange of letters with Herman Wooten to the last-minute securing of financial support. "I could go on all day talking about the miracles which have happened in the development of this work," Warren told the magazine. The article also quoted the pastor of the Crescent church, which had sponsored Warren, as seeming to claim substantial credit for Saddleback's successful start. "At the very outset of this work, we hired Rick on a full-time basis," the pastor was quoted as saying. "He spent time in preparation. We sent out the direct-mail invitations, went door-to-door to invite people to come, and followed up with cards and telephone calls . . . God has blessed our work on every hand." Warren years later would dismiss the article as filled with inaccuracies.

Yet it succeeded in putting him on the map within the denomination. A few months later, a national Southern Baptist publication, *Missions USA*, produced a laudatory five-page spread on Warren and what it dubbed his "mail order church." It described southern Orange County as "one of the nation's fastest growing, most affluent areas," yet one that had "proved a difficult location for Southern Baptist church starting. Then a young seminary graduate began to apply public relations techniques—including direct mail campaigns—to attract visitors." As a result, his Saddleback Valley church had become "the fastest growing congregation in Laguna Hills."

Although the article accurately described some of Warren's strategies and techniques and was decidedly favorable in its tone, it included a photo caption that mistakenly referred to the new congregation as "the Laguna Hills Baptist Church." The misidentification may have been an innocent error, but it touched on a sore spot that had emerged in Warren's dealings with local and state Baptist leaders over his decision not to use "Baptist" in the church's name. Taking a cue from Robert Schuller, Warren had decided early on to name his church Saddleback Valley

Community Church. Like Schuller, he was convinced that a denominational label would add nothing to the church's appeal to unchurched suburbanites. Identifying itself as Southern Baptist, in fact, was more likely to evoke Deep South stereotypes that would repel affluent Orange County residents. Still, Warren insisted that his church would be fully committed to Southern Baptist doctrine and would participate in many of the denomination's state and national programs. Only after people began attending the church would they learn of its affiliations, but by then, Warren hoped, the stereotypes would be shattered.

That strategy did not sit well with lay leaders of the Crescent Baptist Church, which had agreed to sponsor Warren and his work. In negotiating terms of the arrangement, members of the church's missions committee had insisted that the new congregation include "Baptist" in its name as a condition of its support. Warren held his ground and the church's pastor ultimately sided with him. Meanwhile, at the California Southern Baptist Convention headquarters in Fresno, some staff members had begun speculating aloud that Warren's refusal to use the Baptist name indicated a lack of commitment to the denomination. "They took it to mean that he was ashamed of being a Baptist," Harry Williams, the former state director of evangelism and longtime Warren mentor, recalled. "In the first place, they didn't believe his new methods would really work, and if they did work he would probably go independent. They were convinced that the denomination's Home Mission Board would never recoup the support they had given him."

They were proven wrong. By the end of the second year, Warren's church became a regular supporter of the denomination's Cooperative Program, its main financial channel for funding missions and educational programs. Within a year and a half it would become financially self-sustaining and would stop accepting monthly support from the denomination and from other churches.

WARREN WAS DETERMINED TO BUILD SADDLEBACK by winning new converts and then discipling them and training them to take on increasing responsibilities in the church and in its outreach to the community. That was in sharp contrast to the traditional approach of church planting at the time, which involved taking a small group of mature believers from one church and transplanting them into a new community as the committed core of a new congregation.

There were strengths and weaknesses to both approaches. Doing it the traditional way meant that a new congregation was assured of having a steady financial base—a group of people who were accustomed to tithing and could be counted on to keep the church on solid financial footing. The core group of mature believers also could serve as mentors and models of the faith to new converts and could fill slots as Sunday school teachers, choir members, musicians, and so on. The down side, from Warren's perspective, was that it also tended to limit flexibility. Church people usually were accustomed to doing church in traditional ways. Getting them to enthusiastically embrace new approaches could be a problem, one he knew he would not have with more malleable beginners.

Consequently, he turned down an offer from the Crescent church to assign a number of its families to seed the new congregation. A major portion of Crescent's members were transplants from the South, Warren reasoned, and the church itself had a strong southern flavor that he believed would not blend well with the suburbanites he was trying to reach in the Saddleback Valley. He preferred to do it on his own.

EARLY IN JUNE OF THAT YEAR, Warren's former summer evangelism team partner, Steve Williams, who had recently become the pastor of a small church in Fresno, along with his wife, Jean, stopped in for a visit while vacationing in Southern California. The two couples spent hours laughing and sharing memories of their summers traveling around the state with the youth evangelism teams, and Rick and Steve brought each other up to date on their new ministries.

Over dinner at a restaurant one evening, Rick described in some detail to his friend the sometimes nerve-wracking launch of Saddleback and his so-far successful efforts to build a church from scratch by using direct mail to reach behind closed doors and designing services and messages that appealed to nonbelievers. As Williams listened he found himself thinking, "Man, this makes so much sense! This is how we ought to be doing church."

After dinner, as they were driving to an ice cream parlor, Warren shared that he had begun thinking of bringing on an additional pastor. "If we're going to keep growing we'll need more staff," he said, "because a church typically won't go beyond two hundred if it has only one pastor. Who do you think I could get?" They began brainstorming and Williams tossed out several names. One of his suggestions seemed quite promising, but then Williams remembered that the young man had not yet gone to seminary and probably would not want to take a position until he had done so. Warren noted that Golden Gate Baptist Seminary had opened a satellite campus in Southern California a few years earlier and suggested that the man could go to seminary there while working at Saddleback.

Suddenly it was as if a light switched on inside Williams's head. He also had not gone to seminary and for some time had wanted to start, but there was no seminary in Fresno. "You're talking about a full-time position, right?" he asked, "because I might be interested." Warren nearly drove off the road. He couldn't believe what he had heard. "You'd be interested in coming to Saddleback?" The women in the backseat wondered what was going on. "What are you two talking about?" Before the evening was over the two couples had decided that Williams would join the Saddleback staff as Warren's assistant and second full-time pastor. Within two months, Warren raised enough additional financial support, along with growing income from the offering plate, to bring Williams on staff. He started work that fall.

As Warren's assistant, Williams was assigned a variety of tasks including occasional preaching on Sundays and teaching a class on discipleship. His primary duties involved follow-up with visitors and new converts and organizing the growing congregation into small groups—home Bible studies, men's fellowship groups, and the like—which would go on to become such an important part of Saddleback's organizational structure. All of that freed Warren to focus more on his preaching, although he quickly found that as the congregation grew he was spending an increasing amount of time counseling, visiting the sick, and generally caring for the needs of his flock. And in a flock consisting mostly of brand-new converts and not-yet believers, the needs were plentiful.

Shortly after Williams arrived, Saddleback's attendance passed the 150 mark. Roughly two-thirds of the congregation were new believers who needed lots of attention, training, and support, and they looked to Warren to provide it. He confided to Kay one day that he felt like the director of a spiritual orphanage. "There is a sense, when you start a church, that for the first two years the pastor is the glue," he explained. "People relate to you. They don't know each other, so there aren't any real relationships yet. Pretty much you're the glue, and if you leave, the church is going to die. Now that's okay, but the goal is to wean them of that so that they don't need you." Before Williams arrived, Warren carried the entire load. "I literally was doing all the preaching, teaching, praying, baptizing, caring, counseling and it was just all on me."

Even with Williams sharing the burden, the workload itself was expanding. During the week Warren worked out of an office in his home, which meant that on most days his workday never came to a distinguishable end. He soon found himself working sixteen to eighteen hours, Monday through Saturday. Sundays at the school, as busy as they were, often tended to be the least stressful day of the week. He was working hard and fast, but he felt exhilarated—he was doing exactly what he believed he was meant to do. Yet the pace was beginning to take a toll.

By mid-December, Saddleback's attendance surpassed two hundred—a level unheard of at the time in a church less than a year old. On December 28, the last Sunday of the year, attendance slipped slightly from the previous week, which had been expected: at most churches, the Sunday service before Christmas is one of the best attended of the year. Still, the day was no less taxing for Warren. He had arrived at the school early that morning as usual to help with the setup. He taught a membership class at nine o'clock and led a men's Bible study at ten, which was followed immediately by the eleven o'clock worship service. In between those events he had greeted visitors and was stopped in the hallway by church members who had urgent questions or who needed his advice or his prayers. When it came time to deliver the morning message, he felt as though he had been running on a treadmill for hours.

As Warren stood to preach he found himself a little short of breath and, for a moment, felt a bit light-headed. He thought at first that he had stood up too quickly. He gripped the lectern to steady himself and as he started speaking the wooziness seemed to subside. He launched into his message, but within a few minutes another tinge of dizziness swept over him. He paused and glanced down at his notes. He could barely make out the words on the page—the light in the room seemed to have faded as though someone had turned down a dimmer switch. He picked up his notes and held them closer to his face, but the words were blurry and he lost his place. He stammered as he tried in vain to recover his train of thought. Suddenly he felt a wave of panic welling up inside. His temples began throbbing and he felt cold sweat drops rolling down his back. He glanced down at his notes again and tried to force himself to continue, but the pages had gone completely blank. He looked up and the faces of his congregation had disappeared in a gauzy haze. He felt his legs begin to surrender.

"Steve, I need you to come up and finish. I'm not feeling well," he said weakly. "I'm sorry, folks. I'm going to have to sit down." Warren took a seat in the front row and Williams came to the lectern and ad-libbed his way through a truncated version of Warren's message.

The service ended early and the Warrens hurried out of the building and went immediately to their car. Rick still was feeling weak, so Kay climbed into the driver's seat. On the silent ride home, she glanced over at her husband, who sat slouched in the seat next to her, his head leaning up against the window, his eyes closed. She worried about him and wondered if they ever would get to the bottom of these recurring spells that she had come to think of as anxiety attacks. This one had been the worst of them all. He had virtually collapsed. Whatever was causing it, it seemed out of control.

She looked in the rearview mirror at their eighteen-month-old daughter asleep in her car seat and wondered what would become of them—this young family, just starting out in what they believed was a lifelong mission from God, and this fledgling church that had sprung so vibrantly to life so quickly and that seemed to hold such promise. What would become of them all?

Early that afternoon up in Redwood Valley, Jimmy and Dot Warren were just sitting down to Sunday dinner with a new young pastor and his wife when the telephone rang. Jimmy excused himself from the table to take the call. When he returned a few minutes later his face was ashen. "We need to pray for Rick, right now," he said, his voice quivering with emotion. "It looks like his preaching days are over."

# CHAPTER NINE

# Out of the Desert

ON THE MORNING AFTER HIS COLLAPSE in the Saddleback pulpit, Warren loaded his family into the car and drove to Redwood Valley to be comforted by his parents and to recuperate in the quiet isolation of his boyhood home in rural Northern California, far from the demands of his needy flock. After a few days of rest they headed south to the Arizona desert to spend some time with Kay's parents just outside of Phoenix. They would end up staying for nearly a month.

Although physically on the mend, emotionally Warren remained in a fragile state. The spell of dizziness and blurred vision that he experienced was by then a familiar occurrence, although this episode had been the worst. But that was only part of it. For the first time in his life he felt overwhelmed by discouragement and self-doubt—the almost legendary self-confidence he had exuded since childhood suddenly seemed in tatters. Just nine months into a ministry that he believed was God-ordained and would last a lifetime, he had begun to feel that it was more than he could handle. He wasn't sure when—if ever—he would return to Saddleback.

DURING HIS TIME IN ARIZONA, Warren followed a daily routine that would enable him to slowly decompress and begin to heal. He went to bed earlier and slept later than he ever could at home and found that his body craved the sleep—the frantic pace he had been keeping during the previous year had taken a toll. He was just physically exhausted. After breakfast he would take long walks alone in the desert to pray and clear his thoughts and to begin to plumb the crippling emotions that had overtaken him. In those solitary moments of introspection he began to discern that behind the paralyzing panic attacks, which lately had become more frequent, were deep-seated fears that, up to this point, he had been unable or unwilling to recognize.

"What are you afraid of, Rick?" he asked himself aloud one morning in the desert. The answers that came were discomforting. He was twenty-six years old and pastor of a church that had grown from zero to two hundred in less than a year, an amazing achievement that had received wide notice. He earnestly believed that God was blessing the work, and yet he did not fully understand why. "God, I'm not worthy of this," he confessed aloud. "I don't deserve this blessing. I'm not the man of God I ought to be. I have difficulty just being faithful in daily prayer and reading my Bible. What business do I have being a pastor?" He felt like an imposter and it frightened him.

He had seen this "imposter syndrome" at work as he had counseled others, where a person's giftedness exceeded his character—the talented musician whose offstage persona was not competent to accept the accolades of the crowd, the gifted surgeon who received public adoration for his lifesaving skills but whose private life was a shambles, the preacher who was widely acclaimed as a man of God and a stalwart of the faith yet who harbored secret doubts and shame. They could be found everywhere, in every occupation. Each felt like an imposter and lived in fear of being exposed. Some would even sabotage their own careers just to end the charade. Warren shared that fearful sense of foreboding. "I don't deserve to be doing any of this," he said.

Then he recognized a second and related fear: Saddleback was growing so fast that he simply was not equipped for what lay ahead. He knew that at its current growth trajectory the church could number several thousand within just a few years. Perhaps other pastors had the talent and expertise to lead a congregation of that size, but he did not—not at his young age. It was all he could do to lead a church of two hundred, and lately it seemed he was not up to even that. His celebrated vision for a church of twenty thousand now seemed like a frightening delusion. Saddleback was growing much too quickly and it was beyond his personal and professional capability to keep up. "God, this is just more than I can handle," he moaned.

Warren felt unworthy and he felt out of his league, and standing alone in the Arizona desert on a balmy January day he slipped into a deep depression. He longed to hear from God, to receive some immediate knowledge, some intuitive word that he would recognize as God's voice, assuring him that his fears were unfounded, that in fact he *was* deserving and capable of the ministry he had been given, and that all would be well—and the deep funk that had descended over him would be lifted. He had heard from God at pivotal moments in the past. He needed to hear from God again. And so he waited.

And finally one day it arrived, an inaudible inner voice that Warren found soothingly familiar but also relentlessly penetrating and direct.

*"You're right, Rick. You don't deserve it. You never will deserve it. You don't even deserve to be saved."*

It was not exactly what Warren had been hoping to hear. But he recognized the distinct echo of the New Testament book of Ephesians ("For it is by grace you have been saved, through faith—and this not from yourselves, it is the gift of God—not by works, so that no one can boast") and he knew that it was true. Salvation was a gift, fully unmerited, imparted by a loving God who "gave his only begotten son"— in the familiar words of the gospel of John—so that "whosoever believes in him should not perish but have everlasting life." Warren had preached from that passage countless times. He knew that nothing he or anyone else ever could achieve in life could add to or subtract from what Jesus Christ accomplished on the cross on their behalf. Christ had given his life as "a ransom for many," according to the Scriptures, and not because people deserved it. Warren knew that just the opposite was true, that "while we were yet sinners, Christ died for us."

Warren understood that no one was deserving of salvation, least of all himself. And now this inner voice that he sensed was from God was telling him that the same was true of his life's calling.

*"Since when have you deserved anything, Rick? Don't you get it? You don't have to earn my blessing. It's all grace."*

All grace. Just like his salvation, Warren's ministry was unearned and undeserved. It, too, was a gift from God. And in that moment Warren realized that he had nothing to prove—to God, to himself, or to anyone else. The smile of God on his life did not depend upon his personal or professional achievements or even upon his virtue. Everything that God did in him, and through him, and to him, and for him—it was all by grace. It was all God's unmerited favor. Standing alone in the desert, Warren saw starkly that he was just an ordinary, flawed individual whom God had saved and called to the ministry and now was using to accomplish God's purposes in the place where God had set him. He had no reason to be ashamed of his shortcomings or to pretend to be something he was not. What he needed most was to be authentic, to take God more seriously and himself less seriously. His call to the ministry and to Saddleback was all about God. It was not about him.

Warren suddenly felt as though a heavy burden had been lifted. Yet his anxiety was not entirely dispelled. He still felt ill-prepared for the rapid growth of his young congregation and saw no clear way forward; he had no clear notion of how to shepherd such a burgeoning flock. In his seminary research of big churches, and from Robert Schuller and others, he had learned some strategies for getting unchurched people to attend church, and so far those strategies had worked. People were coming to Saddleback's services in surprising numbers and were responding positively to his evangelistic messages—many accepting Christ for the first time. But after that, what? How would Warren continue ministering to potentially thousands of new believers and help them to grow in the faith? How would he turn such a large and disparate crowd of needy individuals into a thriving and cohesive congregation? Nothing he had learned at seminary had adequately prepared him for so great a task.

As Warren wrestled with the uncertainties, a familiar story from the Old Testament came to his mind. The Israelites, after forty years of wandering in the wilderness, were about to enter the Promised Land. Moses had just died and it was left to Joshua to lead God's people as a mighty army into Canaan to take possession of the land. Some of the Israelites were fearful. They had seen the enemy's fortified cities and knew that they were outnumbered. How could they possibly cast out such a powerful foe and take possession of the land as God had commanded? But the Lord reassured them, "Do not be afraid . . . the Lord your God will clear away these nations before you little by little." There was no need to confront the entire enemy in one decisive battle. Victory would come incrementally, by winning many smaller battles spread over time, and the Lord would give the Israelites just the strength and courage they would need to fight each one successfully.

As Warren reflected on the story it occurred to him that perhaps it had been a mistake to focus on the magnitude of his vision—building a church of twenty thousand members—and then to fret about whether or not he was equipped now to reach that goal. Perhaps he needed to focus more on the tasks immediately before him as Saddleback's pastor, not forgetting the overarching vision but trusting God for the strength and ability to handle just this day's challenges, and then tomorrow's, and then the next day's until, little by little, the Saddleback vision would be fulfilled. Was that where he had gotten off track? Was that what it would take to build his church?

Once again Warren sensed that God was speaking to him.

*"Rick, whose church is it?"*

In his mind he responded. "Well, Lord, it's your church."

*"I will build my church. You focus on building people, and I will build the church."*

It seemed so simple yet it made so much sense. Warren had always recognized that his primary role as a pastor was to point people to the kingdom of God both by preaching the Gospel and modeling the spirit-filled life, and then, after people were saved, to move them forward through instruction and mentoring until they became mature Christians capable of ministering to others. He knew that just getting people saved and on the church membership rolls was not sufficient. It was a pastor's job to build his people up, to see that they were growing spiritually. When people grew spiritually the church was strong and healthy, and a healthy church was a growing church. With a great sense of relief, Warren realized that he no longer had to worry about numbers. God would provide the increase. It was a division of labor that he could embrace with enthusiasm.

"Lord, you've got a deal!"

He imagined himself in his study at home, getting up out of his chair and saying to the Lord, "It's your chair now. You are the pastor of this church." He knew that it was not up to his creativity or energy or cleverness to make Saddleback Church happen. Ultimately it was God's responsibility. Warren was responsible for building up people. God would build the church.

AT THE END OF JANUARY Warren went home to Orange County with a renewed commitment to his ministry and a new understanding of his role as pastor. Years later he would look back on his introspective encounter in the Arizona desert and the decisions that came out of it as the seminal event in the formulation of his celebrated Purpose-Driven philosophy of ministry, which he would begin to develop over the next several years. He was convinced now that Saddleback would work regardless of his own relative strengths and shortcomings because he believed that God was in it. He was determined to focus on being a caring shepherd to his flock and let God do the rest.

Warren accepted his new marching orders on faith, and intellectually he was satisfied and reassured. But his ragged emotions were not so easily mollified. As he resumed his pastoral duties that winter, the dark cloud that had enveloped him did not dissipate and he felt powerless against its inexorable downward pull. He would go through the entire year of 1981 in a state of depression.

ON JANUARY 25, HIS FIRST SUNDAY BACK, Warren returned to the pulpit and preached a sermon entitled "How to Pray and Get Answers." The following week he preached on "How to Handle Dry Spells." Both messages were rooted in his own recent experience and in what he felt he had learned as a result. On the third week he had arranged for Billy Hanks Jr., his former ministry supervisor from Fort Worth, to fill in, and Warren was thankful to have a break. It was clear to all that the young Saddleback pastor was not back to full strength. He seemed tentative and subdued in the pulpit as he wrestled with the lingering fatigue and the spells that had gotten the best of him in late December. Prior to each service he confided to Steve Williams that he was not certain he would be able to complete the morning message and said Williams should be prepared to step in if needed.

After a few services, Williams began to lose patience with his friend and coworker. One Sunday he confronted Warren and told him that he was "wimping out"—that he was letting his fear and anxiety get the best of him. This was not the Rick Warren that Williams remembered from their summer youth revival days—the fearless street-corner evangelist who had witnessed boldly to drunken marines as they staggered out of the saloons in Barstow in the middle of the night. It irritated and disappointed Williams that Warren had allowed himself to become so timid, and he let him know it in no uncertain terms. "Come on, Rick. Shake it off, man! You're just psyching yourself out!" Yet no amount of scolding would snap Warren out of his deep funk.

Kay saw the change in her husband as well and it troubled her. She had been aware of his occasional spells since shortly after they became engaged in college and she wrote them off as bouts of anxiety. But now it seemed that he was increasingly unable to cope with situations that had never bothered him before. The panic attacks that often struck on Sundays when Warren was in the pulpit suddenly seemed to occur whenever he stood to speak, no matter how small the audience. Teaching new-member classes and leading Bible studies had become excruciatingly difficult. The person she had known to be outgoing, witty, and self-confident—even cocky—suddenly had become cautious and reserved and was struggling to hold it together, and neither she nor Rick knew what to do about it. Years later she would describe it as a "difficult, depressing time for both of us."

Throughout that year Warren clung tenaciously to the Saddleback vision—that of building a great church with far-reaching missionary impact—and to the promise he brought home from the Arizona desert that God would make it happen. Yet as he labored on week by week, trying to be a good pastor to his growing flock, as he later would recount, his heart's cry was not, "Oh, God, build a great church," but rather, "Oh, God, help me make it through the weekend." After preaching each Sunday he would go home and fall into bed, where he would spend the rest of the day physically and emotionally drained. Occasionally he scheduled Williams or a guest preacher to deliver the Sunday morning message, but he considered it his primary duty as pastor to feed his flock, and so he braced himself each weekend and did what he knew needed to be done despite the stress and discomfort he felt each time he ascended the pulpit. He was determined he would not give in to the panic or the pain. He was reminded of the apostle Paul, who carried

Prophet of Purpose

out his preaching ministry despite having a "thorn in the flesh"—some unspecified physical affliction that the Lord refused to take away. From that experience Paul learned humility and the importance of relying on God's strength rather than his own. "I delight in weaknesses," the apostle was able to declare. "For when I am weak, then I am strong." Perhaps this affliction was Warren's thorn in the flesh. Whatever it was, he was not about to give up.

OVER THE NEXT FEW MONTHS Warren preached a series of messages based on the parables of Jesus and another on "God's Wisdom for Today's Living," in which he presented what was intended as practical, biblical advice on everything from finding fulfillment at work to personal finance and time management. They were exactly the kind of "positive, practical messages" that Warren had promised in his open letter to the community, and people responded to them favorably. After falling back to an average of about 150 immediately after Warren's collapse, church attendance slowly began to recover. It surpassed 200 on several Sundays that spring—including 303 at the Easter service, which had to be moved to the school gymnasium—and by the end of June average attendance had stabilized at around 190.

In August Kay gave birth to their second child, Joshua James, an event that ignited a fresh spark of joy in the Warren household. The oppressive veil of melancholy that had hung so stubbornly over them finally showed signs of lifting.

That fall the church experienced another growth spurt—more than 400 showed up for one early November service—and they added a second Sunday morning service to accommodate the growing crowds. By the end of the year Saddleback's average attendance approached the 250 mark. In the twenty-one months since the church began, more than 310 people had accepted Christ under Warren's preaching. New converts were receiving discipleship training in classes, taught by Williams, which were based on the instruction plan Warren had sketched out as a youth pastor in Norwalk and were designed to guide them through the stages of spiritual growth from new believer to church member to lay minister. Working together, the two young pastors had begun to succeed at what some more seasoned ministers believed implausible—they were

—128—

building a church from the ground up almost entirely of converts. Warren's vision of a "church for the unchurched" was becoming a reality.

The following year, 1982, brought continued growth to Saddleback and renewed energy and optimism to Warren. He was hitting his stride in the pulpit. Each week his messages focused on the problems of everyday life and in many of them he seemed to be preaching to himself as much as to his congregation; his sermon topics addressed a litany of issues that Warren himself had been facing—"How to Handle Discouragement," "How to Survive Under Stress," "How to Feel Good About Yourself," "How to Stay Calm in a Crisis," "How to Keep On Keeping On." He concluded each message by pointing to Jesus as the ultimate answer to all of life's problems and each week two, three, four, or more of his listeners committed their lives to Christ.

By the end of summer Saddleback's weekly attendance had topped three hundred and Warren and Williams believed that God was blessing their work. But they soon recognized that they would need help in training and educating the growing flock. In November, Warren decided it was time to bring on a third pastor.

His leading candidate was Glen Kreun, a retired navy intelligence analyst who was fourteen years Warren's senior and who had recently begun working as an associate pastor at a church in Vallejo, just north of San Francisco. Kreun was just one year out of Golden Gate Baptist Theological Seminary, where he had been a friend and classmate of Warren's brother-in-law, Tom Holladay. (Holladay and Chaundel Warren had met in high school in Ukiah, began dating at California Baptist College, and were married at the seminary in 1978.) Holladay knew Kreun to be an able administrator with a sharp mind for business. Prior to enrolling in seminary, Kreun had planned to study for an MBA after he left the navy. Instead he earned a master's degree in Christian education and, not fancying himself a preacher, felt called to a ministry of providing educational and administrative support to a church's senior pastor. It was exactly the job description that Warren had in mind.

Based largely on Holladay's recommendation, Warren telephoned Kreun in November and asked him to pray about coming to work with him at Saddleback. Kreun, who grew up in rural Minnesota, had turned down other offers mostly because he did not sense a divine call to a new assignment, but also because he was quite contented living in Vallejo, where he was just minutes away from the Solano County farm country. He had absolutely no desire to move to the congested suburban sprawl of Southern California. Nonetheless, he agreed to pray about it and in December Kreun drove down for an interview and to visit Saddleback Church. Recalling that meeting later, Kreun said, "I had to laugh. There I was in an interview—I'm forty-two years old and he's twenty-eight—and he's talking about a church of twenty thousand. I thought, 'I like that. This guy is never going to make twenty thousand. But at least he has a vision. He has a goal he's aiming for. Most pastors don't.'"

They talked about Warren's vision and his plans for the church and both described what they considered to be their strengths and weaknesses as ministers. Both went away from the meeting impressed. A week later, Warren phoned Kreun again and offered him the job. Kreun accepted, and just after Christmas he and his wife, Greta, and their nineteen-year-old daughter, Glenda, moved to Orange County. Kreun started work in January as Saddleback's pastor of education and administration.

Almost immediately, Warren and Kreun developed a synergetic relationship that brought a new spark of creativity and efficiency to the Saddleback ministry. In almost every respect they were exact opposites. Warren, at six foot two, was a big man with a big personality—garrulous and outgoing. He was a visionary preacher and a gifted communicator and motivator, an idea man who had no desire to be bogged down in a project's details. "Rick cruises at the twenty-thousand-foot level," Kreun later would observe. "That's where he works best." Kreun, on the other hand, at five foot ten, was amiable but reserved, with a bespectacled bookish appearance and an analytical mind that relished the challenge of organizing a project and working out the details. They complemented one another perfectly. While they could not have known it at the time, the working relationship they established that year would last for decades.

Kreun quickly set about organizing and staffing an education program covering the entire congregation, from toddlers to adults. It included an expanded Sunday school program with a coordinated curriculum, a restructured class for new members, weeknight Bible studies, and other special classes for training volunteers. As the church's chief administrator, he managed and monitored the church's budget, its use of facilities and equipment, and its paid and volunteer staff. Warren and Williams, meanwhile, were free to focus their energies on preaching and evangelism and on ministering to the special needs of the congregation.

With so much systematic training and mentoring going on, lay members of the church soon began carrying an increasing share of the ministry workload, just as Warren had hoped and intended. Newly trained volunteers were teaching Bible classes, serving as small-group leaders or as mentors to new converts, and performing a host of other ministry tasks. By giving the ministry away to the laity the Saddleback pastors were multiplying the church's outreach in the community and were touching lives that they never could have reached on their own. It was proving to be an effective and productive ministry approach, and by the end of the year, regular attendance surpassed the 350 mark.

In reaching out to the community and inviting new believers to participate in Saddleback's ministry, Warren and his staff were careful to foster an attitude of acceptance of people who, having come from the ranks of the previously unchurched, were not in the least familiar with the cultural expectations of evangelical churches, or with traditional Southern Baptist ways in particular. "We're not here to put people down," Warren reminded his staff, noting that Christ "didn't come into the world to condemn it but to save it . . . We don't expect unbelievers to act like believers until they are. You know, I could have gotten up [in church] and said, 'Everybody who's living together, who's shacking up—get out of here until you get married!' No, they're coming to church. If there's any place I want them, I want them in church."

As laudable as it may have been, that welcoming attitude resulted in a few awkward moments in those early days. One Sunday during the second year, two young men—both recent converts—had been invited to sing a sacred duet in the morning worship service. One of the men showed up wearing a T-shirt with a Budweiser beer label on the front and the words "Damn, I'm Good!" emblazoned across the back. They sang their song with great gusto and sat down, and the service went on without a hiccup. At most Southern Baptist churches, where cussing and beer drinking are reviled as unregenerate behavior, such a scene undoubtedly would have stirred apoplectic protestations. The unruffled Saddleback crowd, however, did not flinch and Warren would take great delight in telling the story for years to come.

THROUGH THE FOLLOWING YEAR, 1983, the churchwide education program that Kreun had organized became a catalyst for a new wave of church growth. By spring the restructured Sunday school had undergone such rapid expansion that Kreun decided to move all adult classes off campus in order to free up more classroom space for children and youth, a move that produced an almost immediate spurt in Sunday morning attendance. Also, as a result of that change, the number of small groups meeting in homes on weeknights began to multiply and soon became the primary means of adult education at Saddleback. Eventually those groups would comprise the structural foundation of a burgeoning regional megachurch and its expanding army of lay ministers. Small groups would provide the interpersonal connections that are difficult to achieve in large congregations. As Warren would often explain later on, the church would grow bigger by becoming smaller.

Early 1984 saw the church's regular weekly attendance break through the 400 mark for the first time, and the numbers continued to roll. In just four years' time, 573 people had accepted Christ at Saddleback and 234 were baptized. Meanwhile, Saddleback had helped to sponsor the launch of four "daughter" churches, most of them in Hispanic neighborhoods of Orange County. Warren and his two ministry partners appeared to be well on their way to fulfilling Warren's vision of building a church of new believers. But all was not going as smoothly as it seemed. Unlike the synergy that had quickly developed between Warren and Kreun because of their complementary talents and personalities, Warren and Williams shared similar gifts. Both were strong and creative leaders who were passionate and opinionated and they often found themselves spinning against each other on matters of ministry. While they got along well on a personal level, it was proving not to be the most productive of working relationships.

Late that winter Warren received a call from a church in San Mateo, just south of San Francisco, inviting him to come and be their pastor. Warren, of course, was not interested and he declined the offer, but he told them about Williams and said he thought he would be perfect for the job. That spring Williams left Saddleback to become senior pastor of the Western Hills Baptist Church in San Mateo. A few years later he would go on to Fresno, where he would build a church of some nineteen hundred members. While Williams and Warren would remain friends, for the next several years Warren and Kreun would carry on the work at Saddleback alone.

CHAPTER TEN

## *Promised Land*

EVEN BEFORE HE LEFT SEMINARY IT WAS Warren's intention to buy land and build his church in the planned upscale community of Aliso Viejo, just next door to Laguna Hills. Most new churches in southern Orange County at the time were built on an acre or less, which usually was more than enough space for a modern church building and adequate off-street parking for a few hundred worshipers. But Warren's plan was much more ambitious. His publicly proclaimed vision called for acquiring fifty acres and constructing a parklike campus that would accommodate a congregation of twenty thousand. Yet his original concept did not include a church building per se. Instead he would begin by building a Christian school, kindergarten through the twelfth grade, and a campus that consisted of an educational building, a recreation center, and a civic auditorium that would be made available to the community throughout the week. The church would use the facilities on weekends.

Warren decided on that approach after learning of a Southern Baptist congregation in Memphis that had gone that unconventional route a few years earlier. He knew of plenty of churches that had added schools to an already established church program, but found few that had attempted the reverse. In February 1979, he went to Memphis to visit the East Park Baptist Church, which had erected a $6 million school and auditorium on twenty-five acres of land. He met with the church's pastor and the architect who designed the buildings and came home with $50,000 worth of blueprints and the intention of duplicating the project in the Saddleback Valley. Financially it just seemed to make sense given the high price of land in Southern California. If successful, a private school would provide a revenue stream and attract community backing that an upstart church on its own would find difficult to match. Building a school first, Warren believed, would help him accomplish his ultimate goal of building a megachurch congregation.

He dropped the idea almost as soon as he arrived in Orange County. While he had anticipated correctly that buying land in the Saddleback Valley would be a challenge, he had no idea just how great the challenge would be until late in 1980 when he learned that a forty-acre parcel in nearby Mission Viejo had just sold for a whopping $40 million. He decided then that his dream of building a fifty-acre church-school campus would have to be put on hold until his congregation, which then was running about 175, grew substantially larger. Meanwhile, as he began refocusing his efforts on "building up people," he became increasingly concerned that in a church-school combination, the operational demands of the school could easily overshadow those of the congregation and the school would become the main priority. He reminded himself that he was called to be a pastor, not a headmaster, and so he jettisoned the school plan entirely.

That important decision was quickly followed by another major change of plans. In July 1981, the nation's economy plunged into the worst recession since the Great Depression. In an attempt to curb inflation, which had soared to 13.5 percent in the aftermath of the 1979 energy crisis, the Federal Reserve raised interest rates, deliberately precipitating a business slowdown and an accompanying spike in unemployment. Especially hard hit were the steel, automobile, and housing industries, and homebuilding in Southern California nearly ground to a halt. In the midst of the economic turmoil, groundbreaking on the planned community of Aliso Viejo was postponed indefinitely. Warren began looking for a new location for Saddleback's permanent home.

His attention quickly turned to the opposite side of the Santa Ana Freeway from Laguna Hills, closer to the mountains in an area surrounding a newly sprouting community called Rancho Santa Margarita. It was hardly more than a cow pasture when Warren first arrived in southern Orange County, but by the early 1980s houses and shopping centers had begun to appear. While construction there had slowed as a result of the recession, at least it was under way. It seemed clear to Warren that the Rancho Santa Margarita area represented the new growing edge of the Saddleback Valley and perhaps held more promise as a potential home for his congregation.

Meanwhile, even though he had set aside any immediate plans to buy land, Warren decided in 1983 that property in Orange County was not about to get any cheaper and that the time had come to begin raising funds for an eventual purchase. In May of that year he hired a professional fund-raising firm from Dallas to conduct a capital campaign within the congregation, which by then numbered about 350. The monthlong campaign was called "Together We Grow" and included a series of motivational messages by Warren in which he offered advice on "how to grow to your greatest potential," "how to accomplish the impossible," and "how to hear God speak." While the campaign was not an overwhelming fund-raising success, it succeeded in raising the general level of enthusiasm within the congregation for Warren's church-growth vision and in heightening the awareness of the sacrifices it would take to become a church of twenty thousand members.

It also opened some fissures within the flock. A handful of church members, including some influential lay leaders, let it be known that they were quite comfortable with Saddleback at its present size. They knew most of their fellow worshipers by name, knew their children, and even knew their pets' names. If anyone was sick and missed a Sunday it did not escape their notice. They saw Saddleback as a caring and intimate congregation and they wanted to keep it that way. Had they wanted to be part of a large church, they complained, they could have gone to one of several that were thriving in the area—Chuck Smith's fifteen-thousand-member Calvary Chapel just thirteen miles away in Costa Mesa, for example, or Robert Schuller's Crystal Cathedral in nearby Garden Grove. Instead they had come to Saddleback because it was new and because it was small, and they announced that if Warren insisted on pursuing a plan to turn it into a megachurch they just might decide to leave. Without hesitating Warren responded: "Well then, good-bye."

At about the same time, the church treasurer and another influential layman objected to a plan to buy a computer system for the church to handle its financial records, keep track of the membership database, and perform other office tasks that were becoming more cumbersome as the congregation continued to grow. Personal computers were brand new on the market and relatively expensive; the three computers Warren and Kreun proposed purchasing would cost about $15,000 total. The two disgruntled lay leaders insisted it was a waste of money—the church would never need three computers—and when the pastors refused to concede they resigned in protest.

In all, several families left the church during that contentious period, including some key leaders and tithers, and despite Warren's firm resolve to stick with what he regarded as a God-inspired plan for Saddleback's future, he harbored some regrets. "My initial thought was, 'What was I thinking?' " he admitted later. "Now when I look back I go, 'Those were some of the smartest decisions I ever made.' You cannot surrender the leadership of your church to whiners or the ship will never get out of the harbor."

While Warren and others later would describe his leadership style as one of open-mindedness and receptivity to the views of his congregants, there was never any question on this or any other occasion that he was the chief decision-maker. Unlike most Southern Baptist churches at the time, which were congregational in their polity and were led by a pastor and a board of deacons, Warren established the church with himself as its CEO. There was no elected church board to which he answered. When Saddleback officially obtained the legal status of a non-profit organization in its second or third year, it formed a board of directors—as was required by law—which consisted of the church's pastors and generally sought to operate by consensus. Years later, Kreun, as the church's chief administrator, would add a board of trustees to advise him on legal and financial matters, including the setting of pastors' salaries. The church held annual membership meetings where budgets were approved, projects were reported on, and members were invited to ask questions concerning the general conduct of church business. But that business always stayed firmly in the pastors' hands. On matters of day-to-day church governance, it was clear from the beginning that Saddleback was no democracy and that Warren had the final say.

Yet, as Warren would insist, neither was it an autocracy. "I have no authority over my church," he maintained in an interview years later. "I just have influence. To me, leadership is influence. If you want to know if you're a leader it's very simple: look over your shoulder. If nobody is following you, guess what. You're not the leader." He subscribed to a leadership style in which, as one observer noted, it may appear to an outsider as if the pastor is a dictator, but "to the people of the church his decisions are their decisions . . . almost as if he had a sixth sense, the pastor knows how to lead the church where the people want to go."

In facing down the early opposition to Warren's megachurch vision, Saddleback had survived its first divisive test. Most of those in the congregation who remained and embraced Warren's plan were steeled in their determination to see it through regardless of the challenges and costs. And in the months and years ahead there would be plenty of both.

SHORTLY BEFORE STEVE WILLIAMS LEFT the Saddleback staff in the spring of 1984, the church added a third weekend service to accommodate the growing number of worshipers who were turning up each week at the Laguna Hills High School theater. When those adjustments proved inadequate to accommodate the burgeoning crowd, Warren and his staff moved worship services into the school gymnasium—a larger but less comfortable venue. It was becoming clear that they needed to find new and larger temporary quarters and they began searching for a suitable site.

In the meantime, Warren had begun doctoral studies at Fuller Theological Seminary in nearby Pasadena. It surprised some who were close to him that he would take on that added workload at such a busy time in his life, especially given the physical and emotional price he had paid earlier for working fourteen- and eighteen-hour days getting the church up and running. But Warren subscribed wholeheartedly to a maxim he had learned from his father and that he would repeat often to his staff and to other pastors over the years: "All leaders are learners. The moment you stop learning you stop leading." The seemingly unquenchable curiosity that had propelled him into so many childhood adventures and wide-ranging academic pursuits as a youth had not abated in adulthood. And so Warren carved out some time and enrolled in the doctor of ministry program at Fuller to continue his study of ministry methods and to strengthen his skills as a leader.

He chose Fuller because of the reputation of its School of World Mission and Institute for Church Growth, which was founded in the mid-1960s by Donald A. McGavran, the former missionary whose writings on church growth had inspired Warren during his summer in Japan. The school was headed at the time by C. Peter Wagner, also a former missionary and a McGavran disciple. Like McGavran, Wagner was a controversial figure in some ecclesiastical quarters because of his emphasis on using pragmatic business management tools—his critics derided them as slick marketing techniques and a carnal obsession with numbers—in order to maximize church growth. Wagner shared McGavran's belief that a church's quantitative growth was an important measure of its faithfulness to God. Multiplying church membership, McGavran had taught, was the very essence of the Great Commission—Christ's command to his disciples to "go . . . and make disciples of all nations." It was not enough for churches to be faithful in biblical preaching, conduct lovely worship services, minister to the needs of its members, and do good deeds in the community. Many churches did all of that and yet had become "static enclaves of comfortable middle-class Christians." It was God's desire that churches grow numerically, and that required making "hard, bold plans" to boost church membership. Pursuing strategies to bring an "increase in countable followers of Jesus Christ," according to McGavran, was an act of Christian stewardship.

Wagner also shared McGavran's controversial view, based on his experience as a missionary in India, that entire "people groups"—tribes, castes, clans, or tightly knit segments of any society—could be converted to Christ at once. This seemed to fly in the face of conventional evangelical belief that Christian conversion was an individual act, a personal decision to repent of one's sins and accept Jesus Christ as savior. Yet McGavran had seen group conversions among Hindu castes and in African villages where a communal assent to Christianity, especially among the leaders of a tribe or village, created a hospitable environment for conversion, making it possible for entire groups to come to Christ without fear of suffering social dislocation. Applying the principle to the West, McGavran and Wagner suggested that American churches were likely to experience greater success in converting nonbelievers if they established their ministries among homogeneous groups within their communities. "Men like to become Christians without crossing racial, linguistic, or class barriers," McGavran had famously written.

The predictable reaction in some church quarters was that McGavran and Wagner were advocating racial and social segregation as a church-growth strategy. One northern Baptist pastor, writing in the *Christian Century* in 1981, charged that their emphasis on homogeneity "encourages sinful prejudices" and "sanctifies the unholy status quo. In regarding the church as 'our kind,' [the] church growth [movement] sees no problem, for example, with apartheid churches in South Africa, regarding them as routine." Wagner vehemently denied that he and McGavran were advocating segregation and insisted that they had merely made a sociological observation about human behavior and about what works in ministry and what does not. The debate would rage for years without a resolution as more and more congregations were attracted to the church-growth strategies taught at Fuller.

Most of what McGavran and Wagner taught meshed perfectly with the strategy Warren was following at Saddleback. When Warren started his church he had one target audience clearly in mind: young, unchurched, white-collar couples. "We focused on them because they were the largest group in the Saddleback Valley, and because that was who I related to best," he explained. Near the end of his studies at Fuller he would expand on that strategy in a doctoral dissertation that contained distinct echoes of McGavran's people-group philosophy: "Explosive growth occurs when the type of people in the community match the type of people already in the church, and the type of person the pastor is," he wrote. "When the people in the community, the people who are already in the church and the person of the pastor match, and they all fit, things happen. There is growth." Later he refined the notion of a target audience and came up with a more personalized composite description of the typical Orange County suburbanites his church was aiming to reach. Warren called them "Saddleback Sam" and "Saddleback Samantha." They were married, in their thirties or early forties, with two children, college degrees, and good jobs. They were self-satisfied—"even smug"—with their station in life, but carried a lot of debt and stress due to the price of their homes. They were into physical fitness and contemporary music and preferred the informal to the formal. They were also skeptical of organized religion. Members of Saddleback would look at those mythical composites and immediately recognize them as their neighbors. By Warren's design they were the central focus of Saddleback's ministry.

Warren's affinity for the teachings of Wagner and McGavran made Fuller seminary the logical place to conduct his doctoral studies. But even before he enrolled, Warren appeared on Wagner's radar screen. As a professor of church growth, Wagner tried to stay closely tuned to trends and developments in the field, so when he learned that an audacious young pastor in Orange County had publicly declared his intent to build a congregation of twenty thousand it immediately piqued his interest. He called Warren and introduced himself and the two began having regular conversations about church planting and church-growth principles and found that they shared many of the same ideas. When Wagner saw that Warren had practical experience and early successes applying some of the principles that he and McGavran had espoused he invited him to the seminary as a guest speaker. "He made me look good," Wagner recalled.

Later he enlisted Warren as a teacher in the Charles E. Fuller Institute for Evangelism and Church Growth, a training institute connected with the seminary that conducted weekend seminars for church leaders around the country. Two or three times a year, Warren would stand up in front of a room full of pastors and share the church-growth lessons he had learned by experience at his own church, often by trial and error. For Warren it marked the beginning of what would become a lifelong ministry of training other pastors, a ministry he had seen modeled by his father in the tiny mission churches of Northern California and that he one day would replicate on a global scale. Meanwhile, in the process of preparing for those sessions and in his studies at Fuller, he began to distill his thoughts about essential biblical principles that define the church's role in the world—principles he would come to recognize and famously write about as the purposes of God.

---

# Prophet of Purpose

ON EASTER 1985, SADDLEBACK'S FIFTH ANNIVERSARY, a record 2,500 worshipers packed into the Laguna Hills High School gym for three weekend services, surpassing the previous attendance record by more than a thousand. Glen Kreun had been busy for months scoping out larger facilities and recently had settled on a new high school under construction some nine miles to the northeast in Mission Viejo, just on the edge of Rancho Santa Margarita. It was substantially larger than the building they presently were using and was situated almost exactly where Warren hoped eventually to build a church. It seemed a perfect temporary home and it was expected to be ready for occupancy in the fall.

Warren was getting anxious to move out of the cramped quarters. In the weeks immediately following the annual Easter attendance surge, Saddleback's weekly turnout settled at a new plateau of over nine hundred—enough to convince Warren that the time had finally arrived to begin looking for property for a permanent church home. At the end of a service in late April, he announced that the search was about to begin and he invited anyone in the congregation who had expertise in real estate, land development, or finance and who would like to help to come to a meeting at his office the following evening.

The next night thirteen men showed up, half of whom he did not know. They went around the room and introduced themselves. One was in charge of acquiring sites for K-mart stores, another was the vice president of a local bank, another was a real estate appraiser for Fortune 500 companies, and another had done $91 million in commercial land acquisitions. It was the most high-powered group Warren could have imagined and all were volunteering their services. He was convinced that God had brought them together for a purpose. Warren turned around and wrote on the blackboard: Fifty Acres. "That's what I believe we should go after," he said. "Your job is to find it. Meeting adjourned."

A week later the men came back and reported that one of the last three major parcels of property available in the Saddleback Valley had just come on the market. It was seventy-two acres in a canyon at the end of the Rancho Santa Margarita Parkway, part of what once had been a pig farm and now was a favorite spot for weekend motocross enthusiasts. The price was $7.2 million. They asked Warren if they should go after it, and he said, "Sure. Why not?" He had no idea how the church would come up with the money.

Within a few days the team negotiated a purchase agreement and put $10,000 in escrow and then set about trying to line up financing. It would prove to be far more difficult than they anticipated. Over the next two years they would approach more than eighty lenders all over the country but would find no one willing to take a chance on a $7 million purchase of raw land by a mostly young and not particularly affluent congregation. In the meantime, the church would spend close to $100,000 to bring electrical service to the property and to obtain zoning changes and land-use and water rights. Everything was ready to proceed, but they needed a loan in order to close the deal, and so they continued looking.

Meanwhile, that summer Kay gave birth to the Warrens' third and last child, Matthew David. It was a difficult pregnancy, with Kay confined to bed and partially paralyzed for the last six weeks. She recovered quickly, however, and the baby was fine.

That important family milestone coincided with the start of a new chapter in Warren's ministry and in the life of the congregation. Late that fall, a little more than five years after it began, the Saddleback Valley Community Church packed up and moved across Mission Viejo to take up residence in its new rented quarters in the brand-new Trabuco Hills High School. The building was so new, in fact, that it had not yet opened for classes; the church moved in before the students did. It was a much larger facility than the school in Laguna Hills, with a larger auditorium and plenty of classroom space for Saddleback's growing Sunday school. But moving to a new location nine miles from the old one also carried some risk, and Warren knew it was likely that some of his flock would drop out rather than make the longer drive to church. He and his staff blanketed the new area with mass mailings introducing the church to the community and inviting residents to a four-week series of messages on "God's Will for My Life," followed by another on "How to Handle Life's Hurts." Weekly attendance quickly shot past the one-thousand mark. Rather than losing members Saddleback began drawing from a larger swath of the county.

The growth continued through the following year, 1986, and as it did the weekly routine of moving in, setting up, moving out, and storing the church's furniture and equipment became much more complicated and labor intensive. Teams of volunteers would show up at the school before 5 a.m. on Sundays to rearrange the building, carefully sketching floor plans of each classroom to ensure that everything was returned to its proper place at the end of the day. The church had access to the school only on weekends, which meant weeknight meetings and services and other special events had to be held at other rented locations—in office buildings, community centers, other churches, or wherever space could be found. It was a logistical nightmare, but Warren managed to make light of it. "If you're smart enough to find us you can go to church here," he joked. Despite the difficulties, there were surprisingly few complaints. For most of the congregation, the hardship only served to heighten the anticipation of having a place of their own. That prospect was about to suffer a setback.

THE FOLLOWING NOVEMBER the owner of the land in Rancho Santa Margarita notified Saddleback that in order to keep the escrow open it would have to begin making nonrefundable monthly payments of $10,000. The church, after all, had tied up the land for a year and a half with just a $10,000 deposit. During that time Warren and his flock had begun to think of the property as theirs. They had conducted some outdoor services at the site and had prayed over it and marched around its perimeter, like the Israelites marching around Jericho, as if to stake a spiritual claim. But after a year and a half the church was no closer to securing a loan and Warren thought it would be an expensive gamble to put out that much money per month. They decided to drop out of escrow and when they were able to raise the money they would come back and buy the property. All of the zoning and other approvals were set, so they would be able then to close the deal quickly. The sellers agreed. The next day a shopping center developer bought the property outright.

Predictably, the entire church was disappointed and discouraged by the turn of events. They had lost nearly two years of time and over $100,000 invested in the property, and it seemed that there was no land of significant size left to buy in all of the Saddleback Valley. They were forced back to square one on the dream of finding a permanent location.

After allowing himself a few days of feeling dejected, Warren quickly went to work, first on himself and then on his crestfallen staff and congregation, to move beyond the disappointment and to reignite a spirit of optimism. He concluded that God had been testing their faith and their commitment to the Saddleback vision and that they would grow spiritually stronger as a result of this apparent setback. "While you are working on the church, God is working on you," he informed his co-laborers. He reminded them of his desert revelation amid his deep depression a few years earlier—that this was God's church and that God had promised to build it. It was their job to minister to people. God would do the rest.

IT TOOK SADDLEBACK MORE THAN A YEAR after it lost the Rancho Santa Margarita property to locate another buildable piece of land. Three hundred acres had come up for sale on Live Oak Canyon Road, about three miles north of the first site, and was listed at $8 million. The front third of the property was gently sloping land that was well-suited for development but the rear two-thirds formed a sharp incline straight up the side of a mountain and was unusable. Warren reassembled his team of financial experts, who immediately went to the owner and offered to buy just the front one hundred acres for $6 million. To their surprise, the owner accepted their bid and said he would donate the rest of the land to the church as a tax write-off.

Warren and his team were elated. They immediately began making plans to raise the money they would need to close the deal. This time, rather than hiring an outside firm, they decided they would stage a fund-raising campaign on their own and they would call it "Possess the Land." They quickly changed their minds on the name when they realized that, given its initials, people might mistakenly associate it with Jim Bakker, the disgraced television evangelist who resigned earlier that year from his PTL ("Praise the Lord") ministry in an illicit-sex and financial scandal. The sordid affair had shaken the evangelical world and dominated the news for months. Warren decided it probably was not wise to use the initials PTL for a church fund-raising effort.

Within a few days they were ready to launch "Possess Our Land"—a monthlong drive that they hoped would generate at least half of the purchase price in cash and pledges. If it was successful, they would borrow the rest. For thirty days Warren and his congregation prayed and fasted and on weekends Warren preached on the power of faith and the importance of sacrificial giving. Many of his people took the messages to heart. Some sold precious jewelry and other prized possessions or took on second jobs in order to raise extra cash. A few sold their homes and bought smaller ones and gave the equity to the church. Warren and his staff and dozens of parishioners cashed in their life savings. By the end of the campaign, more than four hundred Saddleback families had pledged a total of $2 million to be paid over three years and had given a cash offering of $1.2 million. They had succeeded in raising half of the purchase price and they would trust God for the rest. Warren was amazed by the sacrificial outpouring of his congregation. On the final Sunday of the campaign they celebrated the accomplishment in a triumphant closing service.

The next day Warren and his team went to the owner and told him they were ready to buy the property: they had more than one million in cash to put down and two million in commitments and they were ready to sign a contract. The owner told them he had changed his mind. His accountant had advised against donating part of the land and he was raising his price to the full eight million.

Warren's heart sank. He knew there was no way his church could come up with an additional $2 million and they would have to give up the property. He went home angry and depressed and he locked himself in his office. "God, what are you doing?" he prayed. "Our people have just sweat blood. They have given all they have. They've sacrificed everything they could. We're not a wealthy church. It's a bunch of young couples in their twenties and thirties and we just don't have it. What am I supposed to tell them next Sunday when they have made these commitments of such sacrifice? I'll have to tell them there is no land. God, this is not my church. It's your church. What are you going to do with this?"

He didn't have to wait long for an answer. Two days later the third and final major parcel of land came on the market. It was 118 acres on

Santiago Canyon Road, nearly adjacent to the site they had just lost, and it was priced at $3.5 million—half the price of the previous property. Warren had never seen land so cheap in Orange County. He immediately called two of his church members and they rushed over to meet with the seller, William Lyon, a retired air force general and a successful homebuilder in the county. When they arrived at Lyon's office they learned that seven real estate developers already had bid on the land and four of them had offered cash. Warren told the general the church had a million dollars on hand but it could not pay the full amount in cash. He asked what it would take for him to sell the property to the church. "If you can close the deal by the end of the year it's yours," Lyon responded.

It was already late October and so they had a little over two months to come up with nearly $2.5 million. That Sunday Warren reported to his congregation all that had happened that week: the disappointing loss of the first piece of property and the discovery of another at half the price of the first. "Folks, we have an option here," he said. "We either go back to the well—and I don't know how you do that because everyone has already given everything they've got—but either we figure out a way to do deeper sacrifices or we lose the property. What do you want to do?" Without hesitating they gave their answer: "Let's go for it!"

In the final sixty days of that year the Saddleback congregation, which by then had grown to about two thousand, gave another $1.2 million in cash on top of their normal tithes and offerings. They had raised nearly $2.5 million in all, but they still needed a million more to close the deal. When the last business day of the year arrived they were short of their goal.

Two years earlier, when the church was scouring the country looking for a loan to buy the first piece of property, one of the lenders Warren approached was a gentleman by the name of Maurice McAllister, chairman and founder of a savings and loan company in nearby Costa Mesa. McAllister was in his seventies, a down-to-earth, grandfatherly type, and he and Warren, who was then thirty-one, seemed to hit it off well. Sitting in McAllister's high-rise office one summer afternoon they talked about growing tomatoes and growing churches, and Warren spelled out his vision for Saddleback. The financier listened intently, but when Warren finished he broke the disappointing news that his company's policy prohibited lending to churches. Nonetheless, he commended Warren for his commitment and his vision and as they walked out of his office he put his arm around the young minister's shoulder. "I want you to be encouraged," he said. But Warren didn't need encouragement; he needed money.

As they parted company that day, Warren assumed that it would be the last he would hear from the man. He was wrong. At the end of that year, McAllister sent the church a personal donation of one thousand shares of stock in his savings and loan, worth roughly thirty thousand dollars, along with a note to Warren that said, "I believe in the vision of Saddleback Church." The following December he did it again, this time donating two thousand shares accompanied by a similar supportive note, even though he had never set foot in the church.

When Warren launched the "Possess Our Land" campaign in the fall of 1987, he had hoped that God would prompt some wealthy benefactor to make a donation so large that it would challenge the rest of the congregation to see that God was in it and that would encourage them to step out on faith and give sacrificially. But he knew of no one in his church who was capable of doing that. McAllister was the only person he knew who was wealthy enough to give such an amount, but McAllister was not a member of Saddleback, had never visited the church, and did not even live in Orange County; he lived in Los Angeles. Moreover, McAllister had already been generous with unsolicited gifts and Warren was reluctant to hit him up for a big donation to the campaign. Nonetheless, he prayed that if it was God's will that he approach the financier, God would provide an opportunity to do so and would give him the right words to use.

On a steamy autumn day early in the campaign, Warren was preaching in the Trabuco Hills gymnasium on investing in the future and the value of sacrifice. About ten minutes into the message the rear door of the gym opened and McAllister and his family and grandchildren quietly slipped into the gym. They had driven down from Los Angeles to visit the church and Warren was completely caught off guard. Needless to say, he also was thrilled. He finished the message and rushed to greet McAllister outside on the patio. After exchanging pleasantries and making family introductions, McAllister pulled Warren aside. "You know, Rick, I'd be willing to help out on this campaign." Warren could hardly believe his ears. He thanked McAllister profusely and felt relieved that he had not had to broach the delicate subject. Even though the financier had not specified an amount, it was clear to Warren that his prayer had been answered. Yet in the weeks that followed, the campaign came to a conclusion and Warren heard nothing more from the banker.

They had come to the final business day of 1987, the deadline for closing the deal on the Santiago Canyon property, and the campaign was still a million dollars short. Late that morning Warren's telephone rang. It was McAllister calling to inform Warren that his savings and loan had changed its policy and would lend Saddleback the money it needed, and McAllister was personally contributing a quarter of a million dollars to the cause. The final pieces had fallen into place with no time to spare and the church was able to close the deal. In Warren's estimation it was nothing short of a miracle. After years of frustration and wandering from rented site to rented site, he and his flock finally had found a place where they could build a permanent home. On a crisp afternoon early in the New Year they gathered on the property under an azure blue sky and held a Possess Our Land celebration service to give thanks for God's miraculous provision.

While they didn't have the money to begin building immediately, they wasted no time getting started on the design and making other preliminary preparations. Within a few days they posted a sign on the property declaring it the Future Home of Saddleback Valley Community Church and began applying for the various approvals they would need before construction could begin. The original architectural plan called for a 2,886-seat fellowship hall that initially would serve as the sanctuary, two softball fields with lights, three Sunday school buildings with a total of 84 classrooms, a day-care center with room for 200 children, and a double-deck parking garage. A few years down the road the church would add a 4,800-seat sanctuary that would dwarf the Crystal Cathedral in Garden Grove by 1,900 seats. It was an ambitious plan, to say the least, with a total estimated price of $55 million.

Almost immediately the project ran into opposition. Some years before, the Orange County Planning Commission had classified the property—a cluster of low-lying hills covered in patches of green and yellow brush—as part of a "rural transition zone" that stood between a sprawling subdivision on the opposite side of Santiago Canyon Road and the undeveloped slopes that ascended north and west to the mountains. The church's construction plan called for bulldozing the hills, scraping away more than 950,000 cubic yards of earth in order to make a sufficient flat space for its buildings and ball fields. Area residents and local environmentalists vehemently objected. The proposed construction was far too aggressive and would spoil the scenic character of the transition zone, they argued, and they urged the planning commission to block it. Sympathizing with the homeowners, the commission withheld its approval and ordered the church to scale down the project.

Over the next year Saddleback would spend more than $400,000 revising the design in order to satisfy a growing list of county demands which, if carried out, would add significantly to the project's final cost. First, the planners wanted the church to build an earthen mound 90 feet high and 1,200 feet long at the front of the property so that the buildings would not be seen from Santiago Canyon Road, which had been designated a scenic highway. Then they wanted a stand of oak trees moved from the rear of the property and transplanted on top of the mound as an additional visual barrier. Those changes alone would have cost more than $8 million to complete. Warren was baffled by the planners' insistence on hiding the church when houses and retail buildings sat just across the road. "Are they saying homes are scenic and churches aren't?" he asked. Nonetheless, he reluctantly acceded, hoping that the county finally would allow the project to proceed.

Opponents still were not satisfied. Environmentalists wanted the church to install an expensive charcoal-filtered drainage system so that storm water running off the parking lots would be made "Evian pure" before being discharged into a nearby creek. "Wait a minute," an exasperated Warren responded. "Fifty yards downstream at Cook's Corner they're peeing in that creek," he said, referring to a nearby saloon. "You've got bikers taking a whiz out there. Why is anybody

Pastor Rick Warren, 2009.
*(Courtesy of Scott Tokar/Saddleback Church)*

Jimmy and Dot Warren on their tenth anniversary, March 4, 1954, less than two months after Rick was born.
*(Courtesy of the Warren family)*

In his first steps, one-year-old Rick picked up a Bible and ran with it, and he's been running with it ever since. *(Courtesy of the Warren family)*

Jimmy Clyde, Dot, Jimmy, Rick, and Chaundel Warren in Portland, Oregon, 1959. *(Courtesy of the Warren family)*

Rick's senior class photo, Ukiah High School, 1972. *(Courtesy of Ukiah High School)*

Junior Class officers, from the Ukiah High School yearbook, 1971. *(Courtesy of Ukiah High School)*

Rick and Kay Warren in the fifth year of Saddleback Church at Laguna Hills High School, 1985. *(Courtesy of Saddleback Church)*

Home at last! After worshiping in a high school auditorium for nearly thirteen years, Saddleback Church moved to its Lake Forest, California, property on December 3, 1992. *(Courtesy of Saddleback Church)*

Warren at a church celebration in 1993. Says Kay of her husband: "This is a man who will come out in an Elvis costume. He's a ham. He's a goofball." *(Courtesy of Saddleback Church)*

On his fiftieth birthday, Warren dusted off his electric guitar and serenaded his flock. *(Courtesy of Saddleback Church)*

Glen Kreun; Rick's father, Jimmy; and Rick celebrated the dedication of the Jimmy Warren Memorial Bridge at Saddleback in 1999, a few weeks before Jimmy died. *(Courtesy of Saddleback Church)*

Rick teaches a new-members class at the Saddleback Worship Center in 2001. *(Courtesy of Saddleback Church)*

Warren's 1996 lawsuit defending a clergy housing allowance nearly went awry and led Congress to pass a law in 2002 affirming the tax break. The bill was sponsored by Rep. Jim Ramstad, R-Minn. *(Courtesy of Saddleback Church)*

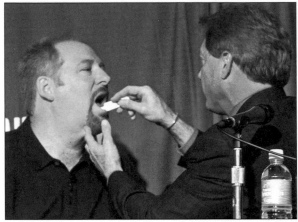

Starting in 2005, Saddleback began sponsoring the annual Global AIDS Summit. At the first gathering, Warren was publicly tested for AIDS. *(Courtesy of Shannon Baker/Baptist Press)*

Saddleback Church celebrated its twenty-fifth anniversary in April 2005, at Angel Stadium, the only venue in Orange County large enough to hold the entire congregation. *(Courtesy of Saddleback Church)*

Rick and Kay joined President Paul Kagame of Rwanda at a stadium rally in the capital city of Kigali in July 2005, marking the launch of the PEACE plan in Rwanda. *(Courtesy of Whitney Kelley/A. Larry Ross Communications and Saddleback Church)*

Rick Warren with President and Mrs. Bush, December 13, 2006. *(Courtesy of Saddleback Church)*

Teaming up against HIV/AIDS in 2006. After Kay first caught the vision, the Warrens became fighters against the AIDS pandemic. *(Courtesy of Allison Cox/Saddleback Church)*

In his final days in office, the Warrens presented President Bush the International Medal for PEACE for his efforts to combat AIDS in Africa. *(Courtesy of Robert Burgess/Saddleback Church)*

Warren quizzed both candidates during a nationally televised presidential forum at Saddleback in August 2008. *(Courtesy of Scott Tokar/Saddleback Church)*

Warren shared a backstage laugh with then senator Barack Obama prior to the presidential forum. *(Courtesy of Scott Tokar/Saddleback Church)*

On the eve of the 2009 Inauguration, Warren delivered the keynote message at the Martin Luther King Day celebration at the Ebenezer Baptist Church in Atlanta. *(Courtesy of Scott Tokar/Saddleback Church)*

worried about 'Evian pure'? It's going to be contaminated in fifty yards!" Then the local residents' association requested that the planning commission shrink the overall construction footprint from thirty acres to nine, which would mean doing away with the ball fields, two of the four support buildings, and the sanctuary. Worship services would be housed permanently in the fellowship hall instead. That, Warren said, was simply unacceptable. "We didn't pay $3.5 million to build on only nine acres," he insisted.

Saddleback and the county would remain at loggerheads for nearly two years as the planning commission and the board of supervisors continued to withhold approval and requested additional revisions. In the meantime, Warren and his flock aggressively lobbied the board of supervisors—which would have the final say on the project—staged letter-writing campaigns, and held peaceful protests outside the county courthouse. At one contentious meeting of the supervisors, a frustrated Warren stood up and told the story of a friend in Leningrad who in the early days of perestroika applied for a government permit to reopen a church that had been shuttered for years. The man received the permit within fifteen minutes and was charged the equivalent of twenty dollars. "Now, I realize that in the People's Republic of Orange County it takes a little longer," Warren told the supervisors, "but this is ridiculous." The local newspaper, the *Orange County Register*, entered the fray and sided with the church in an editorial inveighing against the heavy-handedness of the project's opponents. "What it really amounts to," the newspaper wrote, "is an effort by some people, through the medium of a plan on file in some county bureaucracy, to control other people's property . . . What gives people the arrogance to presume that they have the right to do such a thing?" Still the county would not budge.

Finally, early in 1990, Warren received official word that the board of supervisors had placed the project on indefinite hold. Saddleback's tortuous quest for a permanent location had reached an apparent dead end. When Warren went home and broke the news to Kay, she exploded. "You've been too nice to those county supervisors!" she shrieked at her husband. "You let me go down there! I'll get up on their desk, grab them by the lapels, and go 'You give us that land now!'"

She stormed into her office and closed the door. She had yelled at her husband and now inwardly she began yelling at God. "You know, God, I'm just really tired of playing your game because we have tried to do this with integrity. We have tried to be honest. We haven't tried to break any rules or ask for any favors and you are doing squat about it. If you would just tell me what game you are playing so I can get on the same board with you because this is just . . . I'm sick of this." She began to think of all the pastors she knew of who had succeeded in acquiring big plots of land for their churches. Adrian Rogers, the former Southern Baptist president and pastor of a big church in Tennessee, had just purchased two hundred acres in a Memphis suburb. "What does Adrian Rogers need with two hundred stinking acres? I'm sorry, he doesn't need that. Could you give us some of that?" Bill Hybels, pastor of Willow Creek Community Church outside of Chicago, bought 110 acres just five years after he started his church and paid $450,000 for it. They had virtually no struggle at all. "You must like Bill better than us," Kay complained.

As she sat there stewing she remembered a women's Bible study lesson she had taught recently on the twenty-first chapter of John. It is a passage where the resurrected Jesus turns to his disciple Peter and asks three times, "Peter, do you love me?" and Peter answers, "Yes, Lord, you know I love you," and Jesus commands him, "Then feed my sheep." Then Jesus tells Peter to follow him and that in following him Peter would die. Alarmed, Peter inquires about the fate of the other disciples. Would they also die? Jesus rebukes Peter. "If I want them to remain alive until I return," says Jesus, "what is that to you? You follow me."

Kay recalled that she had taught the lesson with a rather "smug attitude," but now, sitting in her office, she suddenly felt laid low, as if God was asking her the same question: *Kay, what if I let every church on the face of the earth have land and buildings and Saddleback never does? What is that to you? It's none of your business what I do in this church or that church, or what I don't do at Saddleback. The only question that you have to answer is, 'Will you follow me no matter what?'"* Later she would describe that moment as "a huge moment of surrender" that changed her attitude about waiting and believing. "It really is none of my business what God does. Really, my only business is that I have made a commitment that I will follow Him no matter what."

WARREN UNDERSTOOD HIS WIFE'S FRUSTRATION, and he shared it. During the two years that they had battled the county for permission to build, his church had continued to hold its weekend services in the high school and the congregation had continued to expand. By the end of 1989, Saddleback's average weekly attendance topped 2,500 and the total number of baptisms surpassed 1,100. Numerically and spiritually Warren saw his church growing stronger but he knew that his people also were growing weary of the endless weekend routine that was the price of being a transient church. And now, after all of their physical labor and their financial sacrifice to secure a place of their own, they were running out of patience with the government bureaucrats who they perceived were standing in their way.

Warren decided it was time to play hardball. Early that spring he showed up at the office of Gaddi Vasquez, the county supervisor who represented the district where Saddleback was located. He brought with him a copy of the church's directory, which contained more than eighteen thousand names of people who attended Saddleback at least occasionally, and he dropped it on Vasquez's desk. "Sir," he said firmly, "there are eighteen thousand names in this directory. They are all in your district and they all vote. Now, you have a problem. Either get us permission to start using that land or do something else because you're going to have a mutiny on your hands if you don't." Nothing more really needed to be said.

About a week later Vasquez called Warren with some good news. He had met with a major real estate developer in the county, Barry Hon, whose company at the time was developing a mixed residential and commercial community called Foothill Ranch in Lake Forest a few miles to the west of Saddleback's property. One small section of Hon's property was cut off from the rest of the development by a major thoroughfare, the Portola Parkway, and a soon-to-be-built toll road. Hon indicated he would be willing to swap the isolated sixty-acre tract, then worth about $9 million, for Saddleback's land in an even trade. Eventually he would build homes on the site. Since Hon's property was zoned for commercial and industrial use, Vasquez assured Warren that public opposition to putting a church there was unlikely.

Warren quickly agreed to the trade and within a few weeks the papers were signed. The *Orange County Register* caught wind of the deal and wrote a story calling it a boon to both the church and the developer that finally would put an end to the dispute between Saddleback and the Santiago Canyon residents. An officer in Hon's firm told the newspaper that even though the company stood to lose money on the land swap, the benefit to the community would outweigh the loss. "We're doing it because we've been told by people in the county and people in the community that it's a very high priority to find a home for Saddleback Community Church," the official explained. Spared from the political heat of having to choose between offending church members or local activists, Vasquez pronounced himself "extremely delighted" by the deal he had brokered. Speaking for Saddleback, Glen Kreun indicated to the paper that the church hoped to begin construction later that year—although that timetable would prove to be a bit optimistic.

That notwithstanding, Warren and his congregation had reason to celebrate. They had reached the end of a faith-testing ordeal and the beginning of a new phase in the life of the church, and Warren expressed confidence that God's timing had been right all along. Had they succeeded in getting the first piece of land, the church would have been located at the end of a four-lane road, the only way onto the property, and the limited traffic capacity would have severely restricted the church's growth potential. At the second and third properties the traffic bottleneck would have been even worse. Both were located on a two-lane road, and while the county had plans at the time to widen it to four lanes, those plans were never carried out. The property they ended up with, on the other hand, sat at the intersection of two multilane commercial thoroughfares, Portola Parkway and El Toro Road, near what soon would be a toll road off-ramp. Traffic access to Saddleback would be virtually unlimited. Meanwhile, the property they had purchased for $3.5 million had increased in value to $6.5 million and then was traded for land worth $9 million. As a result of the two-year delay they were sitting on equity of nearly $6 million.

All of the waiting and frustration had paid off, and Warren gave all the credit to God. "God knew exactly what he was doing," he reminded his flock. "It's a lesson you must never forget, that God is never late and he is never early. He's always on time."

IT WOULD BE ANOTHER YEAR AND A HALF before the Saddleback congregation moved onto the Lake Forest property. On December 13, 1992, they gathered for the last time at the Trabuco Hills High School. The congregation sang a few songs and Warren spoke briefly, recounting the challenges and accomplishments of the previous twelve years. Then about five thousand worshipers, many carrying balloons and hand-painted placards, lined up behind Warren and Kreun—who took turns pushing a pulpit on wheels—and marched eight-tenths of a mile to the property and their new church home. There they reassembled outside a giant tent that would serve as the worship center until the first buildings were completed. Warren offered a prayer of thanksgiving and, as he concluded, a sign fluttering in the crowd caught his eye. Its hand-printed message seemed to capture the essence of the moment: It didn't come fast but we're home at last!

Saddleback's wilderness sojourn was over.

# CHAPTER ELEVEN

# *Purpose Driven*

DURING THE FIVE YEARS OF DISHEARTENING SETBACKS and false starts in its efforts to establish a permanent home in Orange County, Saddleback Church continued to flourish and Warren continued to refine and expand his ministry seemingly undistracted by the adversity. Between Easter of 1985 when it first ventured into the real estate market and June of 1990 when it finally acquired the Lake Forest property, the Saddleback congregation more than tripled in size to an average attendance of more than three thousand. By the time it moved onto the property in December 1992 it would grow by another thousand and its annual operating budget would surpass the million-dollar mark. "Saddleback people do not give up!" Warren exulted at that first onsite service. "A church is people, not buildings. We've been building a church for thirteen years now, and now we're going to start building the house to put it in."

The secret to Saddleback's growth, Warren would one day write, was in fact no secret at all. From the beginning he had made effective use of direct mail and local-media advertising to promote his messages and the church's seeker-sensitive ministries to the community. But more than that, he would insist, it was the word-of-mouth testimonials of people whose lives had been changed by accepting Christ and through the help they received from the church's various support groups and other Saddleback ministries that attracted newcomers. "Changed lives are a church's greatest advertisement," he would write. "Wherever needs are being met and lives are being changed the word gets out into a community."

An important impetus to the church's growth during the final years in the high school auditorium was Warren's hiring in 1987 of a full-time music minister, a young singer and songwriter named Rick

Muchow. Up until that time, the church generally relied on a small core of volunteers within the congregation to perform musical numbers during worship services and to lead congregational singing. While the music tended to be upbeat it usually consisted of modified hymns or youth choruses sung with a piano accompaniment. Sometimes they would mix in a little jazz or a classical number. "We tried to appeal to everybody's musical taste, from Bach to rock," Warren later would explain, confessing that it often amounted to a confusing musical mishmash that pleased no one. Except on special occasions when Warren brought in outside artists or singing groups—he enlisted Pat Boone for one Easter service and Noel Paul Stookey of Peter Paul and Mary on another occasion—music at Saddleback tended to be regarded as a sidelight and an afterthought rather than an important element in attracting unchurched newcomers and in effectively communicating the Gospel. With Muchow's arrival that quickly changed.

Just three years younger than Warren, Muchow was a mellow-voiced vocalist and a guitar virtuoso who had served as music minister at two Baptist churches in Northern California before accepting a call to Saddleback. Born in California, Muchow had developed a passion for the performing arts while growing up in New York City (his mother worked for the *Village Voice*), where he performed on Broadway as a child and studied acoustic guitar at Juilliard before returning to the West Coast to pursue his musical interests. After accepting Christ as a teenager during a high school production of *Godspell*, he earned a music degree from San Jose State University and immersed himself in the contemporary Christian music scene, writing and performing many of his own compositions in church services, concerts, and youth revival meetings around the country. He studied for a brief time at the Golden Gate Baptist Theological Seminary to strengthen the theological underpinnings of his music ministry. He had just resigned as music minister at a Baptist church in Gilroy in Santa Clara County, where he served for four years, and had set out with his wife and infant son on a solo concert tour when Warren invited him to join the Saddleback staff. He accepted immediately.

Beyond bringing fresh energy to congregational singing at Saddleback with his soft-rock repertoire and energetic style, Muchow set about tapping musical talent within the congregation, and the newly invigorated music program soon began to play a more central role in worship. Shortly after Muchow arrived, Warren began incorporating musical numbers within his Sunday messages, pausing sometimes two or three times during a sermon while Muchow or others performed contemporary songs that were carefully selected to reinforce a sermon point and were accompanied by guitar, drums, electrical keyboard, and other instruments seldom associated with church music. It was an innovative technique at the time and proved so popular with Warren and his baby-boomer flock that it quickly became a permanent feature of Saddleback services.

Measurable results of the music makeover were impressive and almost immediate. Warren began touting the church's music program in regular mailings to the community, and attendance at weekend services doubled during Muchow's first year. Warren later would remark that he had sorely underestimated the power of music within worship at the beginning and that he wished he had integrated it more effectively into his services much sooner. As Saddleback continued to grow and the seeker-sensitive worship format it exemplified continued to catch on in the evangelical world, the easy-listening style of adult contemporary music that Muchow brought to Saddleback soon would become a ubiquitous feature of modern evangelical worship.

ANOTHER IMPORTANT MILESTONE during those years at Trabuco Hills High School was the launch in 1988 of the first Saddleback-sponsored pastors' conference, a training event that marked the beginning of what would become Warren's worldwide Purpose-Driven Network. (Twenty years later, that network would include some 400,000 pastors in 162 countries.) The conference grew out of Warren's involvement in the Fuller-affiliated Institute for Evangelism and Church Growth. As one of the institute's workshop speakers at training seminars held around the country several times a year, Warren had begun to see other churches achieve positive results using the methods he taught that were based on his own experience at Saddleback, and it prompted him to consider new ways of helping other pastors replicate his success. Warren had been especially inspired by one denomination's experience.

After attending the institute's seminars in 1985, leaders of the Christian and Missionary Alliance, a small evangelical denomination based in Colorado Springs, Colorado, initiated an ambitious nationwide campaign to start one hundred new congregations on Easter Sunday in 1987, the denomination's centennial year. The strategies they followed were right out of Warren's playbook. They began with a door-to-door survey to identify a community's needs and the objections people had to attending church, and then designed a program to satisfy those needs and objections. They followed with a mass mailing of attractive brochures geared specifically to the unchurched, inviting them to a new kind of church with relevant sermons and refreshingly contemporary music. Then they designed worship services to be intelligible and user-friendly to non-Christians by steering clear of unfamiliar jargon and traditional religious trappings. Denominational leaders were hopeful that the campaign would reach the unchurched and "yield an evangelistic harvest of unprecedented proportions." They were not disappointed. That Easter saw the launch of 101 new congregations made up mostly of nonchurchgoers, and a year later 94 of them were still flourishing.

"What the Christian and Missionary Alliance did really said something to Rick," Kreun recalled. "He began to see that the system he developed was transferable, that it could work anywhere." At the same time, as a result of the national exposure he had received as a presenter at the Fuller seminars, Warren was becoming widely known in evangelical circles as a church-growth expert. Since his early seminary days Warren had felt it was part of his calling, in addition to pastoring one church for a lifetime, to train and encourage other pastors as he had seen his father do for so many years as a director of missions for Southern Baptist churches in Northern California. It was that sense of calling that had led him as a seminarian to work with the International Evangelism Association and with the Baptist General Convention in Texas training pastors in disciple-making and later to join the Fuller Institute's teaching staff. With his own congregation firmly established and growing stronger, Warren decided it was time to build up the training side of his ministry and to expand his outreach to other pastors, and this time he would do it on his own.

He started out rather modestly. For the first year or so Warren would invite fifteen or twenty pastors from around the country to a Pastors' Day at Saddleback, a daylong conference held every month or two where he would teach his church-growth methods in a small-group setting. Those quickly evolved into a much more elaborate Church Growth Conference, a four- or five-day event held annually that attracted hundreds of pastors from the United States and abroad. While Warren and his recipe for success at Saddleback were the main attraction, other members of Warren's staff and a few outside experts rounded out a program brimming with practical advice for building healthy churches. The second conference in 1989 drew more than six hundred pastors from a variety of denominations and nearly every state of the union, and the numbers continued to grow year by year. "People really enjoyed what they heard," Kreun recalled, "and as we then got feedback from some of these churches—that these things *do* work—Rick began to tweak his strategy both in the way we did things at Saddleback and in what he taught at the conferences."

Having already modified his methods at Saddleback on several occasions—changes in the music program and the addition of Saturday evening services were two noteworthy examples—Warren began to recognize that more important than any particular method or worship style were the guiding principles underlying his church-growth strategies. In 1990, he began work on his doctoral dissertation at Fuller Seminary, a document that, when completed in 1993, would tell the Saddleback story and articulate in a prescriptive way the strategies and principles he had applied in building the church. "Lasting church growth is not built on gimmicks but on the purposes of God," he wrote, adding that defining those purposes was the important first step in starting a new church.

In Saddleback's case, as Warren explained, those purposes were based on two famous teachings of Jesus: the Great Commandment, "Love the Lord your God with all your heart and with all your soul and with all your mind . . . [and] Love your neighbor as yourself" (Matthew 22:37–40), and the Great Commission, "Go and make disciples of all nations, baptizing them in the name of the Father and of the Son and of the Holy Spirit, and teaching them to obey everything I have commanded you" (Matthew 28:19–20). Out of those New Testament passages Warren extracted four purposes around which he said every program and ministry at Saddleback would be built: *worship* ("love . . . God"), *service* or *ministry* ("love your neighbor"), *evangelism* ("go . . . and make disciples"), and *discipleship* ("teaching them to obey"). Later he would add a fifth purpose, *fellowship*—building strong family bonds as members of the church—which he connected to baptism, a ritual symbolizing public identification with Christ and his people. "If an activity or program fulfills one of these [purposes] we do it," Warren wrote. "If it doesn't we don't. We are driven by the Great Commandment and the Great Commission. Together they give us the primary tasks the church is to focus on until Christ returns." While programs and methods may change over time, he said, the purposes would remain constant.

In the process of preparing his dissertation and the teaching materials for his conferences, Warren also sharpened the focus of what he called the "Life Development Process" at Saddleback—a program of instruction designed to systematically move people from a basic faith commitment through stages of spiritual growth until they become mature believers engaged in Christian ministry. The program was based on a plan he developed while working as a youth pastor during college and which used a baseball-diamond diagram to illustrate each of the stages. Initially Warren attempted to lead his entire congregation—most of whom were nonbelievers or were brand new to the faith—through the stages in a series of Sunday morning messages spread over a period of months. The latest refinement involved four classes that were offered each month and were taught sequentially by Rick and Kay and other Saddleback pastors, with each class intended to lead church members to a deeper level of commitment.

While everyone was welcome to attend Saddleback's services, one could reach first base—*membership*—only by taking Class 101, where basic Baptist beliefs were taught, and by signing a covenant committing oneself to Christ and the church. Second base, *maturity*, was reached by completing Class 201 and committing to tithing, daily prayer and Bible reading, and participation in a small group. Third base was *ministry*, and members were taught in Class 301 to serve others and to sign up for one of Saddleback's many lay ministries—from visiting the sick or working with support groups to ushering or working in the church nursery during services. Home base was *mission*, and in Class 401 members were trained and motivated to win others to Christ. At the center of the diamond was *magnification*, where members learned that true worship of God consists in doing all that they had learned in the other classes. "Saddleback is built on a system where we're constantly turning up the heat," Warren said, explaining the Life Development Process. "You meet people where they are but you don't leave them there. We bring them into membership, we build them up in maturity, we train them for ministry, and we send them out in mission . . . That is the whole purpose of the church."

With those refinements in place, in 1990 Warren reorganized his ministry staff—which by then had grown to about a dozen full-time pastors—around the five purposes and the baseball-diamond approach to disciple-making. In doing so he jettisoned traditional ministry titles and job descriptions such as youth pastor or minister of music or adult education and replaced them with pastoral positions focused on worship, fellowship, discipleship, missions, and ministry. In 1991, he hired his brother-in-law, Tom Holladay, to become Saddleback's pastor of spiritual maturity and to work with Kay teaching courses in the church's Life Development Process. Holladay and his wife, Chaundel, Rick's sister, had been living in Maryville, about forty miles north of Sacramento, where Tom was senior pastor of a small Baptist church. Chaundel would become an unpaid lay teacher of women at Saddleback.

A year later, Warren decided he could expand his outreach to other pastors more rapidly if he took his church-growth conferences on the road, as the Fuller institute had been doing for years. So he recruited Fuller's director of operations, Douglas Slaybaugh, to manage the project at Saddleback. By the time they rolled out the first on-the-road seminar in January of 1993 they had settled on a descriptive new label for the program to set it apart from other church-growth gatherings. They called it the Purpose-Driven Church, coining what was about to become a popular catchphrase in religious circles and an international brand.

In June 1993, nearly ten years after he started the doctoral program at Fuller Seminary, Warren completed his dissertation, a largely autobiographical how-to guide bearing the long-winded title *New Churches for a New Generation: Church Planting to Reach Baby-boomers. A Case Study: Saddleback Valley Community Church*. He had vague plans to self-publish it and market it in connection with his conferences to his growing network of pastors, but was in no hurry to do so. Twelve years earlier he had self-published a book on Bible study methods, which he wrote during his years as a youth pastor, and since then had written two other brief books—*Answers to Life's Difficult Questions* (1985) and *The Power to Change Your life* (1990)—both of which were based on sermon series at Saddleback and were published by a small Christian publishing house in Wheaton, Illinois. None of the books achieved more than modest success.

His status in the publishing world was about to change dramatically. Sometime in early 1993, Bruce Ryskamp, the president of Zondervan, a successful Michigan-based publisher of Bibles and other Christian books that was owned by HarperCollins, the book publishing arm of Rupert Murdoch's News Corporation, heard Warren speak at a church leadership conference in Texas, and while he was rather impressed by the California pastor's presentation, he was even more impressed by the enthusiastic response of other pastors who swarmed around Warren afterward to ask questions. When he returned to his office, Ryskamp went immediately to the company's editor in chief, Stan Gundry, and told him about Warren. "There's something there," Ryskamp said. "I think you should go after him."

Gundry was a seasoned veteran in acquiring and editing new authors and he was not exactly bowled over by his boss's suggestion. "Number one, I knew that books by pastors don't sell particularly well," he explained. "And number two, quite frankly, I thought 'What does my boss—who is a business guy—really know about this sort of thing?' So I basically did nothing about it." But Ryskamp was not about to give up on the idea. He continued to talk up Warren over the next month or two until Gundry rather reluctantly agreed to make some inquiries. His initial attempts to reach Warren, however, were unsuccessful—his calls, letters, and e-mail messages went unanswered. "Finally, someone who was close to Rick said, 'You know, Stan, Rick needs two things. He needs to know that you understand him' "— critics of the church-growth movement by then had begun to publicly disparage some of Warren's methods, just as they had earlier with Donald McGavran and Peter Wagner, and it made Warren bristle— " 'and, secondly, he needs to be convinced that he needs a publisher— that he just can't do it all himself.' So this person suggested that several of us attend one of Rick's Purpose-Driven seminars and maybe we would have a chance to meet with him there."

Taking that advice, Gundry and two of his associates from Zondervan showed up at Warren's next conference, which was held in Indianapolis late in 1993. Seeing Warren in action, they were duly impressed but they managed only a brief meet-and-greet conversation with him between sessions. At least it was a foot in the door. Over the next few months Gundry continued to e-mail Warren asking for a meeting and finally he agreed. The following summer, Gundry and his associates flew out to Saddleback and met with Warren for three hours. "We hit it off very well," Gundry recalled. "I think he was convinced that we understood him. I made the case that, 'Rick, you've got something to say that churches and pastors need to hear. But if you self-publish it you need to be aware that the suspicion will always be there that you published it because no one else would. We can add both credibility and value as we edit and market the book on your behalf.' "

Warren apparently bought the argument and in late November he signed a contract for a two-book deal. The first would be a church-growth guide for pastors based on Warren's dissertation and his conference material and would be titled *The Purpose-Driven Church*. That would be followed a year or two later by a second volume that Warren had not yet fully conceptualized but that would be geared toward laypeople and would be called *The Purpose-Driven Life*. Zondervan agreed to pay Warren a respectable $150,000 advance reflecting their belief that the first book would be a winner in its genre by selling as many as 35,000 copies in the first year—far better than most books written by and for pastors.

Gundry wanted to move quickly on the first book and he knew that Warren's writing time would be severely limited by his pastoral duties, so he convinced Warren to allow one of Zondervan's editors, Jack Kuhatschek, to listen to Warren's conference tapes and compose a draft that would replicate Warren's voice. It took Kuhatschek just five weeks to complete the ghostwritten manuscript, but when Warren read it he was not pleased. "Jack, you've done a wonderful job," Warren responded, "but it's not me. I've got to do this myself."

Four months later, in the spring of 1995, he turned in his own manuscript and the book sailed through the editing process and came out that October. "We knew we had something in our hands that was bigger than any of us anticipated," Gundry recalled. It ended up selling close to 100,000 copies the first year, nearly three times what had been projected.

AT ROUGHLY THE SAME TIME that the book deal was being negotiated, Warren decided that his church had worshiped long enough in a weather-exposed tent and that the time had come to build a permanent sanctuary. They had broken ground shortly after they acquired the property in 1990 and immediately began grading the land, laying electricity, water, and gas lines, and pouring concrete pads for the tent and for portable classrooms that would house Sunday school for children and teenagers until permanent buildings could be built—which would have to wait for a major infusion of funds.

In the fall of 1994, Saddleback launched a six-week fund-raising campaign called "Time to Build" with a goal of raising $9 million in cash and three-year pledges. On the first weekend Warren preached a message on "How to Prepare for a Miracle," and members were given pledge cards and were instructed to take them home and pray about their pledge over the next five weeks. To set an example, on that first Sunday of the campaign, Warren announced to the congregation that he and Kay would be pledging $150,000—the full amount of the book advance from Zondervan and the equivalent of three years of Warren's salary. Five weeks later, some 8,800 people turned out for the closing service of the campaign and when the offering was taken the total came to $25 million—$2 million in cash and $23 million in pledges. It was believed to be the largest single church offering in the nation's history at the time.

Less than a year later the occasion arrived that some at Saddleback had begun to wonder if they ever would live to see. The church conducted its first service in its new Worship Center. After nearly three years in the tent and twelve in high schools and other rented facilities, Warren and his congregation finally were in a building of their own.

Like Saddleback itself, the contemporary-designed Worship Center bore little resemblance to a traditional church with steeples and pews and stained-glass windows. It was a glass-and-metal rectangular box that, from the outside, easily could have been mistaken for a commercial building, or perhaps an airplane hangar—which would have been no coincidence since its architect also designed Orange County's John Wayne International Airport. On the inside, the 3,200-seat auditorium had the look of a college gymnasium—a high ceiling with exposed girders and air ducts, a level carpeted floor with moveable interlocking chairs, and a sloping bleacher section in the rear. Across the front, a wide, elevated stage was flanked by two giant video screens with a smaller screen directly overhead. A lone wooden cross was suspended midway between the floor and ceiling just to the left of the stage. "It's an instrument, not a monument," Warren said of the building's decidedly utilitarian appearance. In the first year, nearly ten thousand worshipers would cycle through it each weekend during multiple services.

In the years ahead additional buildings would be added—a children's ministry center, a nursery building, young-adult meeting rooms, an administration building, and eventually a teen meeting and recreation center. The parklike campus would take on the inviting appeal of a southern Mediterranean oasis meticulously landscaped with flowering plants, lush patches of lawn, clusters of pine and towering palm trees, faux rock outcroppings, and a cascading waterfall. Walking trails and paved parking lots would form its perimeter. Warren's original and seemingly elusive vision of building a multipurpose church facility serving twenty thousand people and "set in a peaceful, inspiring garden landscape" on a big piece of land in Orange County was well on its way to being fulfilled.

———

DURING THE INTENSE YEARS of building a congregation and a church home, the Warrens worked hard to balance their personal priorities. While both Rick and Kay considered their Saddleback ministry a lifelong calling and a shared mission—he as pastor and she as supporting partner to her husband and as a teacher of new church members—they saw their role as parents as no less a God-imparted responsibility, and both worked hard to fulfill it. Yet through much of their child-rearing years, with Rick frequently traveling and often consumed by church duties, it was Kay who would assume the greater share of parenting duties. "I was the disciplinarian and the rule-maker," Kay recalled of those early-childhood years. "I'd make sure the homework got done, that everybody got to the doctor, the dog got fed—those kinds of things." While Rick participated when he could, "he has always been what we call the funmeister. I'm the melancholy one and he's the sanguine, happy-go-lucky fun guy. He created some fabulous memories for our kids."

Whenever Rick was not out of town, Monday evenings were set aside as family night, with each member taking a turn on deciding what they would do together. On other nights, Kay recalled, it was not unusual for Rick to arrive home after the children had gone to bed, "and he would just burst into their bedrooms at ten at night and get them up and go, 'Let's go get ice cream!' And I'm screaming, 'What? What do you mean? It's ten o'clock and they have school tomorrow!' And they're just delighted. They'd pile into the car, and he'd take them on what he'd call Daddy's Magical Mystery Tours. We'd just pile in the car and he'd have no plan. It was just, 'Oh, that would be fun. Let's do that.' So I'm the center of gravity that everybody is spinning around, and he is the fun one. He brought just great delight and fun to our family through the years."

As the children grew older and Rick increased his international travel, he would often take his children with him in order to maximize quality time alone with them. When circumstances required it, he seldom hesitated to clear his calendar to make room for family responsibilities. On one occasion in the late 1990s, he cancelled an engagement to speak to 75,000 men at a stadium event in order to go to camp as a counselor with his youngest son, Matthew. "You must never let your professional life outpace your private life," he told an interviewer in 1999. "A spiritual leader whose family life is in shambles is no help to anybody, so my family has always taken first priority over my ministry."

As the pace and success of Warren's ministry continued to accelerate, his parents—watching proudly from afar—became deeply immersed in an important new phase in their own lifelong ministry. After thirty-one years as a Southern Baptist pastor, missionary, and builder of churches, Jimmy Warren retired in 1981 at the age of sixty-two. He and Dot, who was then fifty-nine, sold the Redwood Valley house where they had raised their family and moved into a much smaller house not far away. Four years later they moved again, this time to Pioneer, a tiny Gold Rush–era town in the Sierra Nevada foothills some sixty miles east of Sacramento, where they immediately became involved in a local Baptist church.

Even though they were officially retired, old habits were hard to break and Jimmy and Dot stayed nearly as busy as before with ministry work, only this time as unpaid lay volunteers. Over the next several years they signed on for short-term mission projects in Africa, Asia, Latin America, the South Pacific, the Middle East, and throughout the United States, doing as they had always done—Jimmy using his considerable construction skills to help build or repair churches, schools, and other buildings, and Dot seeing to it that volunteer work crews, or anyone else in need of a hot meal, were properly fed. After the first Gulf War in 1991, they joined a disaster relief team in northern Iraq helping to replenish water supplies in Kurdish villages devastated during the conflict. They performed similar work in the wake of natural or man-made disasters in Israel, Guatemala, Alaska, and elsewhere—sometimes staying months at a time until the job was completed. When the deadly Loma Prieta earthquake struck the San Francisco Bay area on October 17, 1989, they moved to the hard-hit town of Watsonville in Santa Cruz County and lived in a tiny trailer for six months while helping to rebuild houses and churches in the area. Retirement, as Jimmy and Dot saw it, was hardly a time for leisure and self-indulgence. As young newlyweds they had committed themselves to a lifetime of

Christian service together, and as long as they had their health and the means, they intended to honor that commitment.

Jimmy was proud of his son's success at Saddleback, and both he and Dot prayed daily for Rick and Kay and their rapidly growing congregation. Rick cherished his parents' prayer support, and when his father wasn't traveling he often sought him out for advice and counsel on ministry matters, hoping to learn from Jimmy's many years of experience as a church planter and a trainer of other pastors. Sometimes father and son would spend days together at a mountain cabin near June Lake, fishing, praying, and mulling over some new problem Rick had encountered at church or a new sermon series he was contemplating. He considered his dad his first and most important mentor.

During one such outing in 1995, Jimmy mentioned to his son that he recently had been experiencing a bothersome dull pain in his back. He said he didn't think he had injured himself and that he was thinking of seeing the doctor when he went home. Rick encouraged him to do so. A few days later, the call came that doctors had found a mass and it was malignant. Jimmy was diagnosed with lymphoma.

The entire family was shaken by the diagnosis. At the age of seventy-six, Jimmy was spry and active and had seemed the picture of health, having led a wholesome lifestyle his entire life. The sudden onset of cancer came as a complete surprise. Doctors prescribed treating it aggressively: a course of radiation followed by chemotherapy. Radiation treatments began almost immediately at a hospital in Sacramento, but when it was time for chemotherapy to begin the family decided to move Jimmy and Dot to Orange County temporarily so that Rick and Chaundel and their spouses could help their ailing father deal with the debilitating side effects. Over the next several months, as unpleasant as the treatments were, the cancer-fighting drugs worked as intended and the disease went into remission. In early August 1996, Jimmy was declared cancer-free.

During the year of treatment, living in such close proximity to their children and grandchildren, Jimmy and Dot decided they would stay in Southern California permanently and become part of Saddleback Church. They purchased a mobile home and made plans to move in at the end of August. Now that Jimmy had been given a clean bill of health, they were looking forward to beginning an exciting new chapter in their lives.

A week before the scheduled move, on August 16, Rick received an emergency phone call from his dad. Dot had collapsed in the kitchen at their home in Pioneer and was being rushed by ambulance to a hospital in Jackson, some fifteen miles away. Rick relayed the news to Chaundel and told her he did not know their mother's condition, only that she was not doing well. It was well known in the family that Dot previously had some health issues and that she wore a pacemaker, but at the age of seventy-three she had seemed to be going strong.

Chaundel called the hospital but no one could give her additional information. Finally, almost an hour after the initial call, a doctor came on the line. "Your mother had an incident this morning," the doctor said with clinical detachment, "and she did not survive." It took Chaundel a moment to decode the doctor's nearly incoherent euphemism. She would learn later that her mother had an enlarged heart and probably had suffered a sudden cardiac arrest. It happened while she was in the kitchen preparing a picnic lunch for some visiting missionaries. "She died doing what she loved—serving others," Chaundel would recall years later. "Of course, we were all very sad. That was my first reaction. Yet she died exactly how she hoped she would. Her own mother had a stroke and spent the last eight years of her life in a nursing home and Mother was afraid that would happen to her. She prayed she would not go that way, and I believe her prayers were answered."

A few days later the entire family and a wide circle of friends gathered at the tiny Sierra Baptist Church in Pioneer for a memorial service and Rick delivered the message. He would describe it as the most difficult message he had ever preached. They called the service a celebration of life, yet tears flowed freely and Jimmy wept silently as he mourned the loss of his partner in life and ministry—the only woman he had ever loved. Afterward, the family helped him pack his belongings and move to Orange County.

BY THE END OF 1996, *The Purpose-Driven Church* was sitting atop the religion best-seller list and was on its way to selling more than one million copies—a marketing feat that surprised, and obviously delighted, the people at Zondervan. It won that year's Gold Medallion book award, the highest honor in the evangelical publishing world and was about to be translated into some twenty foreign languages. Some evangelical seminaries already had adopted it as a standard text, and church planters and missions departments in some denominations were using it as a training manual.

Much of the book's early sales momentum resulted from its popularity among the thousands of pastors who had attended Warren's seminars or had received other resources from Saddleback over the years. What was coming to be known as the Purpose-Driven Network was proving to be an efficient and lucrative conduit for Warren's books and other teaching materials—one that Warren would tap often. Part of the book's appeal among pastors, by their own admission, was not that it disclosed something new and profound but that it took seemingly common-sense church-growth principles that were grounded in Scripture and laid them out in a way that anyone following the instructions could apply in their own churches in hopes of replicating Warren's success. "What pastors say when they hear the Purpose-Driven principles is, 'It makes sense. I could have written this book,'" Tom Holladay would tell an interviewer.

The book's success also fueled the popularity of Warren's Purpose-Driven seminars. In 1997, the annual conference at Saddleback filled all of its 3,300 slots before the early-bird registration period ended, and some 400 pastors were turned away. That prompted the church to hold a second conference a few months later and it, too, sold out in just a few weeks. Purpose-Driven was becoming a popular brand. Whatever was behind it, the book's unexpected success was expanding Warren's sphere of influence among pastors and was beginning to make his name, in evangelical circles at least, a household word.

IN 1998, JIMMY WARREN'S CANCER RETURNED. He was about to go to Russia on a short-term mission trip when he began having difficulty breathing, so he went in for a checkup and the doctors found a fluid buildup in his lungs. They drained the fluid and told Jimmy to go ahead with his trip. For the next two weeks Jimmy busied himself in St. Petersburg repairing roofs at a church and a school. When he returned home he learned that tests on the fluid had confirmed a recurrence of lymphoma. He immediately began another round of chemotherapy and moved in with Rick and Kay.

Jimmy battled the disease valiantly for several months, but it soon became apparent that this time he would not win. On April 4, 1999, weak and frail, he attended the dedication of a just completed $4.5 million bridge named in his honor that would provide a much-needed second entrance onto the Saddleback property. Within a few weeks of the dedication ceremony he was bedridden and fading fast.

Warren later would describe his father's final days—lying delirious in a semiconscious state, talking in his sleep, replaying in his mind and aloud the building projects he had worked on all over the world. "The night before he died," Warren recalled, "my wife, my niece, and I were sitting in the room with him, and my dad became very agitated. He started trying to get out of bed . . . and Kay said to him, 'Jimmy, you've got to stay in bed.' But he kept trying to get out of bed, and she said, 'Jimmy, you can't get out of bed. You're too frail. What do you want?' My dad said, 'Got to save one more for Jesus! Got to save one more for Jesus!' He kept saying it over and over. 'Got to save one more for Jesus!'

"As I sat there by my father's bed I bowed my head to thank God for my godly parents . . . and my dad reached over and placed his hand on my head, as if commissioning me, and he said, 'Save one more for Jesus! Save one more for Jesus! Save one more for Jesus!' I intend for that to be the theme for the rest of my life."

# CHAPTER TWELVE

# *"It's Not About You"*

As 1999 DREW TO A CLOSE and Saddleback Church approached its twentieth anniversary, Warren and his congregation had every reason to celebrate. During that final year of the century, average attendance at weekend services hovered between 10,000 and 11,000, with more than 30,000 showing up both on Easter and on Christmas Eve. Nearly 1,800 people made decisions for Christ at Saddleback that year, bringing the total saved since the church began to almost 12,000. Meanwhile, Saddleback had just launched its twentieth daughter church in the Los Angeles area, most of them small Latino congregations, and several of those had gone on to plant daughter churches of their own. By nearly every conceivable measure, Warren's audacious dream of building a missionary-minded megachurch that turned unchurched suburbanites into dedicated followers of Christ was being fulfilled.

As the congregation continued to expand, so did Warren's weekend workload. Shortly after they moved into the new Worship Center, the church added a second Saturday service, raising the total number of weekend services to four, and Warren usually would preach at them all. It was a demanding schedule that he hardly could have imagined undertaking years earlier when he battled exhaustion and episodes of panic, blurred vision, and headaches whenever he stood to preach. While he still frequently experienced headaches and blurred vision in the pulpit, Warren had learned to cope with the symptoms by lying down in a cool and darkened room backstage between services. The spells had become so familiar over the years that they no longer triggered the paralyzing anxiety that they once did. Still, they were bothersome, and despite untold numbers of tests and doctor visits they remained a medical mystery.

Early in the year 2000, Warren decided to try once again to get to the bottom of it. He took some time off and checked into the Mayo

Clinic in Scottsdale, Arizona. After running an exhaustive series of diagnostic tests, the Mayo doctors finally came up with an answer. They told Warren that he suffered from a rare brain disorder that prevented his nervous system from properly processing adrenaline, a hormone that is released by the adrenal glands in moments of sudden stress or fear. Normally when adrenaline hits the system it increases heart rate and blood flow, giving a person an extra spurt of energy and mental acuity to handle situations that are perceived as threatening—the biological "fight-or-flight" response. In Warren's case, the doctors concluded, it also produced clouded vision, headaches, and, in some situations, the loss of consciousness that he had experienced as a child. It was an extremely rare syndrome—they told Warren they had seen it only a handful of times—that had no name and no known cure.

Warren and his family and staff were relieved that the mystery finally was solved and they were thankful that it was not a potentially life-threatening condition, but they also realized that it meant Warren would have to deal with the episodes for the rest of his life. As a preacher there was no way he could avoid adrenaline-charged situations; nearly every time he got up to speak in church he experienced an adrenaline rush. "Adrenaline is a public speaker's best friend," he would explain. "If you don't have adrenaline you're boring. Adrenaline gives you passion. But adrenaline also makes it painful for me. The very thing that I need in order to do what I need to do becomes a source of pain. People ask me, 'Rick, do you ever get proud talking to all these people?' I say, 'You have no idea. I'm saying, God get me through this.' It creates a sense of dependency, a sense of humility—what Paul would call a thorn in the flesh. It's been a governor on my life that keeps me focused on God rather than focusing on the crowds."

BETWEEN HIS DUTIES AT SADDLEBACK and his growing national and international involvement with pastors in his Purpose-Driven Network, Warren had little time to think about the second book that he had agreed to write for Zondervan. Under terms of the original agreement, he was to deliver the sequel to *The Purpose-Driven Church* in 1997, roughly a year and a half later. But Warren kept putting it off—mostly because he was too busy, but also, in part, because the book was not coming together in his mind quite as he had anticipated. Although they were anxious to receive the second manuscript, with sales of *The Purpose-Driven Church* continuing to ratchet upward—exceeding one million copies and almost everyone's expectations—the people at Zondervan were not inclined to press the matter. Finally, late in 2001, Warren decided it was time to begin writing.

As originally conceived, his second book, *The Purpose-Driven Life*, would be based on a ten-week sermon series by that title that he had preached in 1993. It would take the same five purposes that he wrote about in the first book—worship, fellowship, discipleship, ministry, and evangelism—and apply them to individuals. Assuming that the book would be an expansion of Warren's sermons and hoping to speed the writing process along, Zondervan had transcripts made of the sermon tapes and sent them to Warren. But Warren had other ideas. When he finally sat down in early December to begin the book, he tossed the transcripts aside and set about writing from scratch.

For the next seven months Warren sequestered himself in a small isolated study backstage in the Worship Center, away from the distractions of home and office, and began crafting what he later would describe as his life's message, the most important book he would ever write. As he worked he followed a disciplined, almost ascetic, daily routine. Getting up in the dark at 4:30 a.m., he would arrive at his office hideaway by five and write until lunchtime, pausing just long enough to shower and wolf down a carried-in meal, and then resume writing until five when he would go home to spend the evening with his family. Except for Christmas and Easter he stayed away from the Saddleback pulpit the entire time. "It about killed me to be alone by myself that long," Warren later would confide, "because I'm wired to be with people . . . It was painful, like birthing a baby." Yet he knew, given his notoriously short attention span, that it probably was the only way he would complete the project without getting sidetracked.

The book that began to take shape in the winter and spring of 2002 was deceptively simple in both its format and content. On its face it appeared to be a rather conventional devotional guide intended to provide daily meditations for personal study and reflection. But Warren saw his book as fulfilling a far loftier role. "This is more than a book," he audaciously announced in the introduction, "it is a guide to a forty-day spiritual journey that will enable you to discover the answer to life's most important question: What on earth am I here for?"

He wasted little time suggesting an all-encompassing answer. From the opening line—"It's not about you"—he set about reassuring readers that everyone has a divine purpose and that finding and living according to that purpose was the key to meaningful living. "The purpose of your life is far greater than your own personal fulfillment, your peace of mind, or even your happiness," he wrote. "It's far greater than your family, your career, or even your wildest dreams and ambitions. If you want to know why you were placed on this planet, you must begin with God. You were born by his purpose and for his purpose."

Warren divided the book into forty relatively short, breezy chapters, brimming with Bible quotations and clustered under five headings, each corresponding to one of the five purposes: "You Were Planned for God's Pleasure" (worship); "You Were Formed for God's Family" (fellowship); "You Were Created to Become Like Christ" (discipleship); "You Were Shaped for Serving God" (ministry); "You Were Made for a Mission" (evangelism). The chapters were chatty and personal, addressing the reader directly, and bore such titles as "You Are Not an Accident," "Becoming Best Friends with God," "Defeating Temptation," and "Understanding Your Shape." In the end, readers would be instructed to "abandon your agenda and accept God's agenda," which boiled down to living for Christ, serving others, and spreading the Christian message.

Warren later would be the first to admit that his book broke no new ground either in its theological insights or its analysis of Scripture. "There's nothing new in *The Purpose-Driven Life* that hasn't already been stated in classic Christian thought over the past two thousand years," Warren told an interviewer. "I just stated it in a simple way. But sometimes as I was writing, I'd break into tears as I typed, because I felt so strongly that God was going to bless these simple truths."

Once it was completed, *The Purpose-Driven Life* would be classified by the publishing industry as part of the "advice and self-help" genre, a label that Warren felt was misapplied. "This is not a self-help book," he insisted in the opening chapter. "It is not about finding the right career, achieving your dreams, or planning your life . . . It is about becoming what God created you to be." Yet the book's introduction did project a decidedly self-help-sounding tone in the benefits it promised readers. "By the end of this journey you will know God's purpose for your life and will understand the big picture—how all the pieces of your life fit together," Warren wrote. "Having this perspective will reduce your stress, simplify your decisions, increase your satisfaction, and, most important, prepare you for eternity."

DESPITE HIS BEST EFFORTS to avoid outside distractions as he labored over his manuscript, Warren was pulled from his isolation early that spring by an unexpected development in a six-year-old court case. What began as a personal challenge by Warren of a relatively routine income-tax audit suddenly had turned into a hotly contested legal battle with far-reaching and potentially catastrophic implications for clergy throughout the country.

At the center of the conflict was a long-standing tax break that exempts ordained clergy from paying federal income taxes on money spent on housing. The so-called "parsonage allowance" had been part of the federal tax code since 1921, and Warren, like some 850,000 other pastors, routinely claimed it each year. In an otherwise uneventful audit of Warren's returns for 1993 through 1995, an IRS auditor disallowed a major portion of Warren's claimed exemptions for those years, asserting that they exceeded the "fair rental value" of the property—a provision in the law that limits the exemption to what it would cost to rent a house of similar value, furnish it, maintain it, and provide it with utilities. In 1995, the Warrens had claimed $79,999 on the four-bedroom house in Trabuco Canyon, which they had purchased three years earlier for $360,000. The IRS set the fair rental value that year at $59,479. Warren asked the IRS agent to provide the basis he had used to determine the value, and when the agent failed to provide a satisfactory answer, Warren sued, charging that there was no objective standard and that the determination was entirely arbitrary.

On May 16, 2000, the United States Tax Court ruled in Warren's favor by striking down the IRS cap and permitting clergy to claim "the amount used to provide a home," however much that might be. It seemed like a clear-cut win for pastors, but the case was far from settled. The IRS appealed, and on March 5, 2002, the Ninth U.S. Circuit Court of Appeals in San Francisco—the same court that a few months later would rule the Pledge of Allegiance unconstitutional because it included the phrase "under God"—raised the stakes, suggesting in a statement that "it is possible that any tax deduction that Rev. Warren receives [for the parsonage] would constitute an unconstitutional windfall at the public's expense." No longer just a matter of caps and objective standards, suddenly the parsonage allowance itself was in jeopardy, and worried ministers around the country began grumbling aloud that Warren had opened a can of worms.

But by then the case had caught the eye of Congress, which quickly set about to defuse the issue. Rep. Jim Ramstad, a Minnesota Republican, introduced the Clergy Housing Allowance Clarification Act, which reaffirmed the parsonage allowance and clarified the standards for determining "fair rental value." Within six weeks the bill passed both houses by overwhelming margins and President Bush signed it into law. Three months later the Ninth Circuit Court of Appeals dismissed the case and the tax break for pastors was preserved.

Looking back on the episode, Warren would insist that "it was not about the money" and that he had taken on the IRS for the sake of other pastors. "I've always had a heart for pastors of smaller churches," he wrote in a letter to his network in 2002. "I dedicated *The Purpose-Driven Church* to bi-vocational pastors who serve with little or no salary. My father and Kay's father were pastors of small churches, and we both spent time living in a 'parsonage' growing up. Our parents could not have served these small churches without the help of a parsonage allowance. . . . We knew a court challenge would actually cost us more than just paying the unfair assessment, but we felt we needed to stand up for what was right and to protect other ministers from abuse."

AS WARREN NEARED COMPLETION of his book, he began to envision a distribution strategy that he believed would all but assure its commercial success. It would involve conducting a churchwide campaign, first at Saddleback and then replicated at other congregations in his Purpose-Driven Network, called "Forty Days of Purpose." During the campaign, members of the congregation would commit to read one chapter a day for forty days and interact with the text by jotting notes in the margins, memorizing an assigned verse of Scripture each day, and considering a "point to ponder" and a "question to consider" that appeared at the end of each chapter. They also would discuss the readings in small groups that met once a week and would listen to book-based sermons at weekend services. With such multilayered reinforcement, it was expected that by the end of the campaign participants would be intimately familiar with the book and its message and would be drawn into a deeper faith commitment and a desire to share their faith with others. Presumably they also would share their enthusiasm for the book with friends and acquaintances, resulting in additional sales momentum.

The key to success, in Warren's estimation, would be enlisting the support of pastors in his network and in getting a sufficient number of copies into the hands of their congregants. Late that spring, while he was still working on the manuscript, he instructed his literary agent, Bucky Rosenbaum, a former executive at Broadman and Holman Publishers in Nashville, to renegotiate his contract with Zondervan. Among other things, he wanted the publisher to make copies available at reduced cost to churches conducting the campaign. He estimated he would need 25,000 copies just for Saddleback and 225,000 more for other churches participating in the first wave of Forty Days of Purpose campaigns. He asked Zondervan to make the books available for just seven dollars, about a third of the suggested retail price. Not surprisingly, the company was reluctant to slash its profit margin so deeply on what would amount to the book's entire first printing and a fourth of the total number of sales of Warren's previous book. But Warren was adamant. "You don't understand," he told the company's representatives. "This book is not going to sell a million. It's going to sell *tens* of millions."

The Zondervan people were not entirely convinced that Warren's plan would succeed. In their experience, the most reliable distribution channel for Christian books was the nationwide network of evangelical retailers—the national and regional book chains and independent stores that made up the Christian Booksellers Association and a $4 billion-a-year industry. Zondervan had a proven track record in the CBA market. What Warren was proposing seemed highly unorthodox—an end run that would bypass the Christian retailers altogether and go directly to the people in the pews, and at cut-rate prices. It seemed like a gamble, but Warren reassured his publisher that the payoff would come in the enormous sales volume that he believed the Forty Days campaigns would generate.

"Rick was absolutely convinced from the get-go that the success of *The Purpose-Driven Life* would be its catching on with pastors who would then have an influence over their congregations," recalls Jeff Slipp, a Saddleback pastor who succeeded Rosenbaum as Warren's agent. "It was not a strategy toward selling it in the general market. It was a strategy to reach those guys who he had spent over twenty years of his life training. He had written his life's work and he wanted it in their hands. In his heart, he knew that its message was going to resonate not just with churches but with the general population."

With some reservation, Zondervan agreed to do it Warren's way. Having finally come to accept at least the potential viability of his church-based distribution plan, the company's marketing people were eager to lend their expertise to make sure it succeeded, but Warren declined their offer of assistance. "If this appears to be a marketing program from Zondervan, pastors will run from it like flies," he told them during a meeting that summer. "All I want you to do is publish the book. You don't need to do anything to promote it to the churches. If you want to promote it to the secular world—put it in the airports and Wal-Mart and Costco—I would love for you to do that. But I don't need you for our market. I already have a relationship with these pastors." He insisted that maintaining a strong firewall between Zondervan and the Forty Days campaigns was absolutely essential to ensure that the campaigns were seen not as a sales gimmick but as one church helping other churches to build their congregations.

Warren completed the manuscript in early July and, after light editing, it went to the printer on August 23, 2002, in an impressive initial pressrun of 250,000 copies. A month later, on September 22, *The Purpose-Driven Life* officially went on sale. That same weekend, Warren launched Forty Days of Purpose at Saddleback and the entire local allotment of 25,000 books sold out almost immediately. Meanwhile, without ever having laid eyes on the book, some fifteen hundred pastors around the country accepted Warren's invitation to do the campaign that fall with their own congregations and they flooded Saddleback with orders for the discounted books and related materials. By the end of October the first run was gone and the book went to its second printing. By December, sales topped 400,000 units and the velocity continued to accelerate.

"Churches couldn't get the books fast enough," Slipp recalls, "and so they went over to the Barnes & Nobles and the Borders and the Amazons and the Christian bookstores to buy them, and then sales just exploded." No longer was it just the churches that were buying. Thousands of church members who had gone through the Forty Days campaign and were smitten by the book's straightforward faith-building message began telling their friends and family about it. Nearly half bought multiple copies at the full retail price and gave them away as gifts, becoming what one Zondervan executive described as zealous "customer evangelists." In a dramatic reversal of conventional marketing wisdom, Zondervan was finding that the best sales prospects for *The Purpose-Driven Life* were not people who had not yet bought the book but those who already owned a copy. "The book had changed their lives," explained Greg Stielstra, Zondervan's senior marketing director at the time, and the enthusiasm they felt "made them a dramatically more powerful force than advertising and the single greatest contributor to the book's explosive growth."

And explosive is exactly what it was. At the end of February 2003, after just five months on the market, the number of copies sold reached 1.7 million and *The Purpose-Driven Life* made its debut on the *New York Times* best-seller list for advice books. It would remain there for 188 weeks, selling at a jaw-dropping pace of more than 800,000 copies a month. In November it edged out *The South Beach Diet* for the number one spot and ended 2003 as the best-selling hardcover book of the year—a feat it would repeat in 2004—with cumulative sales surpassing 10 million units. Over the following twelve months the sales figure doubled again, shooting past 20 million in September of 2004, and showed no sign of slowing. Late that year, *Publishers Weekly* declared *The Purpose-Driven Life* "the fastest-selling book of all time, and the bestselling hardback in American history."

Seemingly out of nowhere, Warren's book emerged as a publishing phenomenon and the nation's news media began to take notice. Despite his growing reputation in the evangelical world as a successful pastor and church-growth expert, Warren at the time was a virtual unknown to most Americans, including journalists. Aside from the religious press and local news outlets in Southern California, he had garnered relatively little media attention over the years. In 1995, PBS's *MacNeil/Lehrer NewsHour* had featured Warren and his church, along with another Southern California congregation, on a piece exploring the spiritual migration of baby boomers. And immediately after the terrorist attacks of September 11, 2001, a few reporters sought him out for comment on the religious implications of the war on terror. But it was the astounding success of *The Purpose-Driven Life* that suddenly thrust Warren into the media spotlight.

On Christmas 2002, just as his book began taking off, he was invited to appear on CNN's *Larry King Live*—it would be the first of many Warren appearances on the popular prime-time talk show—where he was introduced as "author of the best-selling book, *The Purpose-Driven Life*." He appeared along with singer Pat Boone and Boone's family. Boone's grandson, who attended Saddleback with his parents, had been seriously injured in a freak accident and King wanted Warren to explain, among other things, why bad things happen to good people.

"Well, Larry, I don't know that anybody could fully answer that question," Warren responded. "I think nobody knows all the answers. If I did know that, I'd be God. But I do know this, that God is more interested in my character than he is in my comfort. And the Bible teaches that you were—all of us were—made to last forever, that this life is not all there is, that we're going to spend more on the other side of death than on this side . . . If people say, 'What's the meaning of life?' Well, I'll tell you in three words: preparation for eternity . . . And so on earth, we practice what we're going to do forever in eternity. And one of those things is grow in character. And so while not all things are good—that's real clear—God specializes in bringing good out of bad. Anybody can bring good out of good."

Warren seemed to relish being cast in the role of a public theologian, and he projected a genial and comfortable presence on television, a medium he had purposefully avoided throughout his ministry. Unlike Robert Schuller and some other successful megachurch pastors, Warren decided early on that he would not televise his church services, in part because he did not want to compete against the local pastors he was working to train. "If I went on TV or radio," he once explained, "and people would listen to it and go, 'How come my pastor, my minister, doesn't preach like Rick does?'—it doesn't help those churches. It actually becomes a competition." He also was leery of the fact that broadcast ministries often seemed to take on lives of their own and overshadowed the life of the congregation. He had seen it happen with Schuller, Jerry Falwell, D. James Kennedy, and a host of other TV preachers. "I didn't want to be a celebrity," he insisted. "I think always being in the spotlight blinds you."

Yet even without a televised pulpit, Warren was about to become a celebrity whether he wanted it or not. Over the next several months, as thousands more churches signed up to do Forty Days of Purpose, newspapers all over the country began writing about the campaigns and the book and the author behind them. A writer for the *Philadelphia Inquirer* described Warren as a "superstar pastor" whose fast-selling book was "spawning a worship sensation." A *Charlotte (NC) Observer* columnist declared that the title alone was "enough to make lost souls rush to the nearest bookstore." In the spring of 2004, the *New York Times Magazine* gave *The Purpose-Driven Life* a favorable review and remarked that "the book attracts crowds, the crowds buy books, the cycle repeats: Holy synergy!" A few months later, the *Times* carried a front-page story about a successful Forty Days of Purpose campaign conducted among inmates at a medium-security prison in California and called it "a milestone in both spiritual formation and brand expansion." And in the fall, a *Times* political columnist wrote that the surprising popularity of Warren's book reflected a widening cultural "conversation" rooted in Middle American suburban values—a phenomenon that had escaped the attention of the so-called cultural elites.

The sudden groundswell of media attention began to spur demand for the book far beyond church circles. Zondervan estimated in 2004 that for every book purchased as part of a church-based campaign, an additional five were sold at retail. *The Purpose-Driven Life* was demonstrating its appeal to an ever-widening audience and, as a result, millions of Americans were taking their first look at a fresh new face on the religious landscape.

THE BIGGEST PUBLICITY BONANZA for Warren and his book would come quite unexpectedly two weeks before Easter in 2005 while Warren was in Africa. Nearly eight thousand miles away in a suburb of Atlanta, a fugitive named Brian Nichols shot and killed four people during a courthouse escape and then accosted a widowed young mother, Ashley Smith, outside her apartment in the middle of the night and held her hostage for seven hours. When the ordeal was over, Smith would explain how she talked her captor into releasing her and giving himself up peacefully to police.

"I asked him if I could read," she told reporters the day after the incident. "He said, 'What do you want to read?' 'Well, I have a book in my room.' So I went and got it. I got my Bible, and I got a book called *The Purpose-Driven Life*." She said she turned to the chapter that she was due to read that day and began reading it aloud. It was chapter 32, "Using What God Gave You." It opens with a Bible verse: "Since we find ourselves fashioned into all these excellently formed and marvelously functioning parts in Christ's body, let's just go ahead and be what we were made to be" (Romans 12:5); and a Danish proverb: "What you are is God's gift to you; what you do with yourself is your gift to God." That was followed by Warren's message, which began:

> God deserves your best. He shaped you for a purpose, and he expects you to make the most of what you have been given. He doesn't want you to worry about or covet abilities you don't have.

Instead he wants you to focus on talents he has given to you to use. When you attempt to serve God in ways you're not shaped to serve, it feels like forcing a square peg into a round hole. It's frustrating and produces limited results. It also wastes your time, your talent, and your energy. The best use of your life is to serve God out of your shape. To do this you must discover your shape, learn to accept and enjoy it, and then develop it to its fullest potential.

Smith read the opening section and was about to turn the page when Nichols interrupted her. "Stop, will you read it again?" he asked. She read it to him again, and then they talked, for hours—about God and miracles, their families, their pasts. Both indicated that they were born-again Christians. And they talked about purpose. "What do you think mine is?" Nichols wanted to know. She suggested that "maybe it's to minister to people in prison," and urged him to turn himself in so that no one else would be hurt. "Maybe that's what God wants you to do, and he brought you here to my apartment so that you could know that."

As they talked through the night she won his trust. In the morning she served him pancakes and eggs, and then he let her go.

When the story broke, Smith instantly became a media celebrity and was widely hailed as a hero, and Warren's book became the talk of the nation. The dramatic story of faith and survival was media gold in the run-up to Easter, and major newspapers and network news departments clamored for interviews. As soon as he returned from Africa, Warren made the rounds of the major TV news-talk shows: CNN's *Larry King Live*, NBC's *Today*, ABC's *Good Morning America*, CBS's *The Early Show*, and Fox News's *Hannity & Colmes* and *The O'Reilly Factor*. At each stop he delivered similar talking points, that he was "humbled" and "thrilled" that his book had played a role in ending the hostage episode, and he credited the hundreds of Bible passages contained in his book—more than his own prose—for communicating a powerful life-changing message. "Honestly, there's nothing in the book that hasn't been said in historic Christian faith for two thousand years," he told

Larry King. "I just happened to interpret it in a simple way for the twenty-first century."

Meanwhile, the *New York Times*, the *Washington Post*, the *Los Angeles Times*, *USA Today*, and other major publications ran multiple stories recounting Smith's ordeal and the role Warren's book played in convincing a killer to set her free. CNN's Paula Zahn devoted an entire edition of *CNN NewsNight* to the phenomenon of *The Purpose-Driven Life*, relating not only Smith's story but the experience of others—a dying cancer patient and a man addicted to pornography—who found comfort and redemption in the pages of Warren's book. "For those who believe God works in mysterious ways, Ashley Smith and Brian Nichols will long remain a case in point," Zahn concluded. "But the legions of those who have been touched by Rick Warren's teachings will not be surprised."

Predictably, the blanket news coverage sparked a sudden new surge in book sales. On Sunday night, March 13, the day the story broke, *The Purpose-Driven Life* sat in a respectable position at number 79 on Internet bookseller Amazon.com's sales rankings. By 2 p.m. on the following Tuesday it had soared to number 2. Within a few days, it simultaneously hit number 1 on four major best-seller lists: the *New York Times*, the *Wall Street Journal*, *USA Today*, and *Publishers Weekly*—a feat a *Publishers Weekly* editor described as "unprecedented." Warren's Purpose-Driven juggernaut continued to roll.

IN SEPTEMBER 2004, TWO YEARS after *The Purpose-Driven Life* was released, Zondervan commissioned a marketing survey asking readers to describe how the book had affected them personally. The most common response they received: "It changed my life." In the preceding months there had been plenty of anecdotal evidence corroborating that sentiment; thousands of readers had offered testimonials in letters to Zondervan or to Warren himself describing addictions broken, marriages healed, personal faith reaffirmed. In reading the book, people found—or were reminded—that there was more to life than a self-centered pursuit of prominence, pleasure, personal fulfillment, or peace of mind. As Warren told one interviewer: "When [readers] discovered, 'Hey, I'm here for a reason, I am here for a purpose,' it has the power to change people's lives." That life-changing capacity, more than anything else—at least as far as Warren was concerned—explained his book's popularity and its unmatched success. Yet it is difficult to imagine that any life would be changed more dramatically by *The Purpose-Driven Life* than Warren's.

First, there was the matter of money. Warren usually was circumspect when it came to discussing details of his book earnings, seldom venturing beyond the obvious—that it was "in the millions" of dollars. His customary response when conversations turned to royalties was to offer an even more general characterization: "It brought in a ton of money. I mean a *ton* of money."

On at least one occasion, however, he provided a more revealing glimpse of the size of the windfall. In an interview with the multifaith website Beliefnet in 2005, Warren disclosed that his royalty check from Zondervan in one quarter of 2003—the book's first full year in print— came to $9 million, and that was before the book had reached full stride. In 2006, *Forbes* magazine estimated that Warren had pocketed $25 million that year in book royalties and from sales of book-related merchandise, placing him at number 60 in the magazine's annual ranking of the top one hundred celebrity earners. When the list was narrowed to just authors, Warren came in at number 3 behind Dan Brown (*The Da Vinci Code*) at $88 million and J. K. Rowling (*Harry Potter*) at $75 million. Whatever the precise numbers, there was no getting around the fact that *The Purpose-Driven Life* suddenly had made Warren, the son of a poor Baptist minister, an extremely wealthy man.

It also brought him unforeseen national prominence. The blowout sales numbers alone had raised the little-known California pastor's public name recognition at least to the level of other commercially successful authors of the moment. That and the publicity stemming from the Atlanta hostage story had placed Warren squarely on the radar screens of network news producers and other national journalists, many of whom seemed pleased to have discovered a winsome alternative to "the usual suspects"—the dour and aging culture warriors of the Religious Right—as a representative voice of American evangelicalism. At the same time, leaders in business, government, academia, sports, and entertainment also began to take notice, and Warren soon found himself inundated with speaking invitations and interview requests. His circle of influence, centered on his suburban megachurch congregation and an international network of pastors that had taken him more than twenty years to build, appeared to be on the verge of explosive expansion.

For most people, suddenly becoming unimaginably rich and famous at the age of fifty probably would be considered incredibly good fortune and a cause for celebration, but for Warren it presented a quandary. "When you write a book that begins with the line, 'It's not about you,' and it makes millions of dollars, you have to figure that it's not for you." Although Warren chuckled when he made that observation to a group of foreign journalists in 2006, the first royalty payment that showed up early in 2003 was a life-changing amount of money, and as the enormity of the situation sank in, Warren knew that he and Kay would have to make some important decisions. "All my life I planned to simply pastor this church for life and train pastors. That's all I wanted to do," he explained. But the massive infusion of wealth and influence threatened to distort those plans or disrupt them entirely. "I don't think God gives you either money or fame for your own ego—particularly pastors. And so I thought, what am I supposed to do with this?"

As he would later tell the story—and he would tell it often—he turned to the Scriptures for guidance. One of the passages he found was 1 Corinthians 9. "Paul is talking to pastors about money and their salary and he says, 'Those that teach the Gospel should make a living by the Gospel.' In other words, it is okay to pay your pastor. 'But,' he says, 'I will not accept that right because I want the free rein to serve God for free so that I am a slave to no man.' And when I read that, I said that is what I want to do. I want to serve God for free so that I am a slave to no man."

Consequently, he and Kay made four decisions regarding the money. "The first thing we decided was that we wouldn't let it change our lifestyle one bit." They would stay in the same house as before, a comfortable but unpretentious four-bedroom home on a quiet hillside cul-de-sac, which they had bought for $360,000 in 1992, and they would continue driving the same 2000 Ford Expedition. They refused to indulge themselves with luxury cars, yachts, beach houses, and expensive wardrobes.

Second, Warren stopped taking a salary from the church, which was reported at the time to be about $110,000 a year. "Then I added up all that the church had paid me in the previous twenty-five years and I gave it back because I didn't want anybody thinking that I did this for money." (The very next week, a reporter from a national magazine interviewed Warren and immediately asked about his salary. "I was able to say honestly that I've been able to serve my church free for twenty-five years. It felt so good to bust that stereotype.")

Next, he and Kay began to "reverse tithe"—giving back 90 percent of their income to Christian ministry and living on the remaining 10 percent. As dramatic as it sounded, it was not an abrupt change for the Warrens. They had been gradually working their way up toward that ratio, raising their rate of giving back a percentage point each year since early in their marriage, in order, as Warren put it, to "break the grip of materialism" on their lives. Nor did it leave them wanting. Warren once told reporters that they gave away $13 million in 2004 alone—which meant that if they were true to the formula they would have kept about $1.4 million for themselves that year.

Finally, the Warrens formed three charitable foundations: one to train pastors, another to help fund missions work through what later would become the PEACE plan, and a third to help AIDS victims and orphans in Africa. Those three foundations would become the main recipients of their charitable giving as the royalty checks continued to roll in.

As Warren would say often in retrospect, dealing with the sudden wealth was "the easy part." Handling the accompanying notoriety would prove to be a far more daunting challenge.

Sometime in the first half of 2003, as the popularity of his book was accelerating, Warren began to hear from members of Congress, business leaders, entertainers, sports figures, and other celebrities who had read the book and wanted his private spiritual counsel or to talk with him about purpose or simply to share their own personal faith stories. Often they would call him on the phone just to chat. Sometimes they would invite him to fly out to meet with some high-powered group or another—a gathering of business executives in Chicago, a Bible-study group on Capitol Hill, a philanthropists' meeting in Phoenix—and he readily accepted many of the invitations. It was heady stuff suddenly to be in such demand, and as a pastor he welcomed the opportunity to offer spiritual guidance to the high and mighty. Along with the never-ending requests for media interviews, it was becoming clear to Warren that the success of his book—and, ultimately, God—had provided him a new public platform, but for what purpose he was not sure. How was he to use this new avenue of influence that had opened so unexpectedly before him?

Once again, as he would tell the story, Warren turned to the Bible and found guidance in Psalm 72, a prayer of King Solomon. "When you read this prayer it really sounds quite selfish," Warren explained. "Solomon is the wisest and wealthiest and most powerful man in the world, because he is the head of the United Kingdom of Israel when it is at the apex of its power. He prays, 'God, I want you to make me more influential. I want you to bless me and give me more power. I want you to make me famous. I want you to spread the fame of my name to many nations.' It sounds selfish until you understand why. He says, 'so that the king may support the widow and orphan, care for the poor, defend the defenseless, lift up the fallen, release the captive, help the foreigner, the immigrant.'"

Through that passage, Warren said, "God basically said to me, 'The purpose of influence is to speak up for those who have no influence.' That changed my life. I had to repent. I had to say, 'God, I'm sorry. I can't think of the last time I thought about widows or orphans. They aren't even on my agenda.' It wasn't like I was wasting my time twiddling my thumbs. There are 82,000 names on our church roll. We're building a megachurch and baptized 15,000 new believers in the last ten years. So I wasn't just goofing off. But God said, 'But you don't care about the people I care about.' And I said, 'I'm sorry, God, and I will use whatever influence you give me [for] the rest of my life to help those who have no influence.'"

What Warren described as a life-changing moment of repentance in the spring of 2003 would ignite a new personal passion and mark an unexpected turn in the direction of his ministry. In response to his own good fortune, he had committed to a "stewardship of influence" and a "stewardship of affluence" on behalf of the poor and the dispossessed. And yet, as the successful pastor of a comfortable middle-class congregation, he had no clear notion of what it would require of him or where in the world it might take him. The answers would come soon enough, and in ways that he never could have foreseen.

# CHAPTER THIRTEEN

# The Road to PEACE

ON A MILD SPRING MORNING IN 2002, while her husband labored in seclusion on the manuscript of *The Purpose-Driven Life*, Kay Warren sat alone in the comfortable living room of their Trabuco Canyon home and, over a cup of tea, saw her life quietly turned upside down. She had just sent their seventeen-year-old son, Matthew, off to school and had settled onto the couch to spend a few minutes relaxing and reading before launching into her usual busy schedule of church and family-related activities. She picked up a news magazine from the coffee table and was casually thumbing through it when her eyes landed on an article about AIDS in Africa.

AIDS was not a subject that Kay cared or even thought much about. She knew almost nothing about the disease other than that it was deadly, that it seemed to afflict mainly gay men and drug addicts, and that there was no known cure. AIDS had nothing to do with her or her suburban, middle-class, evangelical, "soccer mom" world. But what caught her eye that morning were the horrific pictures of emaciated men, women, and children so weakened by the disease that they couldn't brush the flies from their faces. She found the images deeply disturbing and her first impulse was to toss the magazine aside. Instead, somehow, she felt compelled to read the article, and the more she read the more disturbed she became.

One dramatic phrase, highlighted in a quote box, seemed to leap off the page and grab her by the throat: "Twelve Million Children Orphaned by AIDS in Africa." Her first reaction was stunned disbelief. "No," she said out loud, "there's no way there could be twelve million children orphaned in one place due to one illness at one time. I don't even know one orphan—how could there be twelve million?" She threw the magazine down and went on with her day. That night as she lay awake in bed she was haunted by the images in the magazine and the thought of 12 million children without their parents because of AIDS. Over the next several days she tried to block it from her mind, but it seemed that every newspaper she picked up had an article about AIDS in Africa. As weeks passed there was no escaping the growing awareness of the magnitude of the AIDS pandemic and her own growing anguish over a humanitarian crisis that she could no longer ignore.

With her sense of normalcy disrupted by a killer disease half a world away, Kay felt herself becoming angry with God. "Why are you bothering me with this?" she demanded. "There's nothing I can do about it. I'm just an ordinary person." After about a month of what she described as "intense internal dialogue," she realized that she needed to make a decision. Either she would ignore everything she had learned about the HIV/AIDS crisis and the millions of African orphans and get on with her sheltered suburban life, or she would say "yes" to God and become personally involved in the battle against AIDS—whatever that meant. She decided to say yes, and in that moment, as she wrote later, "my heart broke and I was shattered . . . With lightning speed, God yanked the blindfold of apathy, ignorance, and complacency from my eyes, and I was overcome by the realities of the suffering he revealed . . . I wept as though I was the one who was sick, or it was my child who was dying, or I was the orphan left alone . . . I became a seriously disturbed woman."

Up until that moment, Kay had said nothing to Rick about her sudden and traumatic awakening to the scourge of AIDS. She knew that he was preoccupied with completing his book and she did not want to interrupt his concentration, especially since she was uncertain herself about what it all meant and where it might lead. But once she decided that God was calling her to the frontlines in the fight against HIV/AIDS in Africa she immediately and enthusiastically shared the news with her husband.

"That's great, honey," was Rick's response. "I'm glad you feel so passionately about it, and I support you one hundred percent. But it's not my vision and it has nothing to do with Saddleback." Indeed, with his book nearly finished, Warren already was making plans to launch the Forty Days of Purpose campaign that fall and he expected that to be his church's top priority for the foreseeable future. There would be no room—in his personal thoughts or on Saddleback's schedule—for a competing emphasis on HIV/AIDS.

Kay told him she understood and was fine with that, but added that "as a woman, I cannot get to the end of my life and look back and say that I didn't do anything, that I was just too busy. I couldn't face God like that, not if I ignored what I'd learned." She felt confident that her husband eventually would come around.

In the meantime, she set out to learn quickly all she could about HIV/AIDS—its origins and transmission, its epidemiological distribution around the world, its physiological effects, the available treatments, the state of research, and so on. She read voraciously from books and medical journals, watched videos, searched the Internet, and consulted health care professionals—searching almost frantically for any source she could find that would help her to understand the global AIDS crisis and to make up for lost time. Later that year, while attending a medical conference on HIV/AIDS at UCLA, Kay struck up a conversation with a woman who introduced herself as an AIDS clinician. When Kay identified herself as a pastor's wife, the woman exclaimed with only slightly exaggerated enthusiasm: "Well, hallelujah, the church is finally here!"

To Kay, the reaction to her presence at the conference was an apt metaphor for the long absence of evangelical churches from the fight against AIDS, an absence that reflected the tendency of many conservative Christians to associate the disease with homosexuality, which they considered a perversion. In 1983, Moral Majority founder Jerry Falwell had famously described AIDS as a "gay plague" and called it "the judgment of God" upon a society that tolerated homosexuality. Falwell was not the only conservative preacher to espouse such incendiary views in the early days of the AIDS outbreak, and even though he and others later softened their rhetoric, evangelicals as a group—with a few exceptions—remained largely apathetic to the suffering as the epidemic widened. In a nationwide survey in 2001, only 7 percent of evangelicals said they "definitely" would be willing to donate money to help children orphaned by AIDS. More than half said they "probably" or "definitely" would not. Kay now considered such an uncaring attitude among evangelical Christians to be "sinful" and "not a Christ-like response"—even while admitting that she had been guilty of it herself. She was determined to work to change those attitudes and to nudge her reluctant coreligionists into the fight against AIDS.

In March 2003, almost a year after her personal awakening, Kay decided it was time to go to Africa to see the ravages of HIV/AIDS firsthand. She flew to Mozambique, a small impoverished country on Africa's southeastern coast that had one of the highest HIV infection rates in the world. Some 1.6 million Mozambicans, nearly 17 percent of the adult population, were living with HIV or AIDS and a majority of them were women. Since 1986, when the first cases were reported, a quarter of all deaths in the country were attributed to AIDS and more than 310,000 children had been orphaned by it. Mozambique, it seemed, was a microcosm of the incomprehensible suffering that gripped the entire continent.

Kay was accompanied on the trip by a representative of World Relief, an evangelical humanitarian agency that recently had become heavily engaged in HIV/AIDS work in sub-Saharan Africa. They traveled together by Land Rover to tiny rural villages where Kay, for the first time, was introduced to the human face of AIDS. When she returned home she would tell the story of two people in particular who had made a lasting and haunting impression.

One was a homeless woman whom they found near death lying on a sheet of plastic under a tree. Weak and emaciated, the woman had been banished from her village after people discovered that she and her husband had AIDS. As the woman saw Kay approach she struggled to sit up and straighten her ragged clothing in order to greet her visitor in a dignified manner. Kay was deeply moved and she searched to find some appropriate word of spiritual solace, but nothing came. As she would write later, she knew perfectly well how to counsel people who were stressed about their jobs or their marriages or about losing weight. "But nothing, absolutely nothing, in my experience or my faith had prepared me to speak to a homeless woman dying of AIDS and living under a tree." Finally, she wrapped her arms around the woman, prayed that she would be relieved of her suffering, and whispered in her ear, "I love you." It was all she could think to do.

The other was a young mother whose husband had an affair with a woman who was HIV positive, contracted the virus, and passed it on to her. The mistress became pregnant and the baby was born HIV positive. Then the husband decided to move the mistress and the baby into his family's tiny house. Despite her husband's betrayal and the devastating disease that resulted from it, the woman told Kay her greatest agony was worrying what would become of her children when she was gone. She knew that no one would want them once they learned she had died of AIDS. She asked Kay to pray for her children.

For Kay, the two women had given AIDS a tragic human face and when she returned home she knew her life would never be the same. She shared with Rick what she had seen and felt amid the squalor and suffering in the Mozambique villages, and she informed him that she wanted to start an HIV/AIDS ministry at Saddleback—although she was not yet sure what it would look like or how it would be received. "Here we were preaching a message of God's compassion for the sick, yet we hadn't lifted a finger about [AIDS]," she recalled telling him. While her trip had opened her eyes to the depth of human suffering caused by HIV/AIDS, it also had raised her sights beyond Africa and she realized that people infected by the virus were everywhere, including Orange County—perhaps even in her own congregation—and they needed help. It did not matter how a person contracted the disease, she reasoned. It was enough that they were suffering. "You never find Jesus asking people how they got sick," she noted. "When sick people came to him he simply said, 'How can I help you?' That needs to be the first question out of our mouths."

Rick by then had been reading the articles and listening to the CDs that Kay regularly brought to his attention, and he had begun to share her concern, if not yet her passion. He encouraged her to proceed, and Kay quickly began laying the groundwork for what would become Saddleback's HIV/AIDS Initiative. The new ministry, however, would not get off to a particularly auspicious start. Only six people showed up that summer for the first organizational meeting. Ministering to people who were HIV positive, it seemed, was still an unfamiliar and apparently discomfiting concept at Saddleback, as it was in most evangelical congregations. Kay recognized that it would take some time and determined leadership to move people beyond the common fears and prejudices that had kept them on the sidelines for so long. But at least the new work was under way and she was determined that there would be no turning back.

ABOUT A MONTH AFTER SHE RETURNED from Mozambique, Kay was invited by another evangelical relief agency, World Vision, to visit its HIV/AIDS ministry outposts in Malawi and in South Africa. She eagerly accepted the invitation and immediately began making plans for her second trip to Africa in less than six weeks. This time Rick would accompany her for part of the journey.

In Malawi, Kay was taken to a village, where she visited some of the many thousands of households in Africa that were headed by children whose parents had died of AIDS. It had become such a common living arrangement throughout the continent that government social service and private relief agencies had come up with the official designation "child-headed household"—or CHH—as a euphemism for abandoned AIDS orphans. In a tiny circular mud hut with a dirt floor and thatched roof, Kay was introduced to her first CHH—a fifteen-year-old boy named John, his eleven-year-old brother, George, and three-year-old sister, Nisende. On the floor were a few worn blankets and a dented cooking pot which, besides the tattered clothes they were wearing, appeared to be their only possessions. The boys, she noticed, were "polite but somber" and the little girl never smiled. Kay wondered how they managed to survive on their own, whether they attended school, and who cared for them when they were sick. Her World Vision hosts assured her that their basic needs were met with help from the ministry workers, but they faced a stark future without the nurture and guidance of parents or extended family.

As she turned to leave, Kay began to sob as she considered the harsh sentence that had been meted out on the three young siblings and the thousands of children like them who were left to fend for themselves because of an indiscriminate killer disease and a society that seemed unable to cope. Surely there was more that could be done—that the church could do—on their behalf, she thought. Whatever it was, she was determined to find it.

After a few heart-wrenching days in Malawi, Kay joined Rick in Johannesburg, where they had been invited to speak at a conference on HIV/AIDS. The conference was organized by Bruce Wilkinson, an American preacher and Bible teacher and author of the phenomenally successful book *The Prayer of Jabez*. Published in 2000 by Multnomah Publishers, Wilkinson's little book had sold 9 million copies in its first two years and was on its way to total sales of more than 22 million, making it the fastest-selling book in the world at the time. Suddenly wealthy, Wilkinson had moved his family from Atlanta to Johannesburg in 2002 to put his fortune to work ministering to people with AIDS, promoting abstinence among African young people, and pursuing an ambitious plan to build a self-sustaining village and tourist resort in neighboring Swaziland that would house and support some ten thousand AIDS orphans. That plan would fall through in 2005, however, after the Swazi government turned down his request for some 32,000 acres of prime land located between two popular game preserves where he intended to build his African Dream Village. Disappointed and feeling personally snubbed, Wilkinson abandoned his African aspirations entirely and moved back to Atlanta in what some commentators would describe as a classic case of altruism burnout.

After attending Wilkinson's event, Rick conducted a major conference of his own in Johannesburg; a Purpose-Driven Network training seminar for some eighty thousand African pastors that was broadcast to some four hundred sites throughout the continent via satellite. He later would describe that event as his main reason for going to Africa. "That's what I thought I was there for," he said. "Kay was going to study AIDS, and I was going to go train leaders." His perspective on the purpose of the trip, however, was about to be transformed.

When his conference was over, Warren asked to be taken to a village so he could visit a typical African church and meet some pastors. They took him to Tembisa, a poor rural township just outside Johannesburg where a congregation of about seventy-five people worshiped under a blue-and-white-striped tent that also was home to about twenty-five AIDS orphans. Behind the tent was a garden plot where church members grew food for the orphans. They also provided the children with clothing, schooling, and other basic necessities in addition to caring for their own families.

Seeing that congregation's dedication to the care of the orphans, Warren felt a twinge of guilt. "This church is doing more to help the poor than my megachurch," he remembered thinking. For all of the effective and important ministry that went on at Saddleback—professional marital counseling, recovery programs for addicts, parenting support groups, an array of service projects in the suburban community—there was nothing for the poor. "We're not helping a single orphan," he thought, "and they're helping twenty-five, and all they've got is a tent." He would describe the moment later as "like a knife in my heart, and I said, 'That is going to change.'"

As Warren stood there surveying the scene, a young African pastor came striding toward him smiling broadly and extended his hand. "I know who you are," he proudly announced. "You're Pastor Rick!"

Warren was taken aback. "How in the world do you know who I am?" he asked.

"I get your sermons every week," the pastor replied.

"But you don't even have electricity in this village. How do you get my sermons?"

The pastor explained that the government had placed computers with an Internet connection in every post office in the country. Every week he would walk an hour and a half to the nearest post office, download Warren's sermons from Pastors.com, and preach them on Sunday. "You are the only training I have ever had," he said.

Hearing that, Warren recalled, "I burst into tears, and I thought, 'I will give the rest of my life helping guys like that.'"

LATER THAT NIGHT, SITTING ALONE under the African sky, his conscience already pricked by his long neglect of the poor and of the suffering of millions due to HIV/AIDS, Warren began to wonder what else he had missed. Throughout his twenty-three years of ministry he had focused on two primary objectives that he believed were God-inspired: to pastor one church for life and to train other pastors. He had worked tirelessly on both and, judging from the level of success—his congregation had grown to more than twenty thousand and his Purpose-Driven Network was flourishing—it seemed clear that God had blessed his ministry. Yet now he was gripped by the unsettling realization that his field of vision may have been far too narrow, that the growth of his church and of his Purpose-Driven Network was not an end in itself but was a means to accomplishing something more, something that had not yet occurred to him, or that God had not yet revealed to him, or that in his own inattentiveness perhaps he had simply failed to see.

As he wrestled with those thoughts that night, Warren began to pray for guidance. Thanks to Kay, his eyes finally had been opened to the AIDS crisis and to the needs of the poor in Africa, and the sudden success of his book had provided an unexpected windfall of resources—affluence and influence—that he was willing to place at God's disposal. But how did God plan to use it? What challenges did God want him to tackle? As he prayed, he found his thoughts turning to the biggest problems he could imagine. Over the next several days Warren compiled a list of what he would describe as the five "global giants"—intractable problems affecting not just millions but billions of people all over the world, problems that would take a heroic effort, perhaps a miracle, to address. He jotted them down:

- Spiritual emptiness. ("People lack meaning and purpose to their lives. They're not connected to God.")
- Self-serving leadership. ("The world is full of little Saddams. They are in every nation, they're in every community . . . Give a guy a little bit of power and it goes to his head and he becomes a dictator, and he doesn't understand that the leader exists for the people, not vice-versa.")
- Extreme poverty. ("Half the world lives on less than two dollars a day.")
- Pandemic disease. (Beyond HIV/AIDS, "billions of people are still suffering from diseases that we know the cure for, and that's unconscionable.")

- Rampant illiteracy. ("Half the world is functionally illiterate. How are they going to make a living in the twenty-first century if they can't read or write?")

These were age-old problems that persisted despite the best efforts of governments and the private sector to solve them. Warren was convinced that those efforts had failed because they did not engage the third leg of the stool, the church, which he believed was the only force on earth large enough and distributed widely enough to make a difference. "You could visit millions of villages around the world that don't have a school, a clinic, a hospital, a fire department, or a post office," Warren explained. "But they do have a church." And because local churches were an integral part of their communities they had a degree of credibility and commitment that governments and businesses often lacked.

Shortly after he arrived home from Africa, Warren began to map out an ambitious plan to mobilize the world's 2.3 billion Christians to work through their local churches, in cooperation with business and government, to combat the global giants. He quickly came up with a set of broad objectives to match each of the five problems. Given his preacher's penchant for lists and alliterations, he stated them as an acronym:

- *P*lant new churches (it would change later to "Promote reconciliation")
- *E*quip servant-leaders
- *A*ssist the poor
- *C*are for the sick
- *E*ducate the next generation

They were lofty and laudable goals, but Warren knew that reducing them to a catchy acrostic was a meager first step toward solving global problems. That summer and into the early fall, he and his Saddleback staff worked to flesh out details of the PEACE plan.

The approach they began to envision would be significantly different from traditional public- or private-sector relief strategies that, as they saw it, tended to rely on a model of direct injection of goods or services—food, clothing, medical care, schooling, and the like—into needy areas, mostly by paid professionals. Under the PEACE plan, the bulk of the work would be performed by small groups of unpaid church volunteers working with other church members throughout the world on what Warren would describe as "a reproducible, sustainable, and scalable model of empowering people to do for themselves instead of doing it for them."

Initially it would involve sending small platoons of PEACE workers from the United States on short-term mission trips abroad where they would recruit and train indigenous church members to battle the global giants in their own towns and villages. The locals then would carry on the bulk of the work and multiply the effort by training others. PEACE teams would use professionally designed resource kits to equip locals in such things as church planting, starting a small business or a literacy program, teaching preventative health care, and so on. Warren described the kits lightheartedly as "church in a box," "business in a box," "school in a box," and "clinic in a box." Each would contain ready-to-use teaching materials along with specific tools and supplies needed to accomplish the designated task. "School in a box," for example, might include books and school supplies for students and teaching guides for instructors. "Clinic in a box" might contain basic health and medical supplies along with illustrated pamphlets on personal hygiene, nutrition, and first aid. "Business in a box," in addition to providing rudimentary instruction in financing and running a business, might include small amounts of capital for micro-enterprise loans. The kits were designed to be used by ordinary people with minimal training and to be easily reproduced locally so that churches could do PEACE on their own without relying on outside resources.

Work would be coordinated via a decentralized Internet-based communications network where participating congregations could find and list projects, locate resources, and report results. Once under way, as Warren envisioned it, the PEACE plan would be self-sustaining and would not require centralized direction or control. "Our aim is to mobilize the world's two billion Christians as a huge force of compassion," explained Mike Constantz, a former missionary with

Campus Crusade for Christ, whom Warren hired late in 2003 as Saddleback's PEACE plan director.

Yet, unleashing that army would take time, Constantz acknowledged, and would require overcoming the prevalent mind-set in many churches that "missionary work is for paid professionals"—the denominational agencies and independent parachurch organizations that recruit and support full-time missionaries—"and that the role of the church, as Rick likes to say, is to pay, pray, and get out of the way." The PEACE plan was not opposed to paid professional missionaries, Constantz added. "In fact, we're very much in favor of that. But as long as only paid people are doing it, it's not enough." It was Warren's hope that, through the PEACE plan, the primary responsibility for mission work in both its social and spiritual dimensions would return to local congregations, where it originally resided, and that when positive results were achieved local churches would get the credit.

As the plan continued to take shape, its global significance in Warren's mind took on ever grander proportions. In one e-mailed communication to the congregation that fall, Warren acknowledged that while neither the problems nor the answers identified in the PEACE plan were new, the strategy of mobilizing small groups of local church members around the world was "revolutionary" and would ignite a worldwide spiritual awakening and "a new Reformation." The first Reformation, Warren wrote, "returned us to the message of the original church. It was a reformation of doctrine—what the church BELIEVES. This second Reformation will return us to the mission of the original church. It will be a reformation of purpose—what the church DOES in the world." (Later Warren would sharpen his rhetoric considerably, referring to the first Reformation as "a reformation of creeds" and to the second as "a reformation of deeds." The Church was the Body of Christ, he would observe, "but the hands and feet have been amputated and now we're just a big mouth, known more for what we're against." Through the PEACE plan he hoped to "reattach the hands and the feet to the Body of Christ, so that the whole Church cares about the whole Gospel in a whole new way—through the local church.")

Warren was under no illusion that results would come quickly. "I'm a patient man," he told Constantz shortly after his arrival at Saddleback that fall. "Reformations happen over fifty years, not fifty days. I probably won't be around to see it through." Nonetheless, Warren was eager to get started. He scheduled a six-week series of messages starting in early November to unveil the plan in detail to his Saddleback congregation. That would be followed by months of local training and testing of strategies by church members before the plan's national and international rollout some time later.

Meanwhile, the Saddleback HIV/AIDS Initiative, under Kay's leadership and now with her husband's enthusiastic backing, was moving forward and two churchwide educational events were scheduled for the fall and for early 2004. Kay already had begun establishing connections with local AIDS service organizations and arranging for Saddleback involvement in projects to help Los Angeles–area residents who were affected or infected by the disease. Her vision for mobilizing church members in the global battle against HIV/AIDS was catching on.

The Warrens were about to cross the threshold of an exciting new phase of their ministry, one that neither of them could have anticipated a year earlier prior to the blazing ascent of *The Purpose-Driven Life* and all of the unexpected changes and opportunities that it brought. "I now believe I know why God is blessing this book in such an unusual way," Warren wrote to his flock that fall. "It is more than just a message that God wants to get out to everyone (which is huge). I now also see that God is using this phenomenon to expand the platform for us to mobilize thousands of local churches for global world missions through the PEACE plan . . . God's intention is much bigger than the book. It's all about the global glory of God!"

As Warren would put it later, God had created a wave and he and Kay had merely caught it, and now they were ready to ride it for all they were worth. Their ride, however, was about to be interrupted.

ON SEPTEMBER 24, 2003, SIX MONTHS after her first visit to Africa, Kay was diagnosed with stage-one breast cancer. A routine mammogram a few days before had detected an abnormality, which led to further tests and, finally, to a needle biopsy that confirmed the malignancy. Even though the cancer had been detected early and appeared not to have spread to the lymph nodes, the doctors prescribed an aggressive course of treatment: surgery followed by chemotherapy and radiation.

The diagnosis came as a complete surprise and it hit the Warrens like a kick in the stomach. Rick broke into tears on hearing the news. He could not imagine his life or his ministry without Kay; their lives had become so completely intertwined in twenty-eight years of marriage that the thought of losing her was more than he could bear, and so he focused his thoughts instead on how they would get through it together. After the initial shock subsided, Kay went through a torrent of emotions. "At least it's not HIV; I have a fighting chance with breast cancer," she recalled thinking at first. Her recent awakening to the millions in the world who were suffering with HIV/AIDS had so changed her perspective that her own diagnosis seemed somehow less menacing by comparison. But as the reality of her life-threatening illness and the uncertainty it cast over her future settled in, she began to feel angry and confused. Both she and Rick had just received what they believed were new marching orders and a new vision from God, and now it seemed as though God was yanking it all away. "Why is this happening now?" she demanded to know. Although the question went unanswered, a verse from the book of Job (23:10) came to her mind: "He knows the way that I take; when he has tested me, I will come forth as gold." While she felt no assurance that God would heal her and that her life would return to normal, she felt comforted believing that whatever lay ahead she would not have to face it alone, that God would be with her, and that something good would come out of it.

Early in October Kay underwent a mastectomy and both the surgery and the recovery went smoothly. A month later she would begin a twelve-week course of chemotherapy. In the meantime, based on the successful surgery and the generally favorable prognosis—and at Kay's insistence—Warren decided to go ahead with the scheduled launch of the PEACE plan. On the first weekend of November, he preached the opening message of a six-week series entitled "You Can Change Your

World." In that first sermon he laid out the broad vision of a church-led battle against the five global giants. In the following weeks he planned to spell out the specific strategies aimed at igniting a world-wide spiritual awakening and a new Reformation.

On Monday after that opening weekend Kay went into the hospital for her first round of chemotherapy. Almost immediately she fell violently ill in reaction to the toxic cancer-fighting chemicals that were being pumped into her veins. Palliative drugs to counteract the nausea and other debilitating side effects seemed to bring little relief. Sitting at her bedside, Rick agonized over his wife's suffering and his own powerlessness to alleviate it. Before the week was over, it was clear that Kay was in for a long and difficult ordeal and Rick was determined that she would not go through it alone. He put the PEACE plan on indefinite hold and turned the Saddleback pulpit over to his staff. For the next twelve weeks he would not leave Kay's side.

EARLY IN DECEMBER, MIDWAY through the course of chemotherapy, Warren sat in Kay's hospital room and while she dozed fitfully between treatments he quietly penned a letter to his congregation. In part it was a news update on her condition, in part a reflective personal meditation on marriage and devotion and on plans interrupted.

"Between caring for Kay's basic needs," he wrote, "I sit quietly and think a lot, and thank God for my wife and God's amazing invention of marriage. With all its ups and downs and 'in sickness and health,' I'm certain that marriage is God's primary tool to teach us unselfishness, sensitivity, sacrifice, and mature love.

"We are now halfway through her twelve-week chemo regimen. After this she'll begin six weeks of daily radiation. She healed well from her first surgery, and the pain from the Porta-Cath surgery last Friday has subsided. Yesterday she had a great day here at the hospital UNTIL the chemo effects kicked in about 1 p.m. and she quickly deteriorated into misery and major nausea. The rest of the day was very rough as nurses tried to ease her pain. Finally about 10 p.m., after throwing up, she settled down and fell asleep on the couch that I usually sleep on here in the hospital room. (It felt more comfortable to her than the hospital bed, so I got permission from the nurses for me to sleep in the hospital bed. Don't tell anyone!)

"Today, Kay feels wiped out from all the meds they've given her, along with the expected fatigue and nausea from the chemo. I've kept all visitors away so we can keep the room quiet for hours. The less going on, the better it is for her. Illness always reduces life to its basic level . . .

"I want to thank you for allowing me the freedom to personally take care of Kay during her cancer. My wife is the love of my life, and this is what God intended families to do. I'd want every husband in our church to do the same if the situation arose in their family. God blesses us when we keep our commitments.

"So this year will be the first Christmas Eve services that Kay and I have missed in Saddleback's twenty-three years. I've prepared a message entitled 'When God Messes Up Your Plans.' (How appropriate!) I've always been struck by the fact that EVERYONE at the first Christmas had their plans messed up by God—because God had a bigger and better plan. When life doesn't work out the way we intended, God wants us to trust Him . . .

"Kay and I are both looking forward to 2004 and the beginning of our global PEACE plan. It's going to be a great year, and God is going to use YOU in ways you never imagined. Stay tuned! With great love and appreciation—I wish I could hug each of you—Pastor Rick."

A few months later Warren had another opportunity to reflect publicly on the faith-testing emotional whipsaw he and Kay had experienced during the preceding year. In an interview with *Decision*, a monthly magazine published by the Billy Graham Evangelistic Association, he described 2003 as "the greatest year of my life, but also the toughest . . . I used to think that life was hills and valleys—you go through a dark time, then you go to the mountaintop, back and forth. I don't believe that anymore. Rather than life being hills and valleys, I believe that it's kind of like two rails on a railroad track, and at all times you have something good and something bad in your life. No matter how good things are in your life, there is always something bad that needs to be worked on. And no matter how bad things are in your life, there is always something good you can thank God for . . .

"We discovered quickly that, in spite of the prayers of hundreds of thousands of people, God was not going to heal Kay or make it easy for her. It has been very difficult for her, and yet God has strengthened her character, given her a ministry of helping other people, given her a testimony, drawn her closer to Him and to people—all the five purposes we've been talking about. You have to learn to deal with both the good and the bad of life."

It was a valuable life lesson that the Warrens might have preferred to learn under less dramatic circumstances, yet it was one that they embraced in faith as having come from the hand of God. Out of unimaginable good fortune and unanticipated personal calamity had come an unparalleled opportunity to extend their ministry—and sphere of influence—to "the global glory of God." It was an opportunity that was only beginning to unfold.

# CHAPTER FOURTEEN

# Riding Waves

WARREN RETURNED TO THE SADDLEBACK PULPIT near the end
of February 2004 just as Kay was about to finish the last of her
radiation treatments. With her cancer in remission and having received
a generally positive prognosis, both Kay and Rick were eager to pick up
where they had left off in their new ministry endeavors. It had been
Warren's plan to immediately resume his message series on the PEACE
plan that he had suspended in November when Kay began her
treatments. But during the four-month interregnum it had become clear
to Warren and his staff that additional preparation would be needed to
assure the plan's successful launch, and so they decided to extend the
delay for another full year. "The fact that we're delaying the PEACE
plan series will in no way stop us from moving forward on this
initiative," Warren assured his flock. "God's timing is perfect, and I've
learned from a lot of experience not to worry when things get delayed.
God is in control and we're not."

During his first weeks back, Warren delivered a two-part message
on "Understanding the Passion"—a tie-in and promotion of Mel Gibson's controversial film, *The Passion of the Christ*, which was to be released nationally on Ash Wednesday, February 25, in some 2,800
theaters. Gibson had deftly pitched his independent R-rated film, with
its graphic depiction of the crucifixion of Jesus, to evangelical pastors
around the country as an "outreach opportunity," and thousands of
them, including Warren, responded by buying out entire theaters for
special showings and encouraging their congregations to attend and to
invite their unsaved friends. Warren explained his personal enthusiasm
for the film: "I instantly thought of Jesus' words: 'If I be lifted up I will
draw all men unto me.' That is his promise! Nothing is more magnetic
than the power of the cross. So I knew a huge wave—a spiritual

tsunami—would hit when the film debuted . . . and we began praying and preparing to surf it."

Accordingly, Saddleback booked forty-seven theaters in Orange County and Rick and Kay personally invited over a thousand community leaders, government officials, and other VIPs to be their guests. They also added two worship services to the regular weekend lineup to accommodate an expected crowd of newcomers, and they prepared a three-week study curriculum on the Passion for Saddleback's small groups as a follow-up. The results, as reported by Warren, were impressive: more than 600 unchurched community leaders attended the VIP showing, 892 people were saved during the two-week sermon series, some 600 new small groups were formed, and Saddleback's average attendance increased by 3,000. "That's catching a wave!" Warren exclaimed. Fueled by evangelical fervor nationwide, the movie became an instant blockbuster, grossing more than $117 million in the first five days on its way to a worldwide box-office take of $609 million.

But it was Warren's newly ignited passion for global ministry that would dominate his efforts for the remainder of the year. One weekend late in May, Rick and Kay shared the pulpit and delivered a message entitled "God's Compassion for the Sick: Making a Difference in the Global AIDS Pandemic." Unofficially it marked the public relaunch of the Saddleback HIV/AIDS Initiative, which had been placed on hold during Kay's illness. During his portion of the sermon, Rick presented the battle against AIDS as partial fulfillment of the "C" in the PEACE plan—"caring for the sick"—and he reminded his flock of the staggering worldwide toll: 40 million people infected with HIV/AIDS, 700,000 children infected at birth during the previous year, a child dying of AIDS every minute. "Sometimes when people read statistics like that they get mad at God," he said. "They say, 'Why is God allowing this? Why doesn't God do something about this? What is God's plan for these people?' I'll tell you what God's plan is. It's sitting in your chair. You are God's plan. God wants to use you to make a difference in the lives of these other people."

Kay used the occasion to describe her own initial fear and ignorance concerning the disease and those afflicted by it—how she had mistakenly thought of HIV/AIDS as a gay disease, had stigmatized its victims, and had feared catching the virus through casual contact. "My response was not Christ-like," she confessed. "I was responding with judgment instead of with the compassion that God has toward all He has made . . . [but] what if we as the church of Jesus Christ were willing to lay down our fears and our prejudices and our ignorance and our weakness? What if instead of being the ones that everyone thinks of as being negative and against everything, what if we're actually the people who stand up and be a part of the solution to HIV/AIDS? . . . We can be the ones who lead the fight, not just for the souls of people but for their very lives as well."

That provocative weekend was followed by a churchwide gathering in early June during which hundreds of Saddleback members signed up for local service projects helping HIV/AIDS sufferers and their families in Southern California while hundreds more agreed to donate time and resources to AIDS relief efforts in Africa and elsewhere. The following year, the church would conduct its first national HIV/AIDS conference—a three-day gathering entitled "Disturbing Voices"—that was aimed at pricking the evangelical social conscience and prodding complacent church members around the country into the global battle against HIV/AIDS. The far-reaching Saddleback-led initiative that Kay had envisioned was in full swing and the personal enthusiasm she felt for the long-neglected cause was proving to be contagious.

Meanwhile, even though the PEACE launch had been postponed, behind-the-scenes preparations continued at an intense pace. That summer the church sent out sixty-four small groups on short-term mission trips to forty-seven countries to begin testing the PEACE plan prior to the official rollout. Each group in that experimental first wave conducted a project in each of the plan's five areas—showing an evangelistic film in a village in an effort to win new converts, training local church leaders in the Purpose-Driven paradigm, assessing the needs of the poor and determining whether they would benefit from micro-enterprise loans, teaching seminars on HIV/AIDS prevention, and providing school supplies and basic literacy curricula for children. Afterward, the effectiveness of their work was assessed and adjustments were made as Warren and his staff continued to refine the program.

The major churchwide emphasis at Saddleback that year, however, would come in the fall with a new campaign called "Forty Days of Community." Like the original Forty Days of Purpose campaign, it would involve a seven-week sermon series reinforced in weekly small-group studies. The distinctiveness of the new campaign was its mobilization of 2,600 small groups—some 9,200 people in all—to feed an estimated 40,000 homeless people in Orange County for forty days, three meals per day, with over two million pounds of donated food. For most of the Saddleback suburbanites, Warren would report later, "It was their first experience with a poor person. Touching, helping, smelling. Their lives [were] changed." As such, it was an important first step in preparing them for active duty in the PEACE plan. "So you did it in Santa Ana," Warren would reassure his flock. "Don't you think you could do it in Uganda?" The seeds of his new global ministry, it seemed, were taking hold in the rich Saddleback Valley soil.

THROUGHOUT HIS CAREER, in numerous interviews and sermons and in his own writing, Warren would survey the remarkable successes in his life—building a thriving megachurch from scratch, authoring a mega-bestseller, becoming a counselor and confidant of the rich and powerful—and insist that none of them were the result of his own skills or resourcefulness or of marketing acumen, either his own or others'. In his estimation it was all "a God thing." Using his favorite California metaphor, he would explain: "God makes the waves; surfers just ride them . . , Our job as church leaders, like experienced surfers, is to recognize a wave of God's Spirit and ride it. It is not our responsibility to *make* waves but to recognize how God is working in the world and join him in the endeavor."

Yet if Warren's greatest successes came as the result of riding waves not of his making, there were times when it appeared, at least, that he was roiling the waters around him on his own. In the spring of 1998, nearly five years before *The Purpose-Driven Life* would catapult him to international fame, Warren began making plans to expand his sphere of influence beyond Saddleback and his growing network of churches. His 1995 best-seller, *The Purpose-Driven Church*, by then already had sold hundreds of thousands of copies, bolstering his reputation among pastors and denominational leaders as one of the nation's foremost church-growth experts. As a result of that success, he had found himself increasingly in demand as a conference speaker and commentator and the invitations began piling up. To manage the growing demands on his time, but also to leverage and broaden his outside contacts in order to maximize the reach of his ministry, Warren decided it was time to bring in professional help.

In May of that year he hired the first of several staffers whose primary job would be to hook him in with movers and shakers in business, government, and the philanthropic world—people Warren thought it would be useful to know as his ministry expanded. One of the first to arrive was Forrest Reinhardt, a young fund-development consultant and former staffer for Young Life, a Colorado-based ministry to high school students. At their first meeting, Warren explained his dilemma. "I know a lot of people in the church world," he told Reinhardt, "but I really don't know a lot of folks outside of that world. But my influence—and the opportunity to influence—outside that world is growing, and I need somebody to help me make friends and develop relationships and to help me expand what is coming." Among Reinhardt's professional assets were his connections with Christian businessmen and philanthropists, an influential circle into which he would begin to introduce Warren. As Saddleback's "pastor of strategic resource development," he also would handle media relations and direct internal fund-raising efforts for new construction on the church's campus.

Over the next few years, Warren would bring in additional help. In 2001, he elevated David Chrzan, a young ex-policeman who had been hired to help organize church volunteers, to the new post of chief of staff which, among other things, meant managing Warren's daily schedule and taking over media relations from Reinhardt. Three years later as the PEACE plan began taking shape he retained the services of Billy Graham's longtime spokesman, Texas public-relations executive A. Larry Ross, to handle his press contacts. That same year he recruited Peb Jackson, a former associate of Focus on the Family founder James

Dobson and a veteran in public relations and fund-raising development, to help him forge ties in the international arena and in Washington, D.C., where Jackson was well connected.

"There is no question that Rick was very intentional in wanting to expand his influence, for whatever good could come out of that," one former staffer recalled of that period. In the early years, their efforts were mostly reactive—responding to an invitation to attend a meeting of Christian business leaders, for example, and deciding how Warren could best use the event to build a pastoral relationship with the businessmen and, at the same time, promote his Purpose-Driven ministry. Later, especially after *The Purpose-Driven Life* came out, "there were opportunities to influence at a level he had not had before, and they were coming both reactively and proactively. We would be at an event and we would always be looking for the next opportunity, or how do we leverage that? Frankly, we probably said 'no' to as many things as we said 'yes' to because simply with scheduling we couldn't do them all. But by that point, Rick had really sensed a sacred trust, a sense of stewardship of life. He was not there to ask for their help or their contributions to what he was doing. Often he would mostly just listen and learn. But he also felt like it was a great opportunity to influence that crowd."

After Jackson came on board in 2004, Warren and his staff began making regular forays into Washington, D.C.—Warren once every quarter or so, his staff even more often—for meetings at the White House, on Capitol Hill, and in department and agency headquarters. Warren at the time was no stranger to the nation's capital. He had been among a group of religious leaders invited to the White House early in 2001 in connection with the launch of President George W. Bush's Faith-Based and Community Initiative—a federal grant program to provide social services through religious groups—and had returned in September 2002, also in a group of clergymen, to pray privately with the president at the first anniversary of the 9/11 terrorist attacks.

But now Warren was stepping up his presence in an attempt to leverage his Washington relationships. As he and his staff worked their way around town, their initial points of contact often were prominently placed evangelical Christians, who were plentiful in the nation's capital during the Bush administration and with whom Jackson had cultivated friendships over the years. Most meetings involving Warren, according to his staff, were courtesy calls and get-acquainted sessions with little or no discussion of policy or political agendas. "The first and foremost reason Rick would do these was if he could serve somebody," one staffer explained. Beyond that, his meetings were "basically relational, getting to know people and earning a right to be heard." Warren would characterize his private interaction with government officials more pointedly: "I never talk about politics. It's always, 'How is your family? How are you handling the stress? How can I pray for you?' That's why they're willing to talk with me. They know I'm not going to lobby them." Even so, some of his Washington relationships would pay tangible dividends later on. After getting to know key officials at the U.S. Agency for International Development headquarters in 2005, for example, Warren and his staff found that when they took the PEACE plan to Africa they had easier entrée to USAID offices and to American embassies there because of the contacts they had made in Washington.

Not all of Warren's new relationships in Washington, however, were initiated by Warren and his staff. Shortly after the 2004 election, he received a phone call from Sen. John Kerry of Massachusetts, the unsuccessful Democratic presidential nominee, asking if he could stop by for a visit during a planned trip to the West Coast. The two had never spoken before, but Warren said he would be pleased to meet with the senator and invited him to attend one of Saddleback's weekend services. Kerry, who is Roman Catholic, accepted the invitation. A few weeks later he showed up for church and afterward he and Warren spent about three hours together touring the campus and talking about faith, *The Purpose-Driven Life*, and the election. It was a friendly visit, and when it was over they exchanged e-mail addresses and agreed to stay in touch.

About a year later, Kerry learned that Warren was planning to be in Washington for the National Prayer Breakfast and he invited him to address the Senate Democratic Caucus at its weekly policy luncheon on Capitol Hill. The luncheons, which were closed to the press, typically featured a high-profile guest speaker discussing a current political or legislative issue, and attendance tended to be sporadic—anywhere from a dozen to several dozen Democratic senators, depending on the speaker.

On the day that Warren spoke the room was packed. For nearly two and a half hours he talked about AIDS, the PEACE plan, the environment, and about government programs to help the poor. A former Democratic staff member who attended the meeting described what transpired:

> Warren spoke at length on these topics and then took questions from the senators. The discussion tiptoed around the most contentious social issues until Senator Barack Obama raised his hand and, after graciously thanking Warren for his presentation, said "I think everyone is aware that there's an elephant in the room here. I'd like to hear your thoughts on abortion and gay marriage." A little startled, Warren went on to recommend that those who supported either abortion or gay marriage not try and force their positions on evangelical voters (who were not likely to be persuaded), but instead focus on whatever common ground they may share with these voters. In the end it was refreshing to see Obama go out of his way to cut the crap.

Later that week, Obama invited Warren to a private get-acquainted meeting in his office and, on a personal level at least, the two appeared to hit it off immediately. Obama seemed perfectly at ease discussing his faith, according to a Warren staffer who was present, and the two men quickly discovered that they shared a keen interest in the global HIV/AIDS crisis and in enlisting faith communities to help combat it. At one point in the conversation, Obama confided that he had begun contemplating a run for the presidency although he indicated that he was not yet close to making a decision. He did not ask for Warren's opinion on the matter and Warren did not volunteer it, although he came away from the meeting duly impressed by the young senator. "He just struck me at the time as one of the best communicators I had ever heard," Warren recalled of that meeting. "He just had a winsomeness about him, and I knew that he was going somewhere."

Beyond Washington, Warren's growing reputation as a passionate advocate on HIV/AIDS, poverty, and other social causes seldom associated with religious conservatives helped him to gain entrée among some of the so-called cultural elites—entertainers, artists, media moguls, and other international celebrities. Many of those with whom he established contact had never actually met an evangelical Christian before, let alone a Southern Baptist preacher, and often were astonished to find such a prominent one who shared their social concerns. Whether out of respect or sheer curiosity, they began to welcome him into their circle of acquaintances.

Shortly after Warren conceived the PEACE plan, he began exchanging e-mails with Bono, front man for the popular Irish rock group U2 and an energetic AIDS and antipoverty activist. Bono had been raised a Catholic and was widely known for his gritty, unconventional Christian faith which, like Warren's, informed his philanthropy. Their occasional correspondence consisted mostly of short notes expressing admiration for the work each was doing and keeping one another apprised of their latest efforts. In April 2005, Peb Jackson saw an opportunity to bring the two together for the first time. Bono's band was at the beginning of a worldwide tour and was scheduled to play two nights at the Staples Center in Los Angeles. Earlier in his career, Jackson had worked in the entertainment industry and still had plenty of contacts there. The night before the concert he called Staples Center owner Philip Anschutz and secured two tickets and backstage passes and the use of Anschutz's luxury skybox.

Warren leaped at the opportunity to meet Bono, but he was equally excited to attend the concert. Sitting in the skybox that night, Jackson recalled, "Rick really got into the music," clapping, swaying, and singing along with most of the numbers. "He knew half the words to the songs. I mean, how many Christian leaders do you know who could do that?" Afterward they made their way to the backstage area, where a gaggle of Hollywood glitterati—actors Brad Pitt and John Cusack, comedian Chris Rock, and others—milled about, waiting to meet Bono and his band. Warren stepped into the circle of celebrities and joined their conversation while Jackson slipped outside hoping to intercept Bono. When the singer arrived, Jackson introduced himself. "I told him, 'Rick Warren really wants to meet you,' and he said, 'Oh, I've got to meet him!' So I brought Rick over and Bono took Rick's hands and held them to his chest and closed his eyes, and he just held his hands there almost for an uncomfortable period of time, and finally he said, 'I've always wanted to meet you. I appreciate everything you do.'" They talked for several minutes about their similar commitments and about their faith. Finally, Warren asked the question he often asks of new acquaintances: "How can I pray for you?" Bono closed his eyes and thought for a few seconds. "That I would use my opportunities on stage to appropriately express my faith," he finally responded. Warren assured him that he would. They agreed to stay in touch and both moved on to conversations with others in the room. Three months later, Bono enlisted Warren to serve as unofficial chaplain of the Live 8 concert in Philadelphia, one of ten massive rock fests held simultaneously around the world that summer to draw attention to poverty in Africa. An estimated 1.2 million people turned out on the Benjamin Franklin Parkway in front of the Philadelphia Museum of Art to hear artists ranging from Bon Jovi and Black Eyed Peas to Stevie Wonder and Destiny's Child. "The only thing I remember about that concert is [the rock group] Linkin Park and a sweet smell in the air," Warren joked to his congregation afterward.

THROUGHOUT 2005, WARREN'S "strategic outreach" staff mounted a concentrated effort to forge new connections for Warren among international policymakers, academics, and other influential people outside the church world, and their efforts began producing impressive results. In March, he became the first evangelical preacher invited to address the Harvard Forum at the university's Institute of Politics in the Kennedy School of Government. There, according to a journalist who covered the event, "Warren disarmed the audience with a sense of humor, a passionate exploration of his beliefs and a willingness to answer any and all questions." He called for "more civilized dialogue" in the nation's political discourse and "a return to the old definition of the word 'tolerance.' That word used to mean a respect for those who had completely different opinions and worldviews. But today it doesn't mean that. It means that all ideas have equal value. That's nonsense, irrational and illogical." The Harvard students responded to Warren's remarks with a standing ovation.

That summer Warren continued on the highbrow lecture circuit, speaking at theological conferences at Oxford and Cambridge universities. In July he participated in a panel on leadership and society at the Aspen Institute, a Washington-based think tank, along with such national luminaries as former President Clinton, Colin Powell, William Bennett, and author Toni Morrison. In September, mainly through contacts arranged by his staff, he was invited to join the prestigious Council on Foreign Relations and attended its fall gathering in New York City, where he plugged his PEACE plan and advocated for a larger role for faith communities in addressing world problems.

While in New York for that meeting, Warren was invited to address an interfaith prayer breakfast at the United Nations held on the eve of a UN World Summit on global poverty and human rights. Although advertised as an interfaith gathering, the event was organized by representatives of the North American Mission Board of the Southern Baptist Convention, and its overtones—and Warren's message—were decidedly Christian and evangelical. "I'm not here to talk about religion," Warren told the one hundred or so UN delegates and international dignitaries of various faith backgrounds who attended the unofficial event. "I'm here to talk about a relationship with God . . . The Bible says God is love. It doesn't say He *has* love. Love is the essence of His character. You were created to be loved by God. Being created in God's image, we are to love Him back." He closed his remarks with his standard salvation prayer and invited the audience to pray along silently: "Dear God, thank you for making me, for creating me, and for loving me. I want to fulfill the purposes that you made me for. Starting today I want to get to know you and love you and trust you. And I want my life to bring you pleasure. Thank you for sending Jesus Christ. Help me to understand it more. As much as I know how, I want to open up my life to your love and your purpose. In your name I pray. Amen."

One of Warren's greatest coups in making international connections came the following January when he snagged an invitation to the World Economic Forum, an annual gathering of high-powered bankers, business tycoons, heads of state, philanthropists, and assorted international celebrities in Davos, Switzerland. It is a tony affair where big thoughts are served up with champagne and canapés, but where conversations tend to produce more posturing than progress in solving world problems. It is also a favorite target of right-wing bloggers and conspiracy theorists who see the forum as a sinister cabal pushing a one-world-government agenda. It is not a place where one would expect to find a Southern Baptist preacher. Yet Warren was there and not the least reticent about speaking his mind. Sitting in on an international panel of business entrepreneurs discussing "Innovation and Design Strategy," he described churches and other religious congregations as the world's "most powerful distribution channel." "I can show you 10 million villages where the only functioning institution is the church," Warren said, reiterating a line he used often to tout his PEACE plan.

Warren was one of twenty-three religious figures at Davos that year—an unusually large contingent that included three other American evangelicals: Jim Wallis of the Sojourners Community, Richard Land of the Southern Baptist Ethics and Religious Liberty Commission, and author Anne Graham Lotz, daughter of evangelist Billy Graham. Also there were the Reverend George Carey, the former archbishop of Canterbury; Eastern Orthodox Ecumenical Patriarch Bartholomew; Roman Catholic Cardinal Renato Martino of Italy; and Matthieu Ricard, a Buddhist monk and translator for the Dalai Lama. The presence of so many religious leaders seemed to reflect a growing recognition at Davos of the increasingly important role that religion plays in global affairs. After the event, a representative of the World Bank reported to her superiors on her contact with the religious figures at Davos, particularly the evangelicals. "I was interested to see how the Davos community reacted to U.S. evangelical approaches," Katherine Marshall, the World Bank's director of Development Dialogue on Values and Ethics, wrote. "My sense was of a mutual bewilderment." She took special note of Warren and his staff, with whom she had had a private meeting to discuss the PEACE plan and the World Bank's involvement in Africa. "The contact with Warren and his team is relevant to us primarily because of the rapid step-up of Warren's international work," she reported. "Warren's ambitions are far ranging, as is his influence, and he seems so keen to follow up with us. He also told me that he had talked briefly at Davos with Mr. [Paul] Wolfowitz [president of the World Bank at the time], and plans to meet with him again soon in D.C." A few months prior to the

Davos gathering, members of Warren's staff had met with Wolfowitz in Washington to advocate for debt relief for poor African countries, especially Rwanda. In April 2005, the World Bank and the International Monetary Fund agreed to forgive $1.4 billion of Rwanda's outstanding loans. What role, if any, Warren's intercession may have played in that decision is uncertain. In any event, he was determined to keep the lines of communication open and operating.

THE DETERMINED EFFORTS TO EXPAND Warren's circle of influence clearly were beginning to pay off. In conversations with journalists and others, he and his staff had begun describing his new international role rather immodestly as that of a "global statesman" and, on his personal website, his list of professional credits was expanded to include "pastor, author, global strategist, innovator, and philanthropist." However, it soon became apparent that becoming a global statesman would exact a price. About a year into his new pursuit, Warren discovered that performing on the world stage demanded more time and energy than he, as leader of a megachurch and a network of pastors, could easily spare. If he was to continue on that course, something would have to give.

"Rick began to struggle," his longtime associate, Glen Kreun, recalled of that period. "All of a sudden he was getting these invitations—Congress, the White House—and all kinds of new things were happening, and Rick realized he was going to have to step away from something. He couldn't do it all, and I saw him agonize over it. He would just sit there and cry and say, 'God called me to be a pastor. This is who I am. I'm not this other person. What am I going to do?' And the senior staff prayed with him, cried with him, and we told him, 'Rick, we know you're a farm boy from Ukiah. But God has put you on a new platform now, and you've got to follow God's calling, even though you stay on as a local church pastor. You're always going to be that. But God's got something more for you to do.' "

To allow Warren more flexibility and time away from the Saddleback pulpit, he and his staff devised a preaching rotation using other Saddleback pastors and began looking for other ways for the staff to shoulder more day-to-day responsibility. While that freed some time and relieved some of the pressure, Warren still felt uncertain about the direction in which he was headed and about how to handle his new role as an international figure and confidant of the powerful. He decided to seek advice from someone who had traveled a similar road and who knew firsthand the challenges he was facing. At the end of a hectic week in Washington, Warren and his staff flew down to Montreat, North Carolina, to pay a visit to Billy Graham.

The frail and aging icon of American evangelicalism welcomed his visitors warmly into his modest mountaintop home and for two hours they talked about the hazards and blessings of ministering on a global scale. "I had my list of questions," Warren recalled. "I asked him, 'Billy, how do you deal with politicians without getting sucked in? How do you deal with competing interests? How do you deal with press issues? And how do you handle the demands of that public role without sacrificing your ministry?' " Graham responded patiently to each of Warren's queries, drawing upon his own experience as one who had befriended every U.S. president since Truman and had consorted with scores of world leaders during a ministry spanning more than six decades. Graham had learned many important lessons, some of them the hard way. By his own admission he had mistakenly allowed himself to become politically entangled with President Richard Nixon, sometimes sitting in on Oval Office strategy sessions and offering political advice—his words captured on White House tapes that would be made public years later. But from that episode Graham had learned to steer clear of partisan politics at all costs or risk compromising his ministry and message. It was a lesson, he suggested, that too many contemporary preachers seemed to have ignored. On the demands of fame and influence, Graham cautioned Warren that as he found himself being pulled in new directions, those closest to him—his family and his staff—were likely to suffer the most, and it would take special vigilance on his part to keep those relationships healthy and strong.

Warren listened carefully and jotted notes as the man he had long considered a mentor and a role model of personal integrity described the potential pitfalls of ministering in the public eye. For years Warren had sought to emulate some of the practices that he knew had kept Graham above the scandals that had brought down other famous evangelical ministers. From the very beginning of Saddleback, Warren had followed what he called "the Graham rule"—never allowing himself to be alone with a woman other than his wife—and had imposed it on his staff as well. Graham had carried the rule so far as to never enter a hotel room that had not been checked out first by a trusted male staffer in order to avoid being set up and photographed in a compromising situation—such was his determination to avoid even the appearance of scandal.

As their conversation began to wind down, Warren briefed Graham on the PEACE plan and his vision of precipitating a worldwide revival and a second Reformation. Graham's famous deep-set blue eyes sparkled with enthusiasm as he listened to Warren passionately describe the mobilization of millions of Christians into a vast missionary army that would attack the global giants and bring God's healing mercy to a broken world. When he finished, Warren and his companions stood to leave and Graham, weakened and slowed by Parkinson's disease, placed a trembling hand on Warren's shoulder and prayed a prayer of blessing on Warren and his ministry and for the success of the PEACE plan. "My only regret, Father," Graham prayed, "is that I won't be around to see what it is that you are going to fulfill through Rick come true."

Warren left the meeting deeply moved by Graham's words of encouragement and especially by his prayer which, he would confide to his associates, he had interpreted as Graham's passing of his mantle. "That was the phrase Rick used," one of his aides recalled. "Dr. Graham's prayer confirmed in Rick that this was something that he had not pursued but that was his inescapable duty. It was something that had been decided for him, and that he had slid into a new pair of shoes." Warren apparently was not alone in that assessment. In a year-end summation of the major religion stories of 2005, *USA Today* would note that Graham—"the lion of American evangelism"—had "bowed off the public pulpit" that summer with a final crusade in New York City and had retired to his mountain retreat. The newspaper went on to observe that "Graham's mantle as the star of Christian cross-denominational outreach seemed to rest on California preacher the Rev. Rick Warren, author of the mega-selling Bible-study book, *The Purpose-Driven Life*."

Publicly, as prudence would dictate, Warren in years to come would dismiss the suggestion that he or anyone else stood to inherit Graham's role as "America's pastor" and symbolic leader of American evangeli-calism. "There will never be another Billy Graham," Warren told an in-terviewer in 2008, reiterating a truism expressed often in evangelical circles. Yet he would stop short of disavowing an ambition to be con-sidered among the vanguard of evangelical leadership. "If we are to have a new Reformation there might be multiple leaders, just as there was in the first Reformation," Warren said. "I pray that the Lord will let me be one of those. But I don't think I'll be the only one."

Regardless of how accurately Warren may have perceived Graham's gesture and his own future role as a Christian leader, he left the North Carolina mountaintop reassured in his new global vision and freshly emboldened to pursue it. "After spending time with Dr. Graham," an aide recalled, "Rick's attitude was, 'Okay, here we go. It's time to dive in with all fours.'"

CHAPTER FIFTEEN

# "Global Glory"

BY THE END OF 2004, WARREN HAD BEGUN MAKING final preparations to proceed with the PEACE plan's rescheduled launch in the fall of 2005. His tentative timetable called for reintroducing his vision for PEACE at Saddleback's twenty-fifth anniversary celebration at Angel Stadium in Anaheim in April and then officially kicking it off with a "Forty Days of PEACE" campaign at his church in September. That would be followed by an undetermined period of additional field testing and fine-tuning before the plan was rolled out nationally and internationally through the Purpose-Driven Network.

While his flock would carry the PEACE plan to sixty-eight different countries in the early test stages, Warren wanted to single out one needy country for special attention in order to demonstrate how to successfully combat the global giants on a national scale. There was no shortage of candidates, and Warren and his staff considered a number of distressed nations in Africa, Asia, Central America, and the Caribbean. They quickly settled on a tiny landlocked country in east-central Africa that seemed the perfect test case—a nation ravaged by poverty and disease and struggling to overcome a legacy of violence and corruption and the still-fresh memory of unspeakable human brutality. If ever there was a place where the global giants seemed to stalk the earth unfettered it was the Republic of Rwanda.

To much of the world, Rwanda was a troubled and forsaken land whose image forever would be defined by one hundred horrific days in 1994 when an estimated 800,000 ethnic Tutsis and moderate Hutus— the country's two predominant tribal groups—were systematically slaughtered in a carefully orchestrated genocide. The orgy of killing, instigated by high-ranking officials in the Hutu-led government, was the culmination of decades of ethnic hatred in the former Belgian colony.

The killing had gone largely unchallenged by the international community, which collectively looked away, refusing to intervene in what it considered an internal matter. The country, after all, was locked in a four-year-old civil war at the time, and civilian deaths—reports of which, it was widely assumed, had been greatly exaggerated—were judged to be collateral damage, unfortunate but probably unavoidable in a country the size of Maryland with over 9 million inhabitants.

In point of fact, the mass extermination had been planned for many months. Hutu extremists in the military and the civilian government had whipped up public sentiment among the majority Hutu population against the more affluent and influential Tutsi minority. Under the banner of "Hutu Power," they disseminated hate-filled messages over state-run radio and in newspapers calling for eradication of the Tutsi *inyenzi* ("cockroaches"). In the capital city of Kigali and in towns and villages throughout the country, Hutu militias were organized, equipped, and trained in efficient killing techniques, with the machete as the favored weapon. Once the killing began on April 6, triggered by the death of Rwanda's president in a suspicious plane crash, hundreds of thousands of ordinary citizens were pressed into service and ordered to kill their Tutsi neighbors or be killed themselves. Entire villages were rounded up and shot or hacked to death. Local police, burghers, and even clergy often were complicit, and churches and schools where thousands sought refuge became slaughterhouses.

The carnage stopped only after the Rwandan Patriotic Front, a rebel army composed mainly of Rwandan Tutsi refugees from neighboring Uganda, encircled the capital city in mid-July and toppled the government, dispersing the Rwandan army, the militias, and some 2 million Hutu sympathizers into neighboring countries. The rebels were led by Paul Kagame, a mild-mannered young general whose family had fled to Uganda in 1960 to escape an earlier wave of anti-Tutsi violence. As a young man, Kagame had joined the Ugandan resistance movement and fought as a guerrilla to overthrow the repressive regime of Ugandan leader Milton Obote. Later, he joined with other Rwandan refugees in forming the RPF, which launched an invasion in 1990 to reclaim their homeland from the Hutu government. Kagame, who had been trained in intelligence by the U.S. military, assumed leadership of the rebel army after a close friend who led the invasion was killed in the opening salvo. After three years of intense fighting, the rebels and the government reached a power-sharing agreement—which was never fully implemented—and an uneasy cease-fire took hold. Less than a year later the genocide began, and Kagame and his army resumed their attack full bore.

After the government in Kigali fell to his RPF forces, Kagame quickly installed a transitional government headed by Pasteur Bizimungu, a moderate Hutu who had been a cabinet minister in the previous regime, and named himself the new vice president and defense minister. Bizimungu resigned in 2000, and Kagame ascended to the presidency. Three years later, Kagame ran for election and won in a landslide, drawing more than 95 percent of votes cast. As president, Kagame immediately set about the task of rebuilding his country, not merely repairing it but constructing it anew after the devastation wreaked upon not only its infrastructure and economy—the work of bombs and armaments—but upon the psyche and spirit of its people who had experienced in soul-crushing proportion the human capacity for evil. As Philip Gourevitch, an American journalist and astute chronicler of the Rwandan genocide and its aftermath, would later observe, what Kagame was attempting to accomplish seemed an unattainably radical dream: "I felt tempted, at times, to think of Rwanda after the genocide as an impossible country. Kagame never seemed to afford himself the luxury of such a useless notion. 'People are not inherently bad,' he told me. 'But they can be made bad. And they can be taught to be good.' . . . [He] was convinced that with reason he could bend all that was twisted in Rwanda straighter, that the country and its people truly could be changed—made saner, and so better—and he meant to prove it."

Under Kagame's leadership, the Rwandan government began pursuing an ambitious two-track strategy of building a new society by promoting reconciliation and by bringing thousands of *génocidaires* to justice and by building a new robust economy, welcoming foreign investors and providing a secure and hospitable environment for commerce. Achieving the first would take time and patience. Early steps included opening the door for repatriation of hundreds of thousands of refugees who fled the country during the civil war and enactment of laws banning official ethnic designations. "No more Tutsi. No more Hutu. We are all Rwandan," became the catchphrase. Meanwhile, the difficult but necessary step of bringing genocide instigators to trial would tax the judicial system and clog the country's jails for years to come. To accomplish the second goal would mean rebranding the country to supplant the image of a nation beset by genocide and corruption with that of a new Rwanda—a country of peaceful and industrious people, little crime, and transparent and accountable governance. To help tell the story of Rwanda's rebirth to the international community, Kagame enlisted outside business consultants and well-connected Rwandan expatriates living in Europe and North America. Their efforts paid off quickly and Western investors soon began taking a renewed interest in the tiny nation.

Kagame made frequent trips to the United States to meet with potential business partners and others who he believed might help his cause. On one visit in April 2004, he huddled with Joe Ritchie, a successful Chicago-area businessman and former options trader whom Kagame had tapped as a liaison to the U.S. business community. Sitting in Ritchie's office one evening, the Rwandan leader's eyes were drawn to a book sitting on Ritchie's desk with an attractive cover of faux cordovan leather, gold lettering, and a green etching of a spreading oak tree. It was *The Purpose-Driven Life*. "I am a man of purpose," Kagame remarked, picking up the book. "I would like to read this." Ritchie invited him to take it.

Although they had not yet met, Ritchie knew of Warren's reputation and his interest in Africa and was personally acquainted with Peb Jackson. The next day he called Jackson and suggested that Kagame might be a valuable contact for Warren and offered to set up a meeting the next time the Rwandan president was in the country. The following October, Jackson met Kagame in Denver and brought with him an autographed copy of Warren's book. The two had a friendly and productive chat, with Jackson explaining in some detail Warren's vision for the PEACE plan and his desire to find a country to serve as a national model. "Let us be it," Kagame offered to Jackson. "I want Rwanda to be that model." Shortly thereafter, Warren received a letter from

Kagame inviting him to come to Rwanda. "I am a man of purpose," the president wrote. "Can you come help us rebuild our nation?"— although Kagame later would admit that he had no specific idea at the time of what Warren might actually do to help. "I could tell that this is a man who is very practical and thinks in a very straightforward way and is very forward-looking," Kagame would tell an interviewer. "If he is willing to partner with us—that could be very useful."

Rick and Kay made their first trip to Rwanda in March 2005, accompanied by Ritchie's business partner and an entourage of Saddleback staffers and others. They met with Kagame and other government officials, local businessmen, and Rwandan church leaders and took a whirlwind tour of the country, with its terraced hills and teeming villages. In a little more than a week, they came away with an arresting snapshot of the nation's problems and the beginnings of a vision for two legs of the PEACE plan that they believed were especially needed and might accomplish the most good in Rwanda: assisting the poor and caring for the sick.

Eleven years after the genocide, there were few countries in the world poorer than Rwanda. Almost 90 percent of its population worked in subsistence farming, earning less than two dollars per day, and half the population lived on less than one dollar per day. Coffee, tea, and bananas were important crops but exports were meager. Among other things, Warren hoped to use his connections to help the Rwandan government attract companies that would process and package the country's agricultural products, boosting exports and making the economy more complex. "The old cliché says, 'Don't give a man a fish; teach him to fish,'" Warren explained. "Well, I say even that's not good enough. Do that and all you have is a village of fishermen and nobody buys the fish. What you need is to create a more complex system where somebody says, 'I will build the boats,' and another says, 'I will make the nets,' and another says, 'I will catch the fish,' and another says, 'I will can the fish,' and another says, 'I will sell the fish internationally.' Now you're raising the village beyond subsistence."

In the months to come, Warren would return to Rwanda more than a dozen times, bringing along CEOs and other business experts from his own congregation and from his growing circle of contacts to assist

Rwandan business and government leaders in building their economy. Their focus would range from providing micro-enterprise training in remote villages to supporting multimillion-dollar infrastructure projects in the capital and elsewhere. In one celebrated case, in February of 2006, Warren addressed a business conference on Rwanda in Washington, D.C., and described the country's sore lack of commercial transportation. Sitting in the audience was Matthew Rose, president and CEO of the Burlington Northern Santa Fe Railway Corporation. "When Rick finished speaking," Peb Jackson would later recall, "Matt turned around and said to me, 'Peb, I'd love to be involved in that, and maybe put in some personal money and some of my staff's time in trying to make something happen,' and bingo! It started to fall into place." Within a few months, Rose's company began providing expert technical advice to the Rwandan government and helped shape a joint project with neighboring Tanzania and Burundi to establish a multinational railroad and Rwanda's first commercial rail service, a 720-mile route connecting Kigali with the Tanzanian port city of Dar es Salaam. In April 2009, the three nations signed an agreement to proceed with the $2.5 billion project. "Rick was an important catalyst for that," Jackson observed. "The whole issue for the PEACE plan and for Rick was not just to look at the country from a church perspective but from a total angle—the church, the private sector, and the public sector—in order to bring about some good."

Even more heartrending to the Warrens than Rwanda's dire poverty was its crisis in public health. The country's health care system had been decimated during the genocide, with hundreds of doctors, nurses, and other health workers among the slain; roughly one hundred practicing physicians and some three thousand nurses were all that remained to care for the entire population. Like much of sub-Saharan Africa, Rwanda suffered from the deadly scourge not only of HIV/AIDS, which infected nearly 4 percent of its population and accounted for more than 25,000 deaths annually, but also of such treatable and preventable diseases as malaria and tuberculosis, which killed many thousands more each year. The Rwandan government, with help from the World Health Organization and the U.S. government through the President's Emergency Plan for AIDS Relief (PEPFAR), had taken aim at the pandemic diseases and by 2004 had begun making progress, raising the percentage of HIV-infected Rwandans receiving life-prolonging anti-retroviral drugs from 4 to 64 percent in two years. Yet there were huge gaps in the delivery system. "The problem is not a lack of medicine, but a lack of access to it," Warren observed. In the mostly rural Karongi District on the country's western edge, for example, health care for a population of 650,000 was limited to three small hospitals and a hand-ful of poorly equipped clinics, all of which were located about a two-day walk from many villages. "When you're sick with AIDS and you run out of medicine, getting help under those circumstances is next to impossible," Warren explained. "There just aren't enough doctors, nurses, and clinics to get the job done."

Working with Dr. Robert Redfield, a pioneering AIDS researcher at the University of Maryland School of Medicine, Warren and a team of medical volunteers came up with a plan to enlist the district's churches to step in and fill the gap. Their Western Rwanda HIV/AIDS Healthcare Initiative Project would attempt to recruit and train up to one thousand local church members as community health volunteers capable of per-forming HIV testing and administering and monitoring AIDS medica-tions, along with providing other basic health and nutrition services. As a starting point, working with the Rwandan government's Ministry of Health, they would expand one of the three Karongi District hospitals, a small state-run facility in the town of Kibuye, to serve as a training center for church-based health care workers. The expanded hospital was to be built on the grounds of an infamous soccer stadium where more than eight thousand men, women, and children were rounded up and slaughtered during the 1994 genocide. Speaking at the site to a group of reporters in 2008, Warren announced that "out of the ashes of evil will spring hope and healing to replace hurt as a new and differ-ent kind of hospital will be erected here. A place of betrayal will be-come a place of blessing; a place of pain will become a place of promise; suffering will be replaced by service to the community; and what was once a place of death will become a place of life!"

During an earlier visit, Warren described the health care initiative to Rosemary Museminali, a minister of state in the Rwandan government. "Our goal is to train every church in Rwanda in basic health care,"

Warren explained, sitting across from the government official in a garden café at the Serena Hotel in Kigali. "Let me show you why this is needed." On the table, he spread out a map of the Karongi District, with three dots representing the three hospitals—one in Kilinda in the southern part of the district, another in Mugonero on the shore of Lake Kivu to the west, and the third in Kibuye, also on the lake but farther north—and explained about the two-day walk separating them from most residents. Next he showed a map with eighteen dots spread almost evenly across the page, each representing a clinic located about a day's walk from most people. "If we are going to get health care to everyone in the Karongi District, let me show you what we will need." He flipped to a third map virtually covered in tiny red dots. "These are the 726 churches in the Karongi district. There is at least one in nearly every village, within thirty minutes of most people. Now if I am sick, where would I most likely want to go to get my medicine?"

"Those are all churches?" Museminali said, her eyes wide with astonishment.

"*Yego*," Warren affirmed in the Rwandan language. "And this is just one province. Now do you see why we have to involve the church? When you link the hospitals to the churches and use church members to do home visits and help with nutrition and counseling, you extend the effectiveness of the hospitals into the homes of people. This is what the PEACE plan is all about: using the church for health care, business development, education, leadership training—not just spiritual development, but five things."

"May I take these?" the minister asked, holding the maps.

"Yes, please do." Warren had won another high-level convert to the PEACE plan.

Ever since his first visit in 2005, there was never any doubt that Warren and his team would be warmly received by the Rwandan government. President Kagame had been the PEACE plan's first and most important convert and had declared his intent to make Rwanda the world's first Purpose-Driven country. "When you talk about spiritual emptiness, bad leadership, poverty, disease, and ignorance, we in Rwanda understand you clearly," Kagame told Warren and some nine thousand Rwandan Christians who gathered in Kigali's Amahoro Stadium in July of 2005 for a nationally televised rally launching the PEACE plan. "It was due to lack of spiritual fulfillment that our people set upon each other in the genocide, neighbor killing neighbor, husband killing wife, mother killing son. It was because of egocentric and selfish leadership that by 1990 a quarter of our people lived in exile as refugees, while many of those in Rwanda lived as second-class citizens, deprived of most of their rights. You will be pleased to know that today we are waging a war against poverty, disease, and ignorance, and it is one that we are determined to win . . . We are grateful to you that you have chosen Rwanda as a pilot country, in which the PEACE plan will be tested . . . Now is the time when the church needs to affirm its strategic place in Rwandan society and serve as a real vehicle of reconciliation, and national reconstruction and healing."

Warren and the PEACE plan could not have received a more hospitable welcome. Standing next to the president, Warren told the cheering crowd, "I have looked inside this man's heart and I have seen compassion. I have seen courage, and I have seen humility." He placed his hand on Kagame's shoulder and prayed a prayer of blessing. A lasting friendship had been born.

Despite the warm reception from the Rwandan government and many of the country's religious leaders, Warren's high-visibility presence in Rwanda and his close association with Kagame were met with substantial skepticism in some quarters, even among some of Warren's admirers. "I do not believe that Rick Warren has a bad bone in his body," Alan Wolfe, director of the Boisi Center for Religion and American Public Life at Boston College and a self-described friend of Warren's, wrote in the *Wall Street Journal* a month after the Amahoro Stadium rally. "But I do believe that his remarkable enthusiasm is fueled by considerable naïveté." It was not enough, for example, Wolfe argued, to assert as Warren did at the rally that "spiritual emptiness allows evil acts to occur" when, in fact, some Christian clergy had been among the perpetrators of the Rwandan genocide. "Belief in Christ by itself offers insufficient protection against evil," Wolfe wrote. Moreover, tackling Africa's problems would require addressing complex political and economic questions. "Is there a Christian position on export diversification, energy subsidies, currency convertibility ratios, agricultural overcultivation or civil-service reform? That Rick Warren is serious about overcoming Rwanda's poverty is unquestioned. That he and his volunteers have any expertise or interest in economics and politics is unlikely."

Striking a similar note a few months later, Andrew Paquin, a global studies professor at Colorado Christian University and founder of the 1010 Project, a Denver-based humanitarian organization, wrote in *Christianity Today* magazine that while Warren's motives were commendable, his good intentions and "sudden access to vast resources must not be mistaken for expertise" when it comes to fighting poverty and injustice in Africa. Nongovernmental organizations (NGOs) and international relief agencies, he noted, had been laboring in Africa for years and had "shed blood and tears" for the people of Rwanda. "As Warren's team disperses throughout Rwanda with their 'in-a-box' development plans, they should know that this one-size-fits-all approach has already failed," he wrote. "International development is a complex endeavor . . . It is not enough to teach a man to sell fish. The question of who controls the market must also be addressed."

Both Paquin and Wolfe also expressed concern over Warren's cozy relationship with Kagame, who had been accused by some international human rights observers of military adventurism in the neighboring Democratic Republic of Congo and of squelching political dissent at home. Kagame would describe his army's incursions into Congo in 1996 and again in 1998 as defensive maneuvers against Hutu militias that had fled there after the genocide and that continued to pose a threat to Tutsi civilians on both sides of the border. Whether or not the accusations against the Rwandan president were entirely accurate—and he had plenty of credible defenders—Paquin suggested that, at a minimum, Warren was allowing himself to be used for political purposes. "Years of African corruption in the wake of colonial puppetry have created rifts of distrust between those who are suffering and those with friends in high places," he wrote. "Although Kagame is an improvement from past leaders, his connection to former regimes and to ongoing human-rights concerns should trouble anyone seeking to work with him."

To Warren, the criticism of Kagame and the skepticism regarding the PEACE plan's viability were equally lacking in merit. Citing what he described as one small example of Kagame's transparency and integrity, Warren noted the Rwandan government's efforts to expand access to the Internet for ordinary citizens. "Tinhorn dictators hate the Internet," Warren explained to one interviewer. "They don't want open access of information. They don't want people knowing what's going on elsewhere. They don't want anyone criticizing them." Warren said he was particularly impressed when, during one of his visits, Kagame introduced him to a political opponent who, despite being an adversary, privately spoke highly of the president. "He said, 'I'm actually in the opposition, and I believe [Kagame] is a man of integrity, and I believe he wants what's best for our country,'" Warren explained.

As to the efficacy of the PEACE plan and the preparedness of his army of church volunteers, Warren would yield no ground. "The PEACE plan is an amateur movement," Warren conceded in a 2008 interview. "I'm proud to be an amateur. It comes from the Latin word *amare* . . . It means I do it out of love. I don't do it for the money. I do it for free." To another interviewer, he would explain away the criticism coming from professional relief workers and humanitarian organizations: "Any time you are starting a new way, the existing organization is going to oppose it . . . [But] rather than spending time attacking the PEACE plan or saying, 'Well, it's not going to work,' how about lending your expertise? The role of NGOs has been vital. But it's a drop in the bucket compared to what we could be doing if we had mobilized the entire church. The NGOs need to support the church. Unfortunately, for many years it has been the opposite. The church supported the NGOs, provided money, provided members, provided creativity. The NGO got credit. Get down to the bottom line. Who gets the credit [under the PEACE plan]? Who gets strengthened? Who's the hero? Not Saddleback Church. Not the PEACE plan. We want the local church in a village to be the hero. The more I honor the church, the more God blesses me."

Warren and teams of PEACE emissaries from Saddleback would return to Rwanda often after that opening rally in 2005, with hundreds of small groups each adopting a Rwandan village for special care.

Warren himself would make more than a dozen return trips over the next four years to promote the PEACE plan and monitor its progress and to train Rwandan pastors in the Purpose-Driven paradigm. In March 2008, Warren and Kagame returned to Amahoro Stadium, this time to kick off a nationwide Forty Days of Purpose campaign using a new edition of *The Purpose-Driven Life* printed in the Kinyarwanda language. The campaign initially would involve some 500 Protestant and Anglican congregations throughout the country and would result in more than 21,000 decisions for Christ, some 10,000 baptisms, and an increase in weekly church attendance of more than 61,000.

On the day of the rally, more than 25,000 people crowded into the stadium—which was festooned in light-blue bunting, one of the official Rwandan colors—to hear Warren preach a stirring evangelistic message. Speaking in a rhythmic cadence through a Rwandan interpreter, he declared: "I believe God sent me here from the other side of the world to say this to you: Don't waste your life. Make your life count. And invest your life in the purpose that God created you for." He encouraged his listeners to "accept God's unconditional love," to "overcome evil with good," and to "return love for hatred." He ended his message by inviting the crowd to join him in a salvation prayer. Afterward, Warren and Kagame handed out diplomas to some two hundred Rwandan pastors who had completed an intensive two-year Purpose-Driven training course and who, in Kagame's words, would serve as "foot soldiers of transformation" during the nationwide forty-day campaign. "We have lived in our history without a purpose," the president intoned in English softly, almost inaudibly, as the rally drew to a close. "We cannot afford that anymore. Today we have chosen to be a country with a purpose."

BY WAY OF RWANDA, WARREN HAD MADE his triumphal entry onto the global stage. In the summer of 2006, he set out on an around-the-world tour to find new locales for expansion of his PEACE plan, and to strengthen his global network. Over a period of five weeks he visited thirteen countries in Asia, Africa, and the South Pacific, where he preached evangelistic messages in crowded stadiums and sports arenas and instructed tens of thousands of clergymen on the Purpose-Driven principles. Along the way he would be introduced to the sometimes confounding complexities of international politics.

The highlight of the trip was to have been a scheduled stop in North Korea, where Warren was to meet with government leaders to discuss plans for an evangelistic rally in the communist country the following year. Having learned of Warren's prominence and the popularity of his book among South Koreans, the North Korean government had invited him to preach at a stadium event commemorating the centennial of the Pyongyang Revival, a spiritual awakening that started in the capital and swept the country in 1907, marking a historical milestone in the growth of Protestant Christianity on the Korean peninsula. It was to be the country's first large-scale public religious gathering in over sixty years. During a visit in 1992, Billy Graham had been restricted to preaching in two relatively small state-sanctioned churches in the North Korean capital. Eight years later, Graham's son, Franklin, visited the country but was not allowed to preach at all.

When the invitation was announced just prior to Warren's trip, some human rights activists dismissed it as a propaganda ploy intended to soften the image of North Korean dictator Kim Jong-il, whose repressive regime had long been listed by the U.S. State Department as one of the world's worst violators of religious freedom. By accepting the invitation, some critics charged that Warren was unwittingly abetting a government charade and allowing himself to be used for political purposes. "If Rick Warren goes in there and preaches, Kim Jong-il can say, 'What about our lack of religious freedom? We had Rick Warren,'" Suzanne Scholte, chair of the Virginia-based North Korea Freedom Coalition, said at the time. Added Debra Liang-Fenton, executive director of the U.S. Committee for Human Rights in North Korea: "Maybe [Warren's visit] is another way for the North Korean government to say in its propaganda that, 'We allowed a Christian evangelical to preach to our people. So we must be religiously tolerant.'"

Warren rejected such criticism out of hand. "My policy has always been I go wherever I'm invited, regardless of politics," he insisted in a PBS television interview. "I don't go to places for political reasons. As long as I am not limited on the message, that I can share the Good News of Jesus Christ, I'll go anywhere." In adopting that mind-set, Warren considered himself in auspicious company. "To me, when Billy Graham went to Russia before the communist regime collapsed; when the pope went into Poland to support Solidarity and to preach the Good News; or when [Nelson] Mandela went back into South Africa—there are lots of things that people get criticized for: 'Why are you going there?' My reasoning is, why not? There are people in North Korea that have not heard for sixty years there is a God, he made you, he loves you, and he has a purpose for your life. If I get the chance to do that, I'm there."

But when Warren and his team arrived in Seoul, South Korea, for two major speaking events—a Purpose-Driven conference at the 250,000-member Yoido Full Gospel Church, and a citywide evangelistic crusade in the World Cup Stadium—he learned that the planning meeting in the north had been called off for unexplained reasons, casting a pall of uncertainty over the Pyongyang rally. Yet Warren seemed undaunted. "We are excited about the possibility of getting to preach the Gospel in North Korea," he reported to his flock in an e-mail after receiving the disappointing news, "but right now it's not clear whether that will happen. Pray with us that God's will be done." Providential or not, the meeting was never rescheduled and Warren's opportunity to preach in the communist nation appeared lost, at least for the foreseeable future. Yet as disappointing as it was at the time, the cancellation had spared him from a situation that almost certainly would have engulfed him in controversy just when his nascent PEACE plan was gaining traction. In what may have seemed a misfortune, he had managed to dodge a bullet.

Later that year, however, Warren would find himself in the center of another diplomatic storm, this time involving the hypersensitive politics of the Middle East, and this time he would not escape unscathed. Warren had planned for some time to return to Rwanda in November and had arranged a stopover in Bremen, Germany, to address a pastors' conference and to brief church leaders there on the PEACE plan. Early in the fall another opportunity presented itself, and Warren amended his itinerary to include a five-day visit to Syria and a meeting with its authoritarian president, Bashar al-Assad.

Unlike his ill-fated North Korean venture, Warren's side trip to Syria received little advance notice. As he would explain later to his congregation, he had decided to add the visit at the invitation of his next-door neighbor, a Syrian, who wanted him to see his country and its many ancient Christian sites. "I was touched by this invitation from my friend and promised, 'the next time I'm traveling that direction, I'll visit your home with you.' It was a favor for a friend, not a political statement."

Yet when he arrived in Damascus, he would find political entanglements almost impossible to avoid. After touring several traditional Christian attractions—including the Damascus Road, where the Apostle Paul was converted, and the tomb of John the Baptist—Warren participated in a series of private meetings his neighbor had arranged with some of the country's top Christian leaders, its chief Muslim cleric, the Syrian foreign minister and minister of higher education, and finally with Assad. As soon as he left the president's office, the state-run Syrian Arab News Agency issued a press release reporting that the meeting had "focused on Syrian-American relations" and that "the American delegation stressed that the American administration is mistaken not to hold dialogue with Syria." It said Warren had "hailed the religious coexistence, tolerance, and stability that the Syrian society is enjoying due to the wise leadership of President Al-Assad, asserting that he will convey the true image about Syria to the American people." Later, the government-owned newspaper *Tishrin* quoted Warren directly: "Washington is wrong not to hold dialogue with Syria, which wants peace. I call on the Americans to visit Syria and meet its beautiful people. I will tell the Americans that their idea about Syria does not reflect the truth."

The stories quickly made the rounds on the Internet and caught the attention of a handful of bloggers in the United States, who predictably set about castigating Warren for consorting with a terrorist regime and a sworn enemy of Israel. Joseph Farah, editor of the conservative WorldNet Daily website, wrote on his blog that Warren "had no business traveling to Syria and being used for propaganda purposes" by Assad. "If I were a betting man, I would wager that Warren will come home and allege he was widely misquoted," Farah wrote. "He probably was. I HOPE he was. But here's the problem: When you place yourself in the position of being used—and you ARE used—whose fault is it?" Meanwhile, the Associated Press reported out of Athens that Warren's trip had unleashed a torrent of criticism and quoted an American Christian radio network talk-show host calling Warren a "mindless shill" for Syria and demanding "an apology to Israel, to the American people, and to the victims of Syrian-sponsored terror."

Warren, in an electronic message to his flock while he was still on the road, noted the dustup over his visit and complained that the Syrians had misrepresented him and what he had said. "The official state-controlled Syrian news agency issued some press releases that sounded like I was a politician negotiating the Iraq war by praising the Syrian president and everything else in Syria!" he wrote. "Of course, that's ridiculous, but it created a stir among bloggers who tend to editorialize before verifying the truth. Does it seem ironic to you that people who distrust Syria are now believing Syrian press releases?" At the same time, Warren spokesman Larry Ross released a statement explaining that Warren's visit was "neither official nor political" and that he had gone to Syria "to meet with and encourage the country's key Christian leaders; dialogue with top Muslim leaders; and promote religious freedom." While there, according to the statement, Warren also had sought—and obtained—the government's permission to bring the PEACE plan to Syria. Despite Warren's earlier protestations to the contrary, the statement by his spokesman went on to quote Warren making some decidedly positive comments regarding Syria that did not seem substantially different from those described in the Syrian media.

"The Syrian government has long had a bad reputation in America, but if one considers a positive action like welcoming in thousands of Christian refugees from Iraq, or the protection of freedom to worship for Christians and Jews in Syria, it should not be ignored," Dr. Warren said from Rwanda. He further explained that in terms of religious freedom, Syria is far more tolerant than places like Burma, Cuba, Iran, Iraq, and nations identified in the U.S. Commission Report on International Religious Freedom. "Muslims and Christians have lived side by side in Syria for more than a thousand years, often with mosques and churches built next to each other," he added. "What can we learn from them?

"I believe it is a mistake to not talk to nations considered hostile—isolation and silence has never solved conflict anywhere, whether between spouses or between nations," Dr. Warren concluded.

When the dust began to settle Warren would acknowledge that he could have handled the Syrian visit more effectively. "In hindsight, I wish we'd been better prepared," he wrote to his flock. "We would have handled some meetings differently, watched our words more closely, and been more aware of the agenda of their state press. We wanted to just slip in and out, but that's nearly impossible for me to do anymore. It's been a learning experience." In an interview with CNN's Wolf Blitzer a month after the trip, he would insist that he never intended to play the role of a diplomat. "I'm a pastor, not a politician. And I report to a higher authority, where Jesus said, 'Go into all the world, to every nation.' Does that involve Syria? Yes. Does that involve North Korea? Yes . . . I don't ever go into these places as a politician. I don't go in as a diplomat. I don't go in as trying to take a job that's not my job. But if I get an opportunity to go in and bring hope, encouragement, and the message of the good news, I'm going to do it."

Yet there soon would be other opportunities for Warren to play the role of global statesman, and when they presented themselves, he would not shrink from them.

CHAPTER SIXTEEN

# *Made for Significance*

On a Monday morning early in July 2007, Warren was busy doing what he often did on his only day off—running family errands at a shopping center in Rancho Santa Margarita a short distance from his house in Trabuco Canyon. On this particular morning he had stopped at an Albertson's supermarket to pick up some groceries and was standing in line at a Starbucks kiosk inside the store when his cell phone rang. From the Caller ID he could see it was his deputy chief of staff, Steve Komanapalli.

"What's up, Steve?" Warren asked.

"You need to take this number down," Komanapalli said. Warren pulled out a pen and jotted the number on a Starbucks coffee cup sleeve. "Can you call it immediately?"

"Sure. Who is it?"

"It's Benjamin Netanyahu. He wants to talk with you and he asked that you call him right away."

Warren had never met or spoken with the former Israeli prime minister, although he was well aware of his international prominence and reputation. The handsome, hawkish, American-educated leader of the conservative Likud Party was widely considered to be a pivotal and volatile figure in Middle Eastern politics. He was known as a hard-liner on "land-for-peace" negotiations with the Palestinians and advocated an iron-fisted approach to combating terrorism. As Israel's youngest prime minister—he was forty-seven when elected in 1996—he had taken a tough stance in U.S.-brokered peace talks with Palestinian leader Yasser Arafat but then ultimately agreed to turn over most of the sacred town of Hebron on the West Bank to the Palestinian Authority. That cost him the support of the extreme right in his already fragile governing coalition and resulted in his defeat by Labor Party leader Ehud

Barak in the 1999 elections. After a brief hiatus from politics, he was appointed foreign minister in 2003 and then finance minister under Ariel Sharon but resigned in 2005 in protest over the government's decision to close Israeli settlements in Gaza. Since then he had worked to rebuild his Likud power base in the Knesset and began laying the groundwork for a return to national power.

Netanyahu had called Warren's Saddleback office from his home in Jerusalem and had left his personal number, and when Warren dialed it from his place in line at Starbucks, Netanyahu answered the phone. After a brief exchange of pleasantries, Warren asked: "How can I help you?"

The Israeli leader got immediately to the point. He told Warren that evangelicals had always been among the strongest backers of Israel in America, and that Israeli leaders have long appreciated knowing that they could count on evangelicals for their support. Yet now he recognized that there was "a changing of the guard" in evangelical leadership. Moral Majority founder Jerry Falwell, one of the most outspoken Christian Zionists, had died a month earlier, and other aging lions of the Religious Right—Christian broadcaster Pat Robertson (who once suggested that Ariel Sharon's massive stroke in 2006 was divine punishment for "dividing God's land"), Focus on the Family leader James Dobson, and Texas megachurch pastor and broadcaster John Hagee, among others—were in the twilight of their careers and no longer commanded the influence that they once did. Netanyahu explained that people had been telling him he should get to know Warren and develop a friendship with him, as he had done with the previous generation of evangelical leaders. He asked if they could meet.

"I'd love to," Warren said. "Why don't you come out to Saddleback the next time you're here and I'll show you our campus. I think you'll see that it's not what you think the typical American church is like. I know all of the up-and-coming leaders—many of them I've trained—and I'd be happy to introduce you to the next generation of evangelical Christian leaders in America."

Netanyahu gladly accepted the offer.

Warren took his coffee and moved to a more isolated spot. "Mr. Netanyahu, while I've got you on the phone there are a couple of things I'd like to say."

"Please. Go right ahead," Netanyahu said.

"First, you need to understand that there is a new wind blowing in evangelicalism in relationship to Israel. Now, you never need to doubt that evangelicals are going to support Israel. Israel is the only democracy in the Middle East. They share our Judeo-Christian values. They support us on terrorism. They're our best ally in that part of the world. We are never going to allow the sovereignty and safety of Israel to be threatened. But the days of 'Israel can do no wrong, and everybody else can do no right' are over. The days when you could drop a bomb on Gaza and not even have to say 'Oops'—that's over. People now are looking for a just settlement. They want human rights. Yes, we want to protect Israel's sovereignty, but, yes, we also believe that the Palestinians cannot just be dominated indefinitely and left in a state of transition and tension. And so you just need to figure that into your strategy—that the evangelicals of today are not the evangelicals of twenty years ago."

While Warren had accurately described what was emerging as a new and more nuanced way of thinking within the evangelical world regarding Israel and the Middle East, his characterization of what amounted to a fait accompli was a bit of an overstatement. In an important representation of the approach Warren had described, more than eighty evangelical leaders later that year would sign a letter to President Bush calling for "a fair, two-state solution" to the Israeli-Palestinian conflict that would guarantee the security and economic freedom of both sides. Yet there still were plenty of evangelical leaders who embraced the view that Israel's security trumped all else and that its claim to the land was divinely ordered and, therefore, nonnegotiable. Twenty-two of them—including Falwell, Hagee, and a top Robertson lieutenant—had sent a letter to Bush in 2003 charging that to treat Israel and the Palestinians evenhandedly would be "morally reprehensible." Their view was based in part on their dispensationalist theology, which held that the modern state of Israel was to play a key role in end-times events leading up to the Second Coming of Christ. It was a view that not all evangelicals shared—Warren among them. Meanwhile, the views of ordinary people in the pews seemed somewhat equivocal. Public opinion surveys of evangelicals at the time showed broad support for Israel but also for the just treatment and human rights protections of Palestinians. Like the rest of the country, evangelicals clearly were not of one mind in discerning a road to peace in the Middle East.

Netanyahu listened attentively as Warren spoke. It was not exactly what he had expected to hear. He told Warren that he appreciated his honesty and said he would factor that into his strategy. He gave Warren his cell phone number and private e-mail address and encouraged him to call him any time. He said he needed to hear from people who would tell him the truth.

"I will," Warren said. "I'll tell you the truth." But he wasn't quite finished.

"Since I've got you on the phone, let me say something else. You know, we had an expression in America that said, 'Only Nixon could go to China.'" He explained that when President Nixon visited communist China in 1972—a historic trip that led to normalized relations between the two longtime foes—he was able to succeed because "everybody knew that Nixon was a rabid anticommunist. And even the people here who hated him knew that he wasn't going to surrender the sovereignty of the United States to a communist country. Because Nixon was a hard-liner, they knew he would negotiate from a position of strength.

"It may just be that as only Nixon could go to China, maybe only Netanyahu can bring peace to the Middle East. You're known as a hard-liner. The closest we ever came to peace in the Middle East was when General Sharon was prime minister because he negotiated from a position of strength, and the Israeli people trusted him and it allowed him some flexibility. So maybe you're the guy." Netanyahu took it all in and thanked Warren for his vote of confidence, but otherwise was noncommittal on approaches he might take in future negotiations with the Palestinians.

Warren had one more subject to raise. "There's a man you need to meet," he said. "I believe he's the George Washington of Africa. I think he's a man of rock-ribbed integrity. He has zero tolerance for corruption, and I think, honestly, in the scheme of things, he will be equal to or greater than Nelson Mandela in the history of Africa. His name is Paul Kagame."

Warren briefly sketched out the Rwandan president's life story—his family's exile to Uganda, his rise through the Ugandan military ranks, his leadership role in the Rwandan civil war and in stopping the genocide, and his rebel army's defeat of the murderous Hutu-led regime. After the war, Warren explained, Kagame did two unexpected things. "First, he refused to install himself as Rwanda's president. Anywhere else in the world, you succeed in staging a coup and you're in—you are the new leader. But Kagame said, 'We believe in the rule of law, and I am not elected.' The previous president had been killed, but the vice president was still alive and had fled the country. So Kagame said, 'Let's bring him back because he is now the president.' Then Kagame ran in the next presidential election and he won in a landslide as a national hero.

"The other thing he did," Warren continued, "is he prevented a reverse genocide from taking place—he would not allow retaliatory violence." Instead, he explained, Kagame ordered the arrest of Hutu extremist leaders and tens of thousands of others who had participated in the genocide. Many of them stood trial in traditional Gacaca village courts, an approach that was intended to speed justice but also to promote reconciliation and national healing by bringing entire villages together—witnesses, families of victims, and accused perpetrators and their families—to uncover the truth and begin to bury the hatreds of the past. "You need to meet this guy," Warren told Netanyahu. "When I go to Rwanda, I find ten years after the genocide that Hutu and Tutsi are living side by side without a wall, without barbed wire, and they're not throwing bottle rockets at each other. It's not a perfect country by any means, but they've figured out something about reconciliation that I don't see in the Middle East, because when I go to the Middle East I see barbed wire and fences and walls and people still throwing rocks at each other fifty years later. So I think he has something to teach you."

Netanyahu said he would be pleased to meet with Kagame and he asked Warren to arrange a meeting at Saddleback the next time the

Rwandan president visited the United States. Warren said he would he happy to do so, and with that their conversation ended.

Within a few weeks, Warren had a plan in place and had obtained an agreement from both men to meet on the Saddleback campus on September 23. Warren planned to make a weekend of it by preaching a message on reconciliation at that Sunday's worship services and then hosting a private meeting with the two leaders. A few days before the meeting, however, Netanyahu canceled. Earlier that month Israeli warplanes had staged an airstrike on a suspected nuclear weapons facility in Syria and tensions in the region had escalated as a result, with reports of Syrian troops massing near the Israeli border. Netanyahu told Warren that, given those circumstances, he was unable to leave the country and said that the meeting with Kagame would have to be rescheduled. He reiterated his hope that, in the meantime, he and Warren could arrange a personal get-acquainted session apart from any meeting involving Kagame, but no specific date was set.

Although disappointed that his attempt at brokering a meeting of the two leaders had failed, at least temporarily, Warren was about to receive some welcome and unexpected help in his nascent efforts at global diplomacy. A few days after the canceled meeting was to have occurred, Warren flew to New York City to attend the Clinton Global Initiative, an annual Davos-like international gathering of government and business leaders and assorted intellectuals and celebrities convened by former president Bill Clinton to ponder solutions to some of the world's most perplexing problems. The thirteen hundred attendees at that year's event were a particularly eclectic mix—from media mogul Ted Turner and actress Angelina Jolie to South African archbishop Desmond Tutu, former British prime minister Tony Blair, and President Hamid Karzai of Afghanistan. Warren had been invited to participate in a luncheon panel on alleviating poverty, and he took the opportunity to promote his PEACE plan and to repeat his call for a three-way partnership of government, the private sector, and local faith communities to combat the global giants.

"If we are going to team tackle these big issues like poverty, disease, illiteracy, trafficking, corruption, and so many other issues, we're going to somehow have to tap into the largest pool of volunteer man-power in the world," Warren declared. "It's called people of faiths, plural. There are 600 million Buddhists in the world. There are 800 million Hindus. There are a billion Muslims. There are 2.3 billion Christian members of churches. Now, as a pastor, of course I'm interested in the last one. But they all matter . . . Now, if you want to say, 'Well, we can't have anybody of any faith doing humanitarian [work],' you just ruled out most of the world, because really, outside of Manhattan and Europe, there aren't really that many secularists." The room erupted in laughter. "The fact is most people have some kind of faith. It doesn't matter to me what it is at that point, but if they're willing to work on the issues, that's what matters . . . You see, honestly, I don't care what your motivation is for helping people, as long as you do it. It doesn't have to be my motivation, as long as you do it."

As he often did in front of mainly secular audiences, Warren made a point of emphasizing the PEACE plan's more ecumenical features, touting the efficiencies of a grassroots faith network and broad-based humanitarian partnerships, while making little or no mention of the spiritual awakening or of the "new Reformation" that he believed it would bring to Christianity. Accordingly, his remarks were well received and afterward he found himself surrounded by well-wishers and people requesting more information. One was a handsome young African American man who was impeccably dressed and wearing a long gold chain and medallion around his neck and who Warren thought looked vaguely familiar. "I want in on it," the man announced enthusiastically. "I believe in the 'E'—'Educate the next generation.'" He handed Warren his card and asked that he give him a call. It was the Grammy Award–winning R&B singer Usher.

Later that afternoon Warren received a personal message from Tony Blair asking for a private meeting on the PEACE plan. Like Warren, Blair was a deeply religious man whose interest in humanitarian causes was closely linked to his personal Christian faith. Since leaving office just three months earlier, he had begun work on establishing his own charitable foundation to promote interfaith understanding and to enlist the support of religious communities in combating poverty and other world problems. He also had been appointed a special envoy for an international mediating group seeking peace in the Middle East and composed of representatives from the European Union, the United Nations, the United States, and Russia.

Over breakfast the following day, Warren and Blair compared notes on their projects and both were pleased to discover that the PEACE plan and Blair's soon-to-be-created foundation shared many of the same objectives and were based on the same premise—that the world's most pressing problems would never be solved without involving people of faith. They also found that they shared a similar perspective on Middle East peace. As Blair described his new diplomatic role, he outlined some of the difficulties he faced in attempting to negotiate a two-state solution in the region. Warren, in turn, reported in some detail on his conversation with Netanyahu—how he had informed the former Israeli prime minister that American evangelicals were no longer willing to give the Israeli government a blank check and that they expected more accountability in its dealings with the Palestinians.

"I'm so glad you told him that," a beaming Blair responded. "I can't tell you how much easier that makes my job."

Warren also explained how he had hoped to introduce Netanyahu to President Kagame and how he saw Rwanda as a national model for reconciliation. "You need to meet Kagame yourself," he told his conversation partner. Blair nodded and said he would try to arrange it. As they parted company, both men agreed to stay in touch. In a relatively short period of time they had established a strong rapport and initiated what would become a personal friendship and a close working relationship. Within a few months, Blair would announce the launch of the Tony Blair Faith Foundation and would appoint Warren to its advisory board.

Warren headed back to California feeling that his time in New York had been well spent. His remarks at the Clinton Global Initiative seemed to have resonated well and had helped raise the visibility of the PEACE plan before a broad international audience. He had made hundreds of new contacts with business and government leaders that he believed would prove helpful later on. Between conference sessions he had offered encouragement to a group of local pastors who were preparing for a citywide Forty Days of Purpose campaign later in the fall, and then sat down for an hour of give-and-take with *Time* magazine's editorial board. He was beginning to fit comfortably into his expanding role as a self-described "global statesman" and he was enjoying every minute of it.

Back at his Saddleback office a few days later, Warren received a lengthy e-mail message from Blair. "You're not going to believe this," it began. Blair told how he had arrived home two days after their meeting in New York and had walked into his house and said to his wife, Cherie, "What are we doing tonight?" She responded: "We're having dinner with the president of Rwanda." It was a last-minute arrangement that had not been on his calendar, Blair explained, and Kagame, of course, knew nothing of the conversation that Blair and Warren had just had about him. "It had to be the Providence of God," Blair concluded.

Warren wrote back and said that he agreed with Blair's assessment, and he suggested that perhaps Blair now was in a better position than he to broker a meeting between Kagame and Netanyahu. "If you want to invite me in to make it more comfortable for them, fine," he wrote. "But I have no need to do this or to be there. I'm just glad God saw fit to use me to help put it together."

Warren would learn later that Blair and Kagame held several follow-up meetings after their dinner together in London in the fall of 2007 and struck up a close working relationship. A few months later, Blair would become an official, although unpaid, economic adviser to the Rwandan president. At the same time, Blair was continuing his efforts to bring Kagame and Netanyahu together. Meanwhile, Netanyahu called Warren again in the spring of 2008, hoping to arrange a one-on-one meeting during a planned trip to California, but Warren was scheduled to be on the East Coast at that time and had to decline. As of early 2009, Netanyahu had yet to meet with either Warren or Kagame. In February, his conservative Likud Party came out ahead in a close national election and forged a new governing coalition, and on March 31, 2009, he was sworn in for a second time as Israel's prime minister.

THROUGHOUT HIS RISE TO NATIONAL and then international prominence and through his years of building Saddleback and a global network of pastors, Warren managed to stay in close touch with his extended family. In the years just prior to his parents' passing, he spoke with them at least weekly by phone and went to visit them—or they him—as often as his hectic schedule would allow. After they were gone he sorely missed their wise counsel and their tireless prayer support, which he had come to rely upon so heavily since childhood as a source of spiritual strength. But they had left him a rich legacy of faith and a treasure trove of life lessons that would continue to inhabit his writings and messages throughout his ministry.

He also enjoyed good relationships with both of his siblings, although the relationships were of two entirely different sorts. Rick and his sister, Chaundel, had always been close. Having grown up together in the small-town atmosphere of Redwood Valley and Ukiah, their lives had been shaped by many of the same experiences and they had followed similar faith journeys. Both had dedicated themselves to Christ and to the ministry as young teenagers, attended California Baptist College where they married their spouses, and settled in the Saddleback Valley and raised their families just a few miles apart. Both Chaundel and her husband, Tom, played important roles at Warren's church, Tom as a teaching pastor and Chaundel as a lay minister to other ministers' wives. Chaundel often would refer to her brother as an important spiritual influence in her life. "From the time we were teenagers, I've learned so much from him," she said. "It's been amazing to see how God has used him."

Rick and his older brother, Jim, had not been nearly as close. While they respected and admired each other and shared some common interests—computers, popular music, practical jokes—as adults they had chosen widely divergent paths. Having lived in the San Francisco Bay area since he was a teenager, Jim was a sporadic churchgoer at best and made no pretense of living the kind of dedicated Christian life that he saw modeled in his parents and siblings; he often referred to himself as the black sheep of the family. Since his college days at San Francisco State University, he had pursued a life focused on financial success and the creature comforts that it brought—comforts that he had been deprived of growing up poor in a Baptist parsonage. Right out of college he had landed a job writing software for an upstart company that would become MasterCard. From there he moved to the Federal Reserve Bank and then to the business office of the San Francisco 49ers of the National Football League where, at six-foot-five and over 250 pounds, he moonlighted as quarterback Joe Montana's personal bodyguard. He capped off his career at Bank of America, helping to devise an international system for wire transfers and traveling the world. His seven-year marriage ended in divorce in 1977.

"Jim lived a pretty much typical secular life," Rick recalled, "and that put a strain, for a number of years, between me and my brother, and our family and Jim, because Jim's interests were primarily the 49ers and playing golf. And that was all we had in common to talk about." Then in the early 1990s when personal computers began to become popular, Jim and Rick found that they had a new common interest. "We started building a relationship around technology," Rick said. "I'd call him on the phone and we'd talk about computer problems and issues."

When their mother died suddenly in 1996, it seemed to mark a turning point in Jim's life. "It was a wake-up call for Jim when my mom died." Rick recalled. "We began to talk about spiritual things—things that we hadn't talked about together as brothers in many, many years." Later that same year, Jim, a lifelong smoker, was diagnosed with emphysema and was hospitalized for more than two months, and he and Rick began talking more intensely about the meaning and purpose of life. It would take him seven more years, but slowly Jim began to return to the faith. Finally, in 2003, he left his home and friends in Northern California and moved to Orange County and immediately became an active member at Saddleback. "When he moved down here I just watched the guy get on supercharged spiritual growth," Rick said. "I saw my brother grow spiritually, more in three years than some people I've watched grow in thirty." He immediately became involved in the church's sports ministry, helped out in the office, and participated in disaster relief and international mission trips. Because of his eagerness to serve in so many different areas, Kay jokingly gave him the title "Senior Minister of Small Things." Sometimes he would call his brother on his cell phone between services to offer unsolicited advice. "That joke bombed," he was known to say, never one to mince words. "Change it. Before the next service."

Meanwhile, Jim's health had continued to deteriorate, and as the emphysema worsened he became tethered to an oxygen canister twenty-four hours a day. On January 26, 2007, the three Warren siblings and their families gathered at Chaundel and Tom's house for a birthday dinner for Rick and Tom. It was a lighthearted celebration and the entire clan enjoyed one another's company, although Jim left a little early saying he wasn't feeling well. Afterward he telephoned his sister and told her that when he had gotten into his car to drive home he found that his oxygen saturation level had fallen dangerously low and so he had waited in her driveway until it came up. It was the last she would hear from her brother. Three days later Jim died in his sleep at the age of fifty-nine.

On February 2, Rick conducted Jim's memorial service at Saddleback's packed Worship Center and offered a moving and deeply personal tribute, describing how, in his final years, his brother had moved from a life of chasing worldly success to a life of finding eternal significance in a relationship with Christ. "What's the greatest lesson of Jim Warren's life?" he asked near the conclusion of his message. "The lesson is this, that when you come to Jesus Christ . . . he takes what's good in your life and makes it better, and he takes the negative in your life and diminishes it. I saw that over and over in my brother's life. I saw a guy who was kind and gentle in his life all of a sudden become super kind and super gentle. He'd always been a gentle giant. But after he had Jesus in his life he became effusive in his generosity, effusive in his gentleness, effusive in his kindness. God just took what was there and made it cooler. The rough edges in his life, I started seeing it just get sanded away.

"The other lesson of my brother's life is it is never too late to change. It is never too late to start over." Then, as if pondering the remarkable circumstances that recently had unfolded in his own life, Warren added, "If Jim were here today, I know the thing that he would have me say to you is this: Don't wait any longer in moving from success to significance. Don't waste another second. You are made for more than success. You were made for significance."

# CHAPTER SEVENTEEN

# Weathering the Storm

IN WARREN'S SILVER-ANNIVERSARY YEAR as Saddleback's pastor—the year of the Angel Stadium celebration, the official launch of the PEACE plan, and Warren's personal emergence as a bona fide national and international figure—*Fortune* magazine published a laudatory profile that attempted to explain his meteoric rise to fame and assess his staying power as a leader, thereby posing the question of the story's headline: "Will Success Spoil Rick Warren?" There was little doubt in 2005, when the article was written, that Warren already had attained a level of prominence in the evangelical world and in the culture at large that few American churchmen before him ever had. Next to Billy Graham, he was deemed by a growing number of conservative Protestants, and by many in the media, as the most influential religious figure of his time. He was, as the article aptly described him, "a new brand of evangelical leader—an affable baby-boomer who is savvy about business, comfortable in the mainstream culture, and eager to build coalitions around his major concerns."

But it also was clear by then that Warren was attempting to leverage his considerable influence in the pursuit of two ambitious and seemingly conflicting goals: on the one hand, to rebrand evangelical Christianity by softening its image and expanding its agenda beyond the "culture war" issues of abortion, gay marriage, euthanasia, and stem cell research, while on the other, to strengthen its role in national and global affairs, including on those same social issues that have always mattered to evangelicals. "I want evangelicals to be known not for what they're against, but what they're for," he told an interviewer late in 2006. "Yes, there are some things that I believe are flat out wrong. There is no doubt about it, and I'm not wishy-washy about it. But my agenda is bigger than simply those issues. My agenda is to be as big as the agenda of Jesus."

It was a challenging undertaking, to say the least, and one which, as the *Fortune* article observed, would leave Warren "open to the charge that he is trying to have it both ways." Indeed, by walking that middle path over the years, Warren would gain friends and influence among a widening circle of admirers, but it also would make him a lightning rod for criticism from opposite extremes.

In June of 2005, at a time when Warren was just beginning his work in Rwanda with the PEACE plan, he agreed to help his new rock-star friend, Bono, enlist American evangelicals in a global campaign to pressure the richest Western governments to provide trade and debt relief to Africa. In a widely distributed appeal cosigned by Billy Graham and British evangelical theologian John Stott, Warren urged Christians to write President Bush, who was about to attend a summit of the eight leading industrial nations, encouraging him to support "specific, measurable actions to fight poverty, hunger, and disease" in the world's poorest countries. "I've never been involved in partisan politics and don't intend to do so now," Warren wrote, "but global poverty is an issue that rises far above mere politics. It is a moral issue, a compassion issue, and because Jesus commanded us to help the poor, it is an obedience issue!" Exactly how many evangelicals responded to the appeal is uncertain, but more than a million Americans in all wrote the president and, added to millions in other countries who took up the cause, their voices were heard. Meeting in Scotland that July, the Group of Eight leaders agreed to cancel more than $40 billion of debt for eighteen impoverished countries and promised to provide billions more in economic aid.

The following year, Warren was one of eighty-six evangelical leaders to sign a landmark statement on global warming, calling for federal legislation that would require reductions in carbon dioxide emissions through "cost-effective, market-based mechanisms." Without such action, the leaders warned, "millions of people could die in this century because of climate change, most of them our poorest global neighbors." Many of the signers—who included pastors, college and seminary presidents, leaders of evangelical relief agencies like the Salvation Army, and others—were weighing in for the first time on an issue seldom associated with evangelicals. "For most of us," they confessed, "until recently this has not been treated as a pressing issue or major priority. Indeed, many of us have required considerable convincing before becoming persuaded that climate change is a real problem and that it ought to matter to us as Christians. But now we have seen and heard enough."

Some evangelical leaders, however, remained unconvinced, and a group of them, including such influential figures as James Dobson of Focus on the Family, Prison Fellowship's Charles Colson, and Richard Land, head of the Southern Baptists' Ethics and Religious Liberty Commission, staged a preemptive countermove. A few days prior to the statement's release, they sent a letter to leaders of the National Association of Evangelicals, an umbrella group representing more than sixty evangelical denominations and ministries, declaring that "global warming is not a consensus issue" among evangelicals because science had not yet spoken clearly on it, and they urged the NAE leaders not to sign the statement. The strategy apparently worked and the NAE officials withheld their signatures even though they had helped draft the statement. While Dobson and his allies had prevailed, the public confrontation over the evangelical social agenda had revealed a widening generational rift within the movement that would not soon go away.

As if Warren's involvement in those episodes had not been explicit enough, he soon began making it a point in media interviews and in other public statements to distance himself from the old-line Religious Right and its association with Republican Party politics. "There is a difference between 'evangelicalism' and 'fundamentalism' and 'the Religious Right,'" Warren told journalists at a conference in Key West, Florida, in May 2005. "People use them like they are synonyms and they are not. They are very, very different. I am an evangelical. I'm not a member of the Religious Right and I'm not a fundamentalist . . . and a part of that is because the Religious Right has tended to limit the number of items on the agenda to three or four social issues and missed a bunch of others." He went even further a year later, telling an interviewer in Australia, "I don't think it's really good for churches to get too close to politics. I think that's been one of the big mistakes in America . . . If you identify with either party, you become captive and you can't speak the truth with authority."

It seemed as if he was speaking from experience, and he was. Despite his long-held commitment to abstaining from partisan endorsements, in 2004 Warren had signaled his support for President Bush all but by name in a preelection letter sent to hundreds of thousands of pastors in his Purpose-Driven Network. The letter, he later would insist, was "not an initiative. It was a response to all the guys in the network who were asking me, 'Rick, what do we do?' Well, I wasn't about to tell them how to vote, but I would tell them some issues to consider."

In late October of that year, just a few days before the election, he sent out a blanket e-mail to his network, reminding his pastors that "as church leaders, we know our congregations are not allowed to endorse specific candidates, and it's important for us to recognize that there can be multiple opinions among Bible-believing Christians when it comes to debatable issues such as the economy, social programs, Social Security, and the war in Iraq. But for those of us who accept the Bible as God's Word and know that God has a unique, sovereign purpose for every life, I believe there are five issues that are nonnegotiable." He listed them as abortion, stem cell research, same-sex marriage, human cloning, and euthanasia—issues on which he said Bush and his opponent, Democratic senator John Kerry, "could not have more opposite views." He added: "In order to live a purpose-driven life—to affirm what God has clearly stated about his purpose for every person he creates—we must take a stand by finding out what the candidates believe about these five issues, and then vote accordingly." On November 2, evangelicals turned out at the polls in near record numbers and 78 percent of them voted for Bush, helping to hand the Republican president a narrow reelection victory.

Three years later Warren would be telling reporters that he had come to realize that sending the letter had been a mistake. It was inappropriate, in the first place, to have sent such a message right before the election, he told a *Time* magazine correspondent in the fall of 2007, but it also had been wrong to imply that those five issues were the only ones that mattered to evangelicals. He expanded on that second point in a 2008 interview with National Public Radio:

> If I were sending out a letter today, my view hasn't changed one bit on any of those particular subjects. But my agenda has expanded dramatically over the last four years. And I think one of the things I've tried to do with evangelicals is to get them to not deny their pre-existing agenda but to expand it. I'm still pro-life, but I don't call myself pro-life anymore. What I do is call myself "whole-life." I'm not just in favor of the unborn baby. I'm in favor of her when she's born. Is she a crack baby? Is she an AIDS baby? Is she a baby living in poverty? Is she going to get an education? It's not just concern for protection of the unborn but for protection of the born, too.

Having apparently learned a lesson on partisan entanglements from the 2004 election and having expanded his agenda, Warren renewed his determination to walk a nonpartisan line, and in his frequent forays to Capitol Hill in the ensuing years he was careful to make the rounds of Democrats and Republicans alike so as to avoid any appearance of favoritism. Those efforts at evenhandedness continued to win him new respect and friendships in Washington and the admiration of many in the media who perceived him as a new breed of evangelical leader who stood in contrast to the fiercely partisan old guard of the Religious Right. Whenever reporters asked about his political leanings, he often would resort to a one-line quip: "I'm not left wing and I'm not right wing; I'm for the whole bird."

But Warren's willingness to forge friendships with Democrats and his dedication to the fight against AIDS and poverty and other "liberal" causes earned him far fewer points among religious conservatives, who increasingly complained that he and other like-minded evangelicals were diluting the Christian right's political influence on "family values" issues and thereby were unwittingly playing into the hands of the movement's political and cultural rivals. The ferocity of their criticism reached a fevered pitch late in November of 2006, when Warren invited Democratic senator Barack Obama, along with Kansas Republican senator Sam Brownback and about sixty others, to address his second annual

Global Summit on AIDS and the Church at Saddleback. The two-day summit was to coincide with World AIDS Day and involve more than two thousand pastors, lay leaders, social workers, and medical professionals from around the world who would gather to consider the church's role in combating AIDS. Both Obama and Brownback at the time were known to be considering a run for the presidency in 2008, and Warren considered both of them his personal friends.

But his inclusion of Obama on the program sparked a flurry of vociferous protests from anti-abortion leaders, who vilified the Illinois senator's support of abortion rights and demanded that Warren rescind the invitation. "In the strongest possible terms, we oppose Rick Warren's decision to ignore Senator Obama's clear pro-death stance and invite him to Saddleback Church anyway," eighteen leading abortion foes wrote in a statement released two days before the event. The statement's signers, who included Phyllis Schlafly of the Eagle Forum, Judie Brown of the American Life League, and Tim Wildmon of the American Family Association, declared that "if Senator Obama cannot defend the most helpless citizens in our country, he has nothing to say to the AIDS crisis. You cannot fight one evil while justifying another." Meanwhile, the Reverend Rob Schenck, president of the Washington-based National Clergy Council, sent e-mails to reporters in which he described Obama's political views as "the antithesis of biblical ethics and morality, not to mention supreme American values." And conservative Christian blogger and radio host Kevin McCullough went so far as to describe Obama as "the anti-Christ" and urged his listeners to bombard the church with protest telephone calls.

Warren was unruffled by all of the fuss. "Of course we expect criticism," he wrote in an e-mail to his congregation the day before the summit. "Jesus loved and accepted others without approving of everything they did. That's our position too." And in a statement to the media, he explained that while he and Saddleback Church "completely disagree with Obama's views on abortion" and other issues, "we do not expect all participants in the summit discussion to agree with all of our evangelical beliefs. However, the HIV/AIDS pandemic cannot be fought by evangelicals alone."

The conference went off without a hitch, and while both Obama and Brownback were received warmly during a segment entitled "We Must Work Together," it was Obama who stole the show. "I don't think that we can deny both a moral and spiritual component" to AIDS prevention, he declared, and "in too many places . . . the relationship between men and women, between sexuality and spirituality, has broken down and needs to be repaired." Yet, he insisted, "abstinence and fidelity, although the ideal, may not always be the reality. We're dealing with flesh-and-blood men and women, and not abstractions, and if condoms and, potentially, things like microbicides can prevent millions of deaths, then they should be made more widely available . . . I don't accept the notion that those who make mistakes in their lives should be given an effective death sentence."

Obama received a standing ovation from the conference crowd, but Warren would win the biggest plaudits from the media. Writing in the *Washington Post* a few days after the summit, columnist E. J. Dionne observed that Warren, "one of the nation's most popular evangelical pastors," had "faced down right-wing pressure" by allowing Obama to speak, and in doing so, "he sent a signal [that] a significant group of theologically conservative Christians no longer wants to be treated as a cog in the Republican political machine."

Warren would send a similar message the following November, just a year ahead of the 2008 presidential election, by inviting all of the declared candidates of both parties to that year's AIDS summit. Democrats Obama and former North Carolina senator John Edwards along with three Republicans—Senator John McCain of Arizona, former Arkansas governor Mike Huckabee, and former Massachusetts governor Mitt Romney—all sent video greetings that were flashed to the giant screens in Saddleback's cavernous worship center. But the star of the show without a doubt was New York senator Hillary Rodham Clinton, the Democratic frontrunner at the time and the only candidate to appear in person. Like Obama, her invitation had drawn protests from anti-abortion groups, although they were muted by comparison to the previous year's uproar, and, like Obama, she was greeted enthusiastically by the evangelical audience, who applauded her pledge to boost government spending on AIDS and to encourage abstinence, in addition to condom use, to stop the pandemic. "The fight against AIDS must be done hand-in-hand, building relationships with churches around the world and here at home," she declared, "because if we fail to engage churches in combating AIDS, we will fail to conquer AIDS."

The fact that Clinton had accepted Warren's invitation was widely interpreted as an indication of the Democratic Party's determination in 2008 to close its "God gap" by reaching out to evangelicals—roughly a quarter of American voters, whom it previously had all but ceded to the Republicans—by finding issues on which they could agree, the kinds of issues that were important to Warren. What better place to begin making those new connections than Saddleback? As the election year approached, there was little doubt that Warren's church was fast becoming a requisite stop on the road to the White House for candidates of both parties, and that Warren had emerged as an independent and influential voice of a new brand of American evangelicalism.

If there was any remaining doubt of Warren's rising national stature it disappeared the following summer when he announced that the two presumptive presidential nominees had accepted his invitation to be interviewed on national television in what would be their first joint appearance of the general election campaign. Both McCain and Obama had agreed to submit to Warren's questions on a wide range of topics—most of them related to the candidates' personal faith and values—during an unprecedented two-hour "Civil Forum on the Presidency" to be held at Saddleback just prior to the nominating conventions. Warren had made it clear that the event would not be a debate and that the candidates would be allowed to "speak from the heart—without interruption—in a civil and thoughtful format absent the partisan 'gotcha' questions that typically produce heat instead of light." Rather than focusing just on the candidates' positions on issues, he said, the conversations were intended to reveal the thought processes and values behind the decisions they would make as president.

The forum would turn into a major media event, aired live on several television and radio networks and streamed on the Internet from the Saddleback Worship Center with over two thousand church members and some five hundred journalists looking on. Although it was billed as a joint appearance, Warren interviewed the two candidates separately, each for an hour, posing questions in a relaxed and conversational manner. As determined by a coin toss, Obama went first while McCain waited in isolation offstage. Between the two segments the candidates met briefly at center stage and embraced in an awkward hug, and then it was McCain's turn.

As had been expected, Obama showed himself to be more at ease than McCain in talking about his faith. When asked what Christianity meant to him on a daily basis, he responded, "It means I believe that Jesus Christ died for my sins and that I am redeemed through Him. That is a source of strength and sustenance on a daily basis. I know that I don't walk alone. But what it also means, I think, is a sense of obligation to embrace not just words but also through deeds the expectations that God has for us. And that means thinking about the least of these— acting justly, loving mercy, and walking humbly with our God." Responding to the same question, McCain replied, "It means I am saved and forgiven," and then he abruptly launched into a story about celebrating Christmas with a prison guard when he was held as a prisoner of war in Vietnam.

One of the more poignant moments came when Warren asked each candidate to reveal his "greatest moral failure." Obama told about his youthful experimentation with drugs and alcohol, which he said reflected "a certain selfishness on my part . . . I was so obsessed with me . . . I could not focus on other people." McCain responded succinctly and disarmingly: "The failure of my first marriage." To many evangelicals in the audience, however, the most striking difference between the candidates came in response to an abortion-related question. "At what point is a baby entitled to human rights?" Warren asked. Obama seemed to skirt the issue, saying that determining such a thing was "above my pay grade." He went on to explain that he was pro-choice "because, ultimately, I don't think women make these decisions casually. Rather, they wrestle with these things in profound ways." Asked the same question in the second hour, McCain responded without hesitation. "At the moment of conception," he said, and quickly added, "I will be a pro-life president, and this presidency will have pro-life policies."

While some media observers afterward would give a slight edge to McCain based on the directness of his answers and his deftness in delivering applause lines, the real winner of the event, a number of pundits would aver, was Warren, who they said had acquitted himself as moderator better than many professional journalists in presidential debates. Just getting the two to agree to appear together at his church was widely regarded as a personal coup and an indication of Warren's considerable influence as a bridge builder. The *New York Times* noted approvingly that it had taken "a man of God . . . to do what nobody else has been able to do since the general election season began: Get Barack Obama and John McCain together on the same stage before their party conventions later this summer." And the *Los Angeles Times* added that the feat had demonstrated "the reach that has made the Rev. Rick Warren among the most significant evangelists of his generation." Yet to hear Warren explain it, it was no big deal. "I just got to thinking, you know what? These guys have never been together on the same stage, it would be a neat way to cap the primary season before they both go to the conventions and things go dark for a couple of weeks," he told the *New York Times*. "I've known both the guys for a long time, they're both friends of mine, and I knew them before they ran for office, so I just called them up." Both quickly agreed.

Warren clearly took pride in the fact that he had become close friends with the two presidential candidates. Since meeting Obama in Washington a few years before, the two had communicated often, exchanging e-mails and sometimes praying together over the telephone. While writing his best-selling book, *The Audacity of Hope*, in 2005, Obama had asked Warren to review his chapter on faith. McCain and Warren, meanwhile, had been friends for roughly the same period of time, having met at a dinner in Washington prior to President Bush's State of the Union Address in 2005. "You know, Rick, what we're doing here? None of this is really going to matter," McCain told him at the time, referring to the political gamesmanship in Washington. "What's going to matter most is what you and Kay are doing—the PEACE plan. That's the stuff that's going to make a difference." They had stayed in close touch ever since.

Regardless of who won the election, Warren knew he would have a personal friend in the White House and his continued status as a confidant of presidents would be secure. It was a prospect that he found personally gratifying, and one that did not escape the attention of the national media, which began to pour on the superlatives. The Associated Press soon would hail Warren as "the most influential pastor in the United States," and *Newsweek* would observe that "no evangelical has forged so many alliances with liberals and non-Christians since, well, Billy Graham." *Time* magazine would put an even finer point on it. On the week of the candidate forum it placed Warren on its cover and pronounced him "America's Most Powerful Religious Leader." The goal Warren had set out to accomplish a decade earlier—that of expanding his circle of influence beyond the world of megachurches and evangelical preachers to the international movers and shakers of government and commerce—he had achieved beyond his wildest dreams.

The election results that November came as no surprise to Warren. The polls in the closing days of the campaign had been showing Obama and his running mate, Delaware senator Joe Biden, building a comfortable lead over McCain and Alaska governor Sarah Palin, and the margin was simply too much for the Republicans to overcome. As some analysts had anticipated, the Democrats had succeeded in cutting into the Republicans' evangelical base, although not by much. Roughly 74 percent of white evangelical voters had gone for McCain, about four percentage points fewer than had voted for Bush four years earlier, while Obama picked up a quarter of the evangelical vote compared to 21 percent for John Kerry in 2004. Even the presence of Palin, a born-again and passionately pro-life Pentecostal, on the Republican ticket was not enough to make up for the general lack of enthusiasm that many conservative Christians felt toward McCain, who, as a candidate in the 2000 primaries, had alienated some in the Religious Right by referring to Jerry Falwell and Pat Robertson as "agents of intolerance" and by taking lukewarm positions on abortion and gay marriage in that campaign.

After agreeing to a series of media interviews immediately after the forum, Warren had kept a low profile during the fall campaign, surfacing only once—on a radio talk show in Los Angeles—when he revealed that he had spoken with Palin by phone in September and had asked her, "How can I pray for you?" He said she "asked me to send her some

Bible verses on how do you deal with the unfair, unjust attacks and the mean-spirited criticism that comes in." During the same interview, he declared his neutrality toward the two presidential candidates. "They're different in their philosophy, in their approach to government. They're very different in their personality. But I honestly think that they're both good guys."

Once the election was over, Warren turned his full attention to his pastoral duties at Saddleback and to the PEACE plan and other ministry projects. The campaign season had provided an interesting diversion from the normal routine, but now it was back to business. Whatever new personal opportunities might eventually present themselves as a result of Obama's election, he was perfectly content to wait patiently and let events take their course. He would not have to wait for long.

LATE IN NOVEMBER, WARREN SPENT several days in New York City attending meetings and doing media interviews to generate publicity for his latest undertaking, a glossy new magazine and a related online social network called the *Purpose-Driven Connection*, which was set to debut in February. Three years in the making, the ambitious project—a partnership with the Reader's Digest Association—was designed to broaden Warren's worldwide franchise by reaching out directly to laypeople with "personal growth tools, resources and experiences" derived from the principles taught in his best-selling book. While the quarterly magazine would be the centerpiece, its paid subscribers also would be offered memberships in an Internet-based communications network that Warren confidently predicted would become "a platform for a movement of people to change the world."

It had been a productive few days in New York and everything seemed on track, but by the end of the week Warren was tired and ready to return home. He and his deputy chief of staff, Steve Komanapalli, had just boarded a plane at JFK International Airport for the flight to Orange County and were settling into their seats when Komanapalli's cell phone rang. He took the call and immediately turned to Warren. "It's the president-elect, and he'd like to talk with you," he said, handing the phone to Warren.

Warren and Obama briefly exchanged pleasantries. While the two had traded a few brief e-mail messages and Warren had sent his congratulations after the election, they had not spoken directly since the candidate forum in August, and so the call came as something of a surprise. Obama got quickly down to business. "Rick," he said. "I want you to give the invocation at my inauguration. Will you do it?"

The question caught Warren completely off guard. Although he considered Obama to be a personal friend, he had not supported the Chicago Democrat's candidacy, either publicly or privately, and he was quite certain that Obama was aware of that fact. Moreover, he could think of at least a dozen other prominent clergymen who were much more politically attuned to Obama, including some who had worked for his election. Any one of them, in Warren's estimation, would have been a more logical choice to deliver the inaugural prayer. Yet what Warren had found attractive in Obama, and what he knew they shared, was a passionate commitment to civil public discourse and a desire to transcend partisan disagreements that sometimes needlessly stand in the way of accomplishing worthy goals. Like himself, Obama was a bridge builder, and by inviting him to participate in the historic swearing-in ceremony in spite of their differences, Warren knew that the new president would be setting a tone of civility and unity at the start of his term that would send a powerful message to the nation and the world. How could he possibly decline?

"It would be my honor," he responded. "Of course I'll do it." Obama thanked him and said his staff would get in touch later to make the necessary arrangements, and after chatting for a minute more they ended the call.

As Warren handed the phone back to his aide, an uneasy feeling suddenly came over him. As thrilled as he was to have received the unexpected invitation, he somehow sensed that both he and the president-elect were likely to take some heat because of it from their various constituencies—he for consorting with a supporter of abortion rights and Obama for choosing an evangelical pastor over a more liberal clergyman for the prestigious ceremonial role. Yet he had no inkling of the severity of the firestorm that was about to be unleashed.

NO SOONER WAS THE INVITATION announced on December 17 than the uproar began. The opening salvo came from a handful of conservative bloggers and others, who, just as Warren had anticipated, faulted him for aligning himself with a pro-choice liberal. *WorldNet Daily* editor Joseph Farah, one of Warren's most frequent and virulent critics, expressed "profound and abject revulsion" that Warren had accepted Obama's invitation. "Yes, we are commanded to pray for our leaders," Farah wrote in his online column. "But there is no suggestion in the Bible that we are ever to be used as political pawns by praying at their events—especially when they are promoting the wholesale slaughter of innocent human beings." David Brody, a popular political blogger for Pat Robertson's Christian Broadcasting Network, reported that he was flooded with e-mails from pro-life Christians immediately after the announcement "and most of them absolutely rip[ped] Pastor Warren" for agreeing to pray at Obama's inauguration—some likening him to a Holocaust denier and others questioning the authenticity of his Christian faith.

But the most visceral attacks on Warren—and, by extension, on the president-elect—came from liberals and gay-rights activists who had been among Obama's staunchest supporters and who considered the Warren invitation a slap in the face. Their complaint was based on Warren's support of Proposition 8, a California ballot initiative banning gay marriage in that state, which was narrowly approved by voters that November. In an internal video message to his church eight days before the election—which quickly found its way to the Internet, where it was viewed by tens of thousands—Warren had urged his congregation to vote for the measure.

> By the way, the election is coming up in a couple weeks and I hope you're praying about your vote. One of the propositions, of course, that I want to mention, [is] Proposition 8, which is the proposition that had to be instituted because the courts threw out the will of the people. And a court of four guys voted actually to change a definition of marriage that has been going for five thousand years. Now, let me just say this really clearly. We support Proposition 8. And if you believe what the Bible says about marriage, you need to support

Proposition 8. I never support a candidate, but on moral issues I come out very clear. This is one thing, friends, that all politicians tend to agree on. Both Barack Obama and John McCain, I flat-out asked both of them, "What is your definition of marriage," and they both said the same thing: it is the traditional, historic, universal definition of marriage—one man and one woman for life. And every culture for five thousand years, and every religion for five thousand years, has said the definition of marriage is between one man and a woman . . . So I urge you to support Proposition 8, and pass that word on.

Almost as soon as news of the invitation broke, anti-Warren protestors assembled across the street from Saddleback Church, some carrying signs emblazoned with swastikas, and Warren was labeled a "bigot" and a "homophobe" in angry comments and blog postings on Obama's transition website. The Human Rights Campaign, the nation's largest gay rights organization, called Warren's remarks a sign of intolerance. "We feel a deep level of disrespect when one of the architects and promoters of an anti-gay agenda is given the prominence and the pulpit of your historic nomination," the group's president, Joe Solmonese, wrote in a letter to Obama on the day of the announcement. "By inviting Rick Warren to your inauguration, you have tarnished the view that gay, lesbian, bisexual and transgender Americans have a place at your table." Meanwhile, Rea Carey, head of the National Lesbian and Gay Task Force, called on Obama to withdraw the invitation "and instead select a faith leader who embraces fairness, equality and the ideals the president-elect himself has called the nation to uphold."

Other liberal activist groups quickly chimed in. Kathryn Kolbert, head of People for the American Way, complained that Obama's invitation "elevates someone who has in recent weeks actively promoted legalized discrimination and denigrated the lives and relationships of millions of Americans. Rick Warren gets plenty of attention through his books and media appearances. He doesn't need or deserve this position of honor." And Americans United for Separation of Church and State called the Warren invitation "disappointing news" and described

Warren as little more than "a kinder, gentler Jerry Falwell in a Hawaiian shirt."

Fueling the harsh invective against Warren was a second widely circulated video, this one containing his comments made during an interview with the religion website Beliefnet, in which he seemed to equate gay marriage with incest, pedophilia, and polygamy. The wide-ranging interview, which was conducted by Beliefnet editor Steve Waldman late in November, focused primarily on Warren's latest book, *The Purpose of Christmas*, and also touched on the efficacy of prayer, the state of the economy, and the government's use of torture—which Warren condemned—among other issues. But it was his comments on gay marriage that would attract the most attention.

> **WARREN:** The issue to me, I'm not opposed to [allowing spousal benefits and other legal rights for gay partners] as much as I'm opposed to redefinition of a five-thousand-year definition of marriage. I'm opposed to having a brother and sister being together and calling that marriage. I'm opposed to an older guy marrying a child and calling that marriage. I'm opposed to one guy having multiple wives and calling that marriage.
> **BELIEFNET:** Do you think those are equivalent to gays getting married?
> **WARREN:** Oh, I do.

It was enough to prompt some major media commentators to jump on the anti-Warren bandwagon. *Washington Post* columnist Richard Cohen compared the invitation to Obama's ill-advised refusal in 2007 to denounce his pastor at the time, the Reverend Jeremiah Wright, for giving a lifetime achievement award to Nation of Islam leader Louis Farrakhan. "This time it is not Obama's preacher who has decided to honor a bigot," wrote Cohen, "it is Obama himself." After playing clips of Warren's comments on her nightly news talk show, MSNBC's Rachel Maddow described Warren as an "uncivil anti-gay religious leader" and called the invitation "the first big mistake of [Obama's] post-election politicking." And writing in *The Nation*, investigative journalist Sarah

Posner said Warren's selection was "not only a slap in the face to progressive ministers toiling on the front lines of advocacy and service but a bow to the continuing influence of the religious right in American politics."

Obama was not about to be swayed by the protestations. Asked about the invitation during a news conference in Chicago on December 18, the president-elect held his ground and called on Americans to "come together even though we may have disagreements on certain social issues . . . We're not going to agree on every single issue, but what we have to do is be able to create an atmosphere where we can disagree without being disagreeable, and then focus on those things that we hold in common . . . That's part of the magic of this country, is that we are diverse and noisy and opinionated."

Warren, meanwhile, had decided to decline all news interviews until after the inauguration, believing—as he would later explain—that by answering his critics "I would only be fanning the flames. It was his inauguration. It was not about me." Instead he released a written statement on the same day as Obama's news conference in which he commended the president-elect "for his courage to willingly take enormous heat from his base by inviting someone like me, with whom he doesn't agree on every issue, to offer the invocation at his historic inaugural ceremony. Hopefully, individuals passionately expressing opinions from the left and the right will recognize that both of us have shown a commitment to model civility in America."

The controversy might have begun to fade at that point as the nation turned its attention to the approaching holidays. Both Obama and Warren had addressed the matter—albeit somewhat obliquely—and both were determined that the invitation would stand. Even though the two had not spoken to each other during the uproar, Warren would reveal later that an Obama aide had called him to offer words of encouragement. "Rick, don't worry about the flak," he quoted the aide as saying. "Barack has made his choice and he thinks he did the right thing."

But four days before Christmas, Warren would fan the flames in spite of himself by posting another video message to his congregation, this time giving his personal take on the controversy and insisting that he had been widely misrepresented in the media. It, too, would quickly find its way to the Internet and the eyes of the world. In an unscripted, sometimes rambling, and often defensive-sounding twenty-two-minute talk, Warren asserted that he had been falsely accused of "equating gay partnerships with incest and pedophilia. Now, of course, as members of Saddleback Church, you know, I believe no such thing. I never have. You've never once heard me in thirty years talk that way about that."

Critics immediately pounced on the statement, charging that it was flatly contradicted by his recorded remarks to Beliefnet, even though it should have been apparent to careful listeners that he was referring to his teachings in the Saddleback pulpit and not to an off-the-cuff and imprecise comment made in response to an interviewer's question. He went on to explain his belief that "God created sex to be exclusively a marriage connection between a man and a woman. But I have in no way ever taught that homosexuality is the same thing as a forced relationship between an adult and a child or between siblings, things like that. I've never taught that in thirty years." Referring to the Beliefnet interview, he said: "I was trying to point out that I'm not opposed to gays having their partnerships. I'm opposed to gays using the term 'marriage' for their relationship, and I'm opposed to any redefinition of the definition of marriage."

Taken as a whole, to his followers and admirers for whom it was intended, Warren's video message seemed to present a reasonable, if imperfectly structured, explanation of the controversy from his perspective. But once in the public domain and the hands of his critics, dozens of shortened versions began appearing on the Internet that were carefully edited to present Warren in the least favorable light. Predictably, as a result, the media drumbeat and the potshots against him continued and Warren himself had inadvertently provided the ammunition.

After the holidays the torrent of criticism finally began to subside. As trying and sobering as the controversy had been, throughout the ordeal—a period Warren later would laughingly refer to as "my forty days of persecution"—Warren had not lacked friends and allies in high places. Beyond the Obama transition team, his defenders had included some influential voices in Washington, members of the media and the entertainment industry, and even the gay community, who were quick to remind Warren's critics of his record as a global humanitarian and AIDS relief advocate. Appearing on PBS's *NewsHour with Jim Lehrer*, Michael Cromartie, vice president of the Ethics and Public Policy Center, a Washington-based think tank, defended Warren as "a compassionate man" who "is in dialogue with people of all kinds of faiths. He's gotten a lot of criticism for the people he talks to and the people he's in dialogue with. So this attempt to brand him as some sort of right-wing fanatic and nut, it just won't work."

Writing on the liberal news website the Huffington Post in late December, openly gay rock singer Melissa Etheridge described a private meeting she had recently had with Warren during which she discovered that he was not the "gay hater" that he had been made out to be. "He explained in very thoughtful words that as a Christian he believed in equal rights for everyone. He believed every loving relationship should have equal protection. He struggled with Proposition 8 because he didn't want to see marriage redefined as anything other than between a man and a woman. He said he regretted his choice of words," regarding pedophiles and incest because "in no way is that how he thought about gays . . . Sure, there are plenty of hateful people who will always hold on to their bigotry like a child to a blanket. But there are also good people out there, Christian and otherwise, that are beginning to listen."

Meanwhile, in reporting on the controversy, the *New York Times* had glowingly suggested that receiving the inaugural invitation "positions Mr. Warren to succeed Billy Graham as the nation's preeminent minister and reflects the generational changes in the evangelical Christian movement." Just before the inauguration, the *Washington Post* and ABC News would release a nationwide poll showing that 61 percent of Americans supported the Warren invitation and fewer than a quarter opposed it. Sixteen percent registered no opinion. Moreover, the levels of support were nearly identical among Democrats, Republicans, and independents. For all of the attention it had garnered, and for all of the frustration it had caused Warren and those around him, it appeared that the controversy over his selection had barely registered with the public, and that, perhaps more than anything else, had enabled Warren to weather the storm.

ON SUNDAY, JANUARY 18, RICK AND KAY set out from Southern California for the nation's capital and the historic inauguration. Their flight itinerary included a stopover in Atlanta, where Warren was to participate in a Martin Luther King Day celebration at the Ebenezer Baptist Church where King had been pastor. Almost lost in the media din over the prayer controversy during the preceding weeks was the fact that Warren had been invited to deliver the keynote message at the official commemorative service, a rare honor for a white minister. When he ascended the pulpit the following day and looked out over the crowded sanctuary, he felt awed by the historical significance of where he was standing and of what was about to transpire in Washington. "This means more to me personally [than praying at the inauguration]," Warren asserted rather surprisingly at the outset of his message. "Martin Luther King was a mighty tool in the hand of God," he said, eliciting shouts of "Amen!" from the congregation. "But God isn't through," he continued. "Justice is a journey, and we're getting farther and farther along."

# CHAPTER EIGHTEEN

# *Higher Ground*

ON THE MORNING OF THE INAUGURATION, the crowds began arriving on the National Mall long before sunrise in the bone-chilling cold—families and couples and people of all ages, races, and creeds—hoping to stake out a spot for the momentous swearing-in ceremony that would begin shortly before noon on the West Front of the Capitol. By 6 a.m., every security entrance to the Mall, from the Capitol to the Washington Monument, was glutted and nearly at a standstill and by 11:30 a.m. they were closed. Officials estimated the crowd at more than 1.8 million, most of whom would view the proceedings on giant TV screens placed strategically around the Mall.

Rick and Kay began the day by attending a private prayer service for the president-elect and invited guests at St. John's Episcopal Church, known as the "church of the presidents," just across Lafayette Square from the White House. Every U.S. president since James Madison had worshiped there at least once during his tenure, and five—Franklin Roosevelt, Harry Truman, Ronald Reagan, and both Bushes—had prayed there on the morning of their swearing in. Between the prayers on this inauguration morning, Texas megachurch pastor and best-selling author T. D. Jakes, a bear of a man and one of the nation's most prominent African American clergymen, delivered a brief but spirited homily, at one point looking Obama squarely in the eye and declaring that the problems awaiting him "are mighty and the solutions are not simple. Everywhere you turn there will be a critic waiting to attack every decision that you make. But you are all fired up, sir, and you are ready to go. And this nation goes with you. God goes with you."

After the service, the Warrens boarded a bus along with the other dignitaries for the brief two-mile ride to the Capitol, past the White

House and the bundled and shivering crowds lining the inaugural parade route along Pennsylvania Avenue. On the way, Warren struck up a conversation with Oprah Winfrey, who was sitting nearby with her longtime companion, Chicago businessman Stedman Graham. Warren had met the famous talk-show host and media mogul four years earlier at the Houston Astrodome, where they both had gone to meet with victims of Hurricane Katrina. He knew that she had been an enthusiastic backer of Obama's candidacy since the early primaries, had helped raise funds for the campaign, and had stumped with Obama and his wife, Michelle, in Iowa and New Hampshire. And now she was about to witness the swearing in of her fellow Chicagoan as the nation's first African American president. "Oprah, what's going through your mind in all of this?" he asked, gesturing out the window at the milling crowds and the street lamps festooned with American flags. She closed her eyes and smiled faintly. "It's a dream come true," she said, shaking her head slowly. "It's a dream come true."

Warren could have said the very same thing. In a matter of minutes he would be standing on the inauguration platform before a sea of humanity and the eyes of the world, not just as a witness but as a participant in the historic ceremony, invoking God's blessing on the nation and its new president, a man he counted a personal friend. Even for one who had become accustomed to consorting with the high and the mighty, it was heady stuff. He had long ago put away his boyhood dream of one day taking the oath of office himself, having come to believe—as he still very much did—that politics and government could never solve the world's problems. The transforming power of the Gospel, Warren was convinced, was far greater than the power of any government or nation, and only when human hearts were changed, one by one, through a personal encounter with Jesus Christ, would the world become more peaceful, more just, more secure, more humane. That was the task to which he had committed his life as a pastor. And now, thrust onto the international stage by his unexpected fame and fortune, he had been given an opportunity to advance the Gospel on a global scale and in the highest circles. It was an opportunity few preachers in history had been granted and one he could not have dared to imagine just a few years before. When he stepped before the TV cameras at the Capitol shortly before noon that day, he would be stepping into the history books.

WARREN HAD BEGUN PREPARING for the inauguration weeks beforehand by writing an early draft of the prayer he would deliver and giving some thought to a wardrobe for the trip. Having attended George W. Bush's second inauguration four years earlier, he knew how cold it could be in the nation's capital late in January and that he would need a warm hat and overcoat for the outdoor ceremony—items he seldom needed in sunny Southern California. He didn't own a hat suitable for the occasion, so he made some inquiries and found a store in West Hollywood that specialized in them. He found one he liked and bought it but then inadvertently misplaced it. He wasn't sure when he would have time to buy another.

A week before the inauguration an unexpected package arrived in the mail at Warren's home. Inside, carefully wrapped, was a charcoal-colored Homburg hat made of crisp fur felt with a stiff narrow brim and a satin band. It was stylish and expensive looking and reminded Warren of the hat Al Pacino wore in *The Godfather*. Tucked inside was a note from Billy Graham. "This is the hat I wore at all the inaugurations," wrote Graham, who had prayed at four of the events, more than any other modern churchman. "It's your turn, Rick. It's your hat now." Warren felt humbled by the gesture and could think of no more appropriate attire for the occasion.

As he stepped off the bus at the Capitol, he slipped Graham's hat on his head and adjusted it. Then, offering Kay his arm, they made their way inside.

THEY HAD ARRIVED AT THE CAPITOL shortly after 10:30 a.m. and were escorted through the rotunda to the West Front entrance and the platform where the ceremony would begin in less than an hour. When they stepped outside, the United States Marine Corps Band was playing and guests were milling about, visiting with one another and finding their seats. Former secretary of state Colin Powell stopped and chatted briefly with the Warrens, and Chief Justice John Roberts, who would be administering the presidential oath, paused to say hello. Out of the corner of his eye, Warren spotted the Reverend Joseph Lowery, who would be giving the closing prayer, sitting nearby in a wheelchair, and went over to greet him. The eighty-seven-year-old Methodist minister was an icon of the civil rights movement, having cofounded the Southern Christian Leadership Conference with Martin Luther King in 1957, and had been at King's side during the March on Washington in 1963, when King delivered his famous "I Have a Dream" speech from the steps of the Lincoln Memorial. And now, nearly thirty-six years later, he had returned to participate in the inauguration of the first African American president. Warren posed the same historical-moment question he had asked Oprah Winfrey. "What must you be feeling right now?" he asked. Lowery did not hesitate. "I'm cold," he said with a shiver. Warren laughed and returned to his seat.

A few minutes later the incoming and outgoing presidents and vice presidents and their families arrived and took their seats, and the ceremony was about to begin. Dianne Feinstein, the senior Democratic senator from California and chair of the inauguration committee, offered a few welcoming remarks and then introduced Warren. When she spoke his name, a scattered chorus of boos could be heard in the distance, along with a smattering of applause, and Warren stepped quickly to the lectern. He had removed the hat he had received from Graham and left it at his seat and his hair was slightly askew. "Let us pray," he said, and bowed his head.

"ALMIGHTY GOD, OUR FATHER," he began, spreading his arms in a sweeping gesture of supplication, "everything we see and everything we can't see exists because of you alone. It all comes from you, it all belongs to you. It all exists for your glory. History is your story.

"The Scripture tells us, 'Hear, O Israel, the Lord is our God; the Lord is one.' And you are the compassionate and merciful one. And you are loving to everyone you have made.

"Now today we rejoice not only in America's peaceful transfer of power for the forty-fourth time. We celebrate a hinge-point of history with the inauguration of our first African American president of the United States. We are so grateful to live in this land, a land of unequaled possibility, where the son of an African immigrant can rise to the highest level of our leadership. And we know today that Dr. King and a great cloud of witnesses are shouting in Heaven.

"Give to our new president, Barack Obama, the wisdom to lead us with humility, the courage to lead us with integrity, the compassion to lead us with generosity. Bless and protect him, his family, Vice President Biden, the Cabinet, and every one of our freely elected leaders.

"Help us, O God, to remember that we are Americans, united not by race or religion or blood, but by our commitment to freedom and justice for all.

"When we focus on ourselves, when we fight each other, when we forget you, forgive us. When we presume that our greatness and our prosperity is ours alone, forgive us. When we fail to treat our fellow human beings and all the Earth with the respect that they deserve, forgive us.

"And as we face these difficult days ahead, may we have a new birth of clarity in our aims, responsibility in our actions, humility in our approaches, and civility in our attitudes, even when we differ.

"Help us to share, to serve, and to seek the common good of all.

"May all people of goodwill today join together to work for a more just, a more healthy, and a more prosperous nation and a peaceful planet. And may we never forget that one day all nations and all people will stand accountable before you.

"We now commit our new president and his wife, Michelle, and his daughters, Malia and Sasha, into your loving care.

"I humbly ask this in the name of the one who changed my life—Yeshua, Isa, Jesús [hay-SOOS], Jesus—who taught us to pray:

"Our Father who art in heaven, hallowed be thy name. Thy kingdom come; thy will be done on Earth as it is in heaven. Give us this day our daily bread, and forgive us our trespasses as we forgive those who trespass against us; and lead us not into temptation but deliver us from evil, for thine is the kingdom and the power and the glory forever. Amen."

As Warren concluded the invocation with the words of the Lord's Prayer, hundreds of thousands across the Mall and on the platform recited it along with him and applauded when he was finished.

He took his seat, and as he settled in for the remainder of the ceremony the thought occurred to him that with nearly 2 million people on the Mall and many millions more watching at home and around the world, it may have been the largest number of people ever to recite the Lord's Prayer together at one time. "Jesus has got to be pretty pleased with that," he thought to himself. Later, he would tell his Saddleback flock that leading the Lord's Prayer that day, more than praying the words he had written, was "one of the greatest privileges of my life."

Given the furor of the preceding weeks, reaction in the media and elsewhere to Warren's five-minute prayer would be surprisingly subdued. He had carefully avoided mentioning any divisive political or cultural issues and had presented a respectfully straightforward petition on behalf of the nation and its president. As he expected, some would fault him for praying "in the name of Jesus"—a customary way of ending Christian prayers—at a national event, even though Warren had not been as rigidly dogmatic about it as some ministers had been in the recent past. At George W. Bush's first inauguration in 2001, Franklin Graham, filling in for his ailing father, concluded his invocation by saying, "We pray this in the name of the Father, and of the Son—the Lord Jesus Christ—and of the Holy Spirit," while Houston pastor Kirbyjon Caldwell, delivering that year's benediction, prayed "in the name that's above all other names, Jesus the Christ." Those prayers stirred up fevered protests in some secularist circles and even prompted a lawsuit—which later was dismissed—attempting to ban inaugural prayers altogether.

Warren had signaled his intentions in that regard weeks before the event. "I'm a Christian pastor," he told the Associated Press in late December, "so I will pray the only kind of prayer I know how to pray." Yet, even though his was an unequivocally Christian prayer, he had attempted to give it an inclusive flavor by quoting from a traditional Jewish prayer, the Sh'ma Yisrael ("Hear, O Israel, the Lord is our God; the Lord is one"), and from a Muslim invocation found in the Qur'an ("the compassionate and merciful one"), and by pronouncing Christ's name in Hebrew, Arabic, and Spanish. As Richard Mouw, president of Fuller Theological Seminary, Warren's alma mater, would tell an interviewer later on Inauguration Day: "It was as ecumenical a prayer as an evangelical could give."

While a few conservative bloggers would chide Warren for quoting the Qur'an, his prayer, for the most part, had been well received, and once it was over, the tumult that had enveloped him for weeks finally seemed to dissipate. He had had his glittering moment in the international spotlight and had emerged, in the footsteps of Billy Graham, as America's most famous evangelical.

WITH THE INAUGURATION BEHIND HIM, Warren returned to Southern California and to what he hoped would be at least an approximation of the normalcy that had been lost in the preceding two months. Because of the dismal state of the nation's economy at the time, and the distress and uncertainty it was creating for many people, Warren had decided that for the remainder of the year he would refocus his efforts on shepherding his own congregation, cutting back on overseas travel and other outside engagements in order to spend more time at home. While many in his congregation had lost or were fearful of losing their jobs, both weekly attendance and plate offerings at Saddleback had continued to grow in the several months since the recession began. "Bad times are good times for churches," he would explain later that spring in a webcast to pastors in his network. "A recession is not a time to hunker in the bunker. It is a time to reach out because people are hurting and are looking for connection, and they're going to be more open to spiritual truth."

On his first weekend back in the Saddleback pulpit, worship attendance spiked by about two thousand, an indication that the local impact of all of the publicity surrounding Warren's participation in the inauguration had been mostly positive. As he took the stage he was greeted with a sustained standing ovation, and after thanking his congregants for their prayers and support, he launched into a message entitled "My Prayer for the Nation," using his inaugural invocation as an outline. The following week he would begin a seven-week series on "Connecting with God," based on seven key phrases of the Lord's Prayer, and as Easter approached, he would do a series on "Making Sense of Life's Great Mysteries." All of the messages were intended to remind his flock of the basics of the faith and to rekindle their fervor in difficult times. "Our nation, and really each of us, stands at a crossroads right now," he declared on that first Sunday back. "Either we're going to have extended recession or we're going to have revival. So it's my prayer that we'll have revival."

A few days before Easter, however, Warren would briefly reignite the inaugural prayer controversy by agreeing to a number of media interviews, as he often did during the holiday seasons. Since the inauguration was over, he felt free to talk about the criticisms that had been leveled against him over his gay-marriage remarks and he was eager to set the record straight. But, appearing on *Larry King Live* on April 6, he seemed to muddy the waters even more by offering a somewhat disjointed and off-the-cuff-sounding explanation.

During the whole Proposition 8 thing, I never once went to a meeting, never once issued a statement, never—never once even gave an endorsement in the two years Prop 8 was going. The week before the—the vote, somebody in my church said, "Pastor Rick, what—what do you think about this?" And I sent a note to my own members that said, I actually believe that marriage is—really should be defined, that that definition should be—say, between a man and a woman. And then all of a sudden out of it, they made me, you know, something that I really wasn't. And I actually—there were a number of things that were put out. I wrote to all my gay friends—the leaders that I knew—and actually apologized to them. That never got out.

Liberal critics immediately accused Warren of lying about having "never once issued a statement" on Proposition 8 since he clearly had issued one to his church, and conservatives accused him of backpedaling on gay marriage by indicating that he had apologized to his "gay friends" for his publicized remarks. The next day, Warren's press aide, Larry Ross, rushed out a statement attempting to clarify Warren's clarification. In claiming that he had never campaigned for Proposition 8, the statement said, Warren "was referring to not participating in the official two-year organized advocacy effort." He had made only one internal statement to his church members, in response to queries, "confirming where he and Saddleback Church stood on this issue." His mea culpa to gay leaders, moreover, the statement explained, "was not with respect to his statements or position on Proposition 8, nor the biblical worldview on marriage," but was an apology for his comments to Beliefnet in which he "unintentionally and regrettably gave the impression that consensual adult same sex relationships were equivalent to incest or pedophilia."

The statement notwithstanding, the media buzz continued unabated through the remainder of Holy Week. On Easter morning, Warren was scheduled to appear live on ABC's *This Week with George Stephanopoulos*, but he canceled at the last minute, saying he had been sickened by fumes from his freshly varnished pulpit and needed to conserve his energy for a marathon of thirteen Easter weekend services.

THAT EASTER MARKED THE BEGINNING of Saddleback's thirtieth year, and Warren had made plans to commemorate the milestone with a celebration of biblical proportions. "Two thousand years ago," he wrote in an electronic newsletter to his church late in March, "the Day of Pentecost was the first day of the Christian Church. Acts 2:41 tells us, 'About 3,000 people were baptized and joined the church that day.' . . . I was asked, 'Rick, if you could wish for anything to celebrate your thirty years of service at Saddleback, what would you dream of?' I said, 'To experience a repeat of Pentecost and see three thousand people affirm their faith and join our church family on a single day.'"

Even for Warren, a man not known for thinking small, setting out to replicate the first spiritual outpouring upon the Christian church seemed an ambitious goal, and even though he would fall short, he would come amazingly close to achieving it. After a series of evangelistic messages and a concerted effort to sign up recruits for a special weekend membership class, over a three-week period that April more than 2,600 people accepted Christ at Saddleback and over 1,200 were baptized, including 800 in one day. On Easter weekend the church received more than 2,600 new members—more than had joined Saddleback in its first ten years. Warren would call it the greatest spiritual harvest his church had ever seen.

The phenomenal growth that had characterized Saddleback from the beginning was showing no signs of slowing. Midway through 2009, average weekly attendance reached a new all-time high of 25,000, helped along by the addition of four satellite congregations meeting in rented auditoriums in San Clemente, Corona, Irvine, and Laguna Woods, each with its own worship leader and musicians but with Warren's sermons beamed in live from the Lake Forest campus. Plans for two more regional venues were in the works. Meanwhile, work on the PEACE plan continued apace with hundreds of short-term-mission teams being dispatched from Saddleback and other churches to towns and villages on every continent to battle the "global giants" of poverty, disease, ignorance, oppressive leadership, and spiritual emptiness. And after a respectable launch in early February, Warren's latest ministry venture, the *Purpose-Driven Connection* quarterly magazine and Internet social network, appeared to be gathering momentum, although it was far from certain whether it would reach its ambitious circulation target of one million subscriptions by the end of its first year. Three decades after it all began, a callow young minister's audacious dream of reaching unchurched suburbanites by the tens of thousands with the gospel of Jesus Christ still was being fulfilled, and the missionary-minded megachurch he had built from scratch was leaving a widening imprint around the world.

THROUGHOUT THE YEARS Warren would seldom speak of retirement and tended to dismiss questions regarding pastoral succession at Saddleback. Like his parents, he considered his divine call to the ministry to be a lifelong commitment, and as long as he had his health he intended to continue serving God in whatever capacity he could. In one notable exception to his reticence to discuss the matter, he opened one Saddleback staff meeting in 2007 with the startling announcement that he had chosen his successor as the church's pastor. After a pregnant pause for dramatic effect, he popped a picture of his newborn grandson onto the overhead screen and then burst into raucous laughter.

Levity aside, the question of succession was a legitimate one—not just for Saddleback but for hundreds of other megachurches that had known only one leader. What would happen to those congregations of tens of thousands of worshipers and their multimillion-dollar budgets when the founder left or died? Like Saddleback, most of the thriving megachurches were relatively new and were led by men of Warren's generation, so there was little experience to draw upon in making a transition. In more serious moments of contemplation, Warren would express a simple confidence that Saddleback belonged to God and that God would raise up a new leader when the time was right.

In March 2009, Warren gave a rare public indication of when that time might be. In a webcast to his network, Warren recalled the vow he had made to God as a young man to spend his entire ministry pastoring one church. Speaking to his pastors that day, he described that vow as a forty-year commitment, and now the end of it was just ten years away. "When I am sixty-five I will let go of the church," he said almost matter-of-factly. "I'll never retire from the ministry," he quickly added, saying that he planned to "spend more time with you" and on working on the PEACE plan. "But I intend to turn the church over. That means I've got ten years left. And I started thinking, what would I say to my church if I only had ten years left? That's 520 weekends. What I am *not* going to do is waste that time. I'm going to do everything I can to make it count the most."

However many years remained, given Warren's history, it seemed a safe bet to those around him that the time would be filled with even more of the innovative strategies and ambitious outreach programs that had characterized his ministry from the start and that had propelled him to such prominence as a religious leader. It was equally likely, given his irrepressible proclivity toward unguarded talk and his willingness to flout convention, that he would one day again find himself embroiled in controversy. But that was a place where Warren had seemed to thrive over the years and he knew it was part of the price to be paid for making one's way as a spiritual entrepreneur and visionary.

Whatever changes lay ahead, one thing Warren was certain would never change was the purpose that was driving him—the overarching theme that had guided his ministry from its earliest days, imbuing it with meaning and with a sense of exigency that had been impressed upon him so poignantly by his father, and that, in its simplicity, had provided the motivation underlying all he had ever sought to accomplish as a minister of the Gospel. At the end of his life, Warren knew that his success would not be measured by his personal renown or the size of his church or the number of books he sold or the power and prestige of the company he kept, but in the steadfastness of his commitment to continue laboring on in obedience to a plaintive inner voice calling him to an urgent task—to "Save one more for Jesus! Save one more for Jesus! Save one more for Jesus!"

# Acknowledgments

I owe a tremendous debt of gratitude to a host of people whose help and encouragement made this book possible. First and foremost, I would like to thank Rick Warren for his gracious cooperation and generosity of spirit throughout this project, for subjecting himself to my many hours of interviews, and for granting access to his family, staff, and other valuable sources of information. Thanks to Kay and Josh Warren for offering their personal insights into the family and the early years of Warren's ministry, and especially to Chaundel Holladay, Rick's sister, who provided a priceless trove of family history, including the unpublished written remembrances of her father, Jimmy Warren.

I want to give special thanks to the staff at Saddleback Church, especially to David Chrzan, Warren's chief of staff, and to David's assistant, Anne Krumm, who was a model of patience and a frequent source of help and information. Thanks, too, to Glen Kreun, Saddleback's executive pastor, and to many others on the church staff whose names appear in the preceding pages. I also am grateful to Larry Ross and his public relations staff for their valuable assistance at several key points along the way.

I would also like to express thanks to Sheila Strobel Smith for her help on the Warren family genealogy, to Harry and Steve Williams and to Pratt Dean for recounting the early years of Warren's ministry, and to Warren's former classmates, ministry partners, and myriad other acquaintances who provided useful information and biographical background.

As always, I am deeply indebted to my agent, Gail Ross, for helping to make this book happen, and to my editor at Doubleday, Gary Jansen, for guiding it to completion. I am especially thankful for the encouragement and helpful critiques provided by my most trusted editor and adviser, my wife, Doreen, who abided my many absences and long periods of self-imposed isolation with utmost grace. Her prayerful support throughout the project made a world of difference.

*—Jeffery L. Sheler, July 10, 2009*

# Notes

### CHAPTER ONE: *America's Pastor*

2 **It sold over a million copies:** As reported on Warren's website, http://www.rick warrennews.com/bio_rwarren.htm.

2 **best-selling nonfiction hardcover of all time:** Daisy Maryles, "A Big Fete for a Big Feat," *Publishers Weekly*, September 27, 2004.

3 **as *Fortune* magazine would describe him:** Marc Gunther, "Will Success Spoil Rick Warren?" *Fortune*, October 31, 2005, 108.

3 **the evangelical flagship magazine *Christianity Today* declared him:** *Christianity Today*, November 18, 2002. The coverline reads: "Rick Warren: Just a regular guy who may be America's most influential pastor."

3 **Two years later, a nationwide survey of pastors found:** "Pastors Reveal Major Influencers on Churches," the Barna Group, a survey taken in December 2004 and reported on January 14, 2005. See http://www.barna.org/barna-update/article/ 5-barna-update/187-pastors-reveal-major-influencers-on-churches.

5 **Warren's wife, Kay, put it more bluntly:** Tim Stafford, "A Regular Purpose-Driven Guy," *Christianity Today*, November 18, 2002.

6 **"the inventor of perpetual revival":** Peter F. Drucker, "Management's New Paradigm," *Forbes*, October 5, 1998, 152.

6 **"the best public speaker I have ever heard":** Michael Cromartie, "Salvation Inflation? A Conversation with Alan Wolfe," *Books & Culture*, March/April 2004.

7 **"If Rick believes God is in it":** Glen Kreun, interview with the author, October 9, 2007.

### CHAPTER TWO: *"A Peculiar People"*

11 **"poor, uneducated, and easy to command":** Michael Weisskopf, "Energized by Pulpit or Passion, the Public Is Calling," *Washington Post*, February 1, 1993, Al.

12 **a shared set of convictions and emphases:** David Bebbington, *Evangelicalism in Britain: A History from the 1730s to the 1980s* (London: Unwin Hyman, 1989), 2–17, as summarized by Mark A. Noll, *American Evangelical Christianity: An Introduction* (Oxford: Blackwell, 2001), 13.

13 **It is a corrective impulse:** I am deeply indebted to Mark Noll, history professor at the University of Notre Dame, whose authoritative published works and generous personal communication inform much of the historical section of this chapter. Of particular help were Noll's *The Rise of Evangelicalism: The Age of*

*Edwards, Whitefield, and the Wesleys* (Downers Grove, IL: Inter-Varsity Press, 2003), and *American Evangelical Christianity: An Introduction* (Oxford: Blackwell, 2001). Other sources, including specific citations from these two works, will be noted where appropriate.

13    "rediscovery of the Gospel": Randall Balmer and Laura F. Winner, *Protestantism in America* (New York: Columbia University Press, 2002), 11.

14    "a new style of leadership": Mark Noll, *The Scandal of the Evangelical Mind* (Grand Rapids: Eerdman's, 1994), 61.

14    While "ecclesiastical life remained important": Ibid.

15    Finney believed revival could be deliberately induced: Randall Balmer and Laura F. Winner, *Protestantism in America* (New York: Columbia University Press, 2002), 18.

15    "infused with postmillennial optimism": Mark Noll, telephone interview with the author, January 5, 2006.

16    charitable organizations in New England exploded during this period: Balmer and Winner, *Protestantism in America*, 59.

16    The slavery debate had opened deep fissures: Ibid., 18. Baptists, Methodists, and Presbyterians all divided into separate northern and southern entities in the 1840s.

16    what it meant to be Baptist: David E. Garland, "Baptist Distinctives," *Baylor Magazine Online*, accessed on May 2, 2009, at http://www.baylormag.com/story.php?story=006209.

17    In 1844, the Society threw off any pretense: Nancy Ammerman, *Baptist Battles: Social Change and Religious Conflict in the Southern Baptist Convention* (New Brunswick, NJ, and London: Rutgers University Press, 1990), 31.

17    It would take the denomination 150 years: On June 20, 1995, the Southern Baptist Convention adopted a resolution declaring that messengers, as delegates to its annual convention are called, "unwaveringly denounce racism, in all its forms, as deplorable sin" and "lament and repudiate historic acts of evil such as slavery from which we continue to reap a bitter harvest." It offered an apology to all African Americans for "condoning and/or perpetuating individual and systemic racism in our lifetime" and repentance for "racism of which we have been guilty, whether consciously or unconsciously." Although Southern Baptists previously had condemned racism, this was the first time the predominantly white convention had dealt specifically with the issue of slavery. ("SBC Renounces Racist Past," *Christian Century*, July 5–12, 1995, 671–72.)

17    "teeming, squalid tenements populated by immigrants": Randall N. Balmer, *Encyclopedia of Evangelicalism* (Waco, TX: Baylor University Press, 2004), 246.

18    the theology's growing appeal had an important twofold impact: Joel A. Carpenter, *Revive Us Again: The Reawakening of American Fundamentalism* (New York: Oxford University Press, 1997), 78.

19    "No longer was the goal": George M. Marsden, *Fundamentalism and American Culture*, New Edition (New York: Oxford University Press, 2006), 31.

19    The Social Gospel: Ibid., 91–92. See also Balmer and Winner, *Protestant America*, 62–63.

20    "Conservative victories turned out to be largely illusory": Ibid., 104.

20    a twelve-volume series of booklets entitled *The Fundamentals*: Marsden, *Fundamentalism and American Culture*, 119.

20    In 1919, the World Christian Fundamentals Association met: Ibid., 158.

21    organizing . . . to battle the "false apostles" of "false science": Ibid., 158–59.

21    As a pastor in Michigan declared: From a sermon by the Rev. Oliver W. Van Osdel, *Baptist Temple News* IX (January 3, 1920), cited in Marsden, *Fundamentalism and American Culture*, 157.

21    Between 1923 and 1928: John C. Green, "Seeking a Place: Evangelical Protestants and Public Engagement in the Twentieth Century," in Ronald J. Sider and Diane Knippers, eds., *Toward an Evangelical Public Policy* (Grand Rapids: Baker Books, 2005), 19.

22    "the good life was the separated life": David Gushee and Dennis P. Hollinger, "Toward an Evangelical Ethical Methodology," in Sider and Knippers, eds., *Toward an Evangelical Public Policy*, 118.

22    a renewed focus on revivalism and missionary work: Noll, *American Evangelical Christianity*, 16.

23    By the end of the 1930s, observes Christian Smith: Christian Smith, *American Evangelicalism: Embattled and Thriving* (Chicago: University of Chicago Press, 1998), 9.

24    Carl Henry . . . published *Remaking the Modern Mind*: Balmer, *Encyclopedia of Evangelicalism*, 276–77.

24    teamed up to found Fuller Theological Seminary: Quoted in Smith, *American Evangelicalism*, 11.

24    Graham envisioned a magazine: Billy Graham, *Just As I Am: The Autobiography of Billy Graham* (New York: Harper Collins, 1997), 286.

24    In 1949, at the age of thirty, he launched: Noll, *American Evangelical Christianity*, 44.

25    "He came to prominence": From an interview with the author in Toronto, Ontario, November 23, 2002.

25    "the most attractive public face that evangelical Protestantism has offered": Noll, *American Evangelical Christianity*, 53.

26    Beginning in the late 1970s the number of megachurches began to surge: Stephen Ellingson, "The Rise of the Megachurches and Changes in Religious Culture," *Sociology Compass* 3, 1: 16–30. Published online December 12, 2008.

## CHAPTER THREE: *Roots of Faith*

29   **On a cool, overcast January morning:** Much of the information in this chapter is based on an unpublished journal kept by Warren's father, James R. Warren, which Warren made available to the author.

30   **Though he would later insist:** Rick Warren, interview with the author, April 27, 2007.

30   **His great-grandfather on his mother's side:** Attempts to corroborate this family story through genealogical research were unsuccessful. E. M. Armstrong was born in Claysville, Pennsylvania, in 1836, and spent most of his adult life in Illinois and Kansas. Later in life he was ordained to preach and may have been a circuit rider. It is possible that he traveled to England, although there is no record of it. It is more likely that the story of a conversion under Spurgeon confuses Armstrong with another of Warren's great-grandfathers, Edward Gould, who was born in England in 1852 and moved to Oklahoma in 1871.

## CHAPTER FOUR: *"Huck Finn"*

45   **Members of the Charles Manson family:** Vincent Bugliosi and Curt Gentry, *Helter Skelter: The True Story of the Manson Murders* (New York: W. W. Norton, 2001), 315.

45   **"the one that shaped me most":** Warren writing in John Edwards, ed., *Home: The Blueprint of Our Lives* (New York: HarperCollins, 2006), 156–59.

46   **"In many ways I enjoyed a Huck Finn childhood":** Ibid.

46   **"I literally was":** Rick Warren, interview with the author, April 27, 2007.

47   **It was a warm and inviting place:** Edwards, *Home*, 157.

47   **"My parents modeled":** Warren, interview.

47   **"At home he was":** Chaundel Holladay, interview with the author, February 21, 2008.

48   **"We had this family shtick":** Ibid.

49   **Older brother Jim was a different story:** Ibid.

49   **Rick would describe his brother's turn:** Warren, interview.

49   **Rick grew up idolizing his older brother:** From Warren's message at a memorial service for his brother on February 2, 2007, at Saddleback. He apparently misspoke in his reference to the Beach Boys album since there was no album by that title. He may have been referring to *All Summer Long*, which was released by the Beach Boys in July 1964, roughly six months after *Meet the Beatles*.

52   **On one occasion he conducted:** Rick Warren, video interview with Sally Quinn, "Divine Impulses," washingtonpost.com, February 20, 2008. http://www .washingtonpost.com/wp-dyn/content/video/2008/02/20VI2008022001639.html ?hpid=topnews>

52   **"I never got into drugs":** Warren, Quinn interview.

52    **Rick started to become "pretty tuned in to politics":** Gwendolyn Driscoll, "A Call to Faith," *Orange County Register*, September 3, 2006, Special 4A.

52    **One of his favorites was:** Ibid.

52    **"The building we were in":** Rick Warren, interview with the author, May 25, 2008.

53    **"People kept telling me, 'You're a natural leader'":** Warren, interview, April 27, 2007.

55    **The prayer he prayed that night:** Ibid.

55    **"I don't know if I was expecting":** Ibid.

CHAPTER FIVE: *Boy Preacher*

56    **"My parents and I were very excited":** Chaundel Holladay, interview with the author, February 21, 2008.

56    **That fall he crafted a basic salvation message:** From Warren's unpublished sermon notes.

57    **"It wasn't that I thought":** Rick Warren, interview with the author, May 25, 2008.

57    **"like an anxiety attack":** Rick Warren, interview with the author, October 12, 2007.

58    **When Rick returned to Ukiah High School:** Rick Warren, "Northern California High School High on Jesus," *Hollywood Free Paper*, September 21, 1971, 3, 19.

59    **"Fishers of Men was life-changing":** Mark Pardini, interview with the author, January 16, 2008.

59    **"Because of the Holy Spirit's work":** Warren, "Northern California High School High on Jesus."

60    **Jones reportedly had chosen:** Tim Reiterman and John Jacobs, *Raven: The Untold Story of the Rev. Jim Jones and His People* (New York: E. P. Dutton, 1982), 95.

60    **The *Ukiah Daily Journal* carried an admiring story:** Ibid., 98.

60    **The transplanted congregation:** Denice Stephenson, ed., *Dear People: Remembering Jonestown* (Berkeley: Heyday Books, 2005), 21.

61    **he began teaching a night civics class:** Reiterman and Jacobs, *Raven*, 98–99.

61    **he would forge strong ties:** David Chidester, *Salvation and Suicide: Jim Jones, the People's Temple, and Jonestown* (Bloomington: Indiana University Press, 1988), 31.

61    **It was an opinion that:** Reiterman and Jacobs, *Raven*, 94.

61    **Christians in town were much more appalled:** Chidester, *Salvation and Suicide*, 7.

61    **There were reports:** Ibid.

61    **"You couldn't get in":** Holladay, interview.

61    **seventeen or eighteen busloads:** The number is likely inexact, but it is how Rick Warren remembers it. Warren, interview, May 25, 2008.

61    **"And so all the Christians were saying":** Holladay, interview.

62     **"They were the sweetest, kindest people"**: Warren, interview, May 25, 2008.

62     **the Warrens mistakenly received mail intended for Jones**: Chaundel Holladay interview, Febuary 21, 2008.

62     **Mark Pardini remembers that**: Pardini, interview.

62     **Dot Warren became acquainted with**: Holladay, interview.

62     **Sitting on the platform**: Warren, interview, May 25, 2008.

63     **"They were afraid"**: Holladay, interview.

63     **Seven years later**: Tim Reiterman, "Hell's 25-Year Echo: The Jonestown Mass Suicide," *Los Angeles Times*, November 19, 2003, B1.

63     **"I remember sitting and watching the TV coverage"**: Holladay, interview.

64     **At Wednesday night prayer meeting**: From an unpublished family history written by James R. Warren.

65     **"These kids who were becoming Christians"**: Harry Williams, interview with the author, October 25, 2007.

66     **"I was in for a surprise"**: Ibid.

66     **All the hard work seemed to pay off**: Ibid.

66     **"Rick and I were really on fire"**: Steve Williams, interview with the author, October 23, 2007.

67     **Rick would describe those summers**: Warren, interview, May 25, 2008.

67     **But, as he later observed**: Ibid.

67     **"It is by the Holy Spirit"**: Jack R. Taylor, *The Key to Triumphant Living* (Nashville: Broadman Press, 1971), 11.

67     **But he warned that God**: Ibid., 190.

68     **He exorted his readers**: Ibid., 195.

68     **Sitting in his room**: Warren, interview.

CHAPTER SIX: *Kay*

71     **"There was a talent contest"**: Kay Warren, interview with the author, February 27, 2008.

72     **"Because I was a pastor's daughter"**: Kay Warren, *Dangerous Surrender: What Happens When You Say Yes to God* (Grand Rapids: Zondervan, 2007), 26.

73     **"While no one has told me I'm ugly"**: Ibid.

73     **She headed off**: Ibid.

73     **He and some like-minded friends**: From Jimmy Warren's unpublished family history.

74     **"Rick just figures"**: Kay Warren, interview.

74     **In a radio interview**: Kay Warren, interview on "FamilyLife Today," a daily radio broadcast of the FamilyLife ministry, www.familylife.com, June 27, 2007.

74     **Then, as she recalls**: Kay Warren, interview.

75    **As they finished praying:** Ibid.

75    **"I instantly said to God":** Kay Warren, "FamilyLife Today" interview.

75    **"The way I explain it":** Rick Warren, interview with the author, April 27, 2007.

76    **True to form, Criswell's sermon:** Criswell's preaching style is described in "W. A. Criswell, a Baptist Leader, Dies at 92," *New York Times*, January 12, 2002, C18.

76    **as he exorted his audience:** Warren summarized Criswell's sermon during an interview with the author on May 25, 2008. The quotations are a paraphrase of 2 Timothy 4:7.

77    **(By the time Criswell retired in 1994):** "W. A. Criswell, a Baptist Leader, Dies at 92," *New York Times*.

77    **"God spoke personally to me":** Rick Warren, *The Purpose-Driven Church: Growth Without Compromising Your Message and Mission* (Grand Rapids: Zondervan, 1995), 26.

77    **Sitting in that hotel ballroom:** Ibid.

77    **But as Rick tells it:** Ibid.

77    **"Did he pray what I think":** Ibid., 27.

77    **Nevertheless, "that holy experience confirmed":** Ibid.

78    **"Rick Warren, our 'Praise-the-Lord!' summer missionary":** Pratt Dean, letter to his supporters, June 13, 1974.

79    **"I noticed that when":** Rick Warren, interview with the author, October 12, 2007.

80    **As he read the article, he would write later:** Warren, *The Purpose-Driven Church*, 30.

80    **"I got some fantastic shots":** Rick Warren, letter to Pratt and Rita Dean dated August 27, 1974.

81    **"Our letters were just always off":** Kay Warren, interview.

82    **"I remember standing":** Kay Warren, "FamilyLife Today" interview.

82    **The honeymoon was a disaster:** Kay Warren, interview.

82    **"I did my best to block it":** All quoted material in this paragraph is from Warren, *Dangerous Surrender*, 122–23.

83    **"People would say":** Kay Warren, "FamilyLife Today" interview.

83    **"I wasn't going to go back on the commitment":** Ibid.

83    **"I was so sick from the stress":** Ibid.

84    **"It was the beginning of teaching us":** Kay Warren, interview.

84    **"There are times now":** Ibid.

CHAPTER SEVEN: *The Texas Years*

88    **But as the century wore on:** James C. Hefley, *The Conservative Resurgence in the Southern Baptist Convention* (Hannibal, MO: Hannibal Books, 1991), 15.

88    Leading the Texas uprising was: Ibid.

88    On one side were: Nancy Tatom Ammerman, *Baptist Battles: Social Change and Religious Conflict in the Southern Baptist Convention* (New Brunswick, NJ, and London: Rutgers University Press, 1990), 64.

88    Like the early twentieth-century fundamentalists: Ibid., 69.

90    As one observer noted: Jesse C. Fletcher, *The Southern Baptist Convention: A Sesquicentennial History* (Nashville: Broadman & Holman, 1994), 248.

91    "You know, son, when you're not reaching people": Rick Warren, interview with the author, May 25, 2008.

91    "I just wasn't interested in denominational politics": Ibid.

93    "This man was passionate": Ibid.

93    "Rick turned out to be": From an interview with the author, May 2, 2007.

94    "I didn't think the name 'Reformed'": Robert H. Schuller, *Your Church Has Real Possibilities!* (Glendale, CA: Regal Books, 1974), 160.

95    "I have sometimes described": Ibid., 29.

95    Kay, many years later, recalled: Tim Stafford, "A Regular Purpose-Driven Guy," *Christianity Today*, November 18, 2002.

95    "He had a profound influence on Rick": Ibid.

95    "That was life-changing for Rick": Steve Williams, interview with the author, October 23, 2007.

96    While pastoral longevity did not guarantee: Warren, *The Purpose-Driven Church*, 31.

96    "I don't care where you put me": Ibid.

96    After about six months, Warren recalled: Ibid.

96    Kay remembers feeling somewhat disappointed: Kay Warren, interview.

97    Kay at the time was nine months pregnant: Warren, *The Purpose-Driven Church*, 34.

97    Describing the moment years later, Warren said: Ibid.

98    In his letter, he told of his desire: Ibid.

98    Unbeknownst to Warren: Herman Wooten, interview with the author, June 5, 2008.

98    "When I saw his letter": Ibid.

98    "When I opened the mailbox": Warren, *The Purpose-Driven Church*, 35.

98    "If Kay had felt any reluctance": Ibid.

CHAPTER EIGHT: *Saddleback*

102    "They came in and wanted to rent a house": Don Dale, interview with the author, January 8, 2008.

102    Warren asked Dale if he attended church: Warren, in *The Purpose-Driven Church*, would tell the story slightly differently: "While driving to the condo,

I asked Don if he attended church anywhere. He said he didn't. I replied, 'Great! You're my first member!' And that is exactly what happened. I began Saddleback Church with that realtor's family and mine." The difference between the two versions, though seemingly minor, is symbolically noteworthy. Depending upon which version is more accurate, the first member of Warren's "church for the unchurched" either was a nonchurchgoer or was recruited from another congregation. Warren, *The Purpose-Driven Church*, 37.

104 **"We wrote out on little cards every single detail":** Warren told this story during a staff meeting at Saddleback Church on June 6, 2007.

105 **"When we got home":** Ibid.

106 **"What we discovered":** Rick Warren, interview with the author, September 20, 2005.

106 **"It's a passing fad":** Danny Akin, vice president for academic administration and dean of the School of Theology at Southern Baptist Theological Seminary, Louisville, Kentucky, during an October 29, 1997, address at Southeastern Baptist Theological Seminary, Wake Forest, North Carolina, as quoted in L. Weeks, "Seeker-Sensitive Approach Is Passing Fad, Akin Maintains," *Baptist Press*, November 3, 1997. Retrieved from http://www.bpnews.net. Akin was voicing a criticism that had been leveled for years against the "felt needs" approach to ministry.

106 **In an interview with a Baptist magazine:** Frank Halbeck, *The California Southern Baptist*, June 5, 1980, 7.

107 **Years later he would reflect on it further:** Warren, *The Purpose-Driven Church*, 40.

108 **"We'll practice singing the songs":** Ibid., 42.

108 **"It is the dream of a place":** Ibid., 43.

110 **Warren made his way to the main entrance:** Ibid., 42.

111 **"Would you like a fresh start with God?":** While the first Saddleback service was not recorded, Warren saved his notes from the first message and preached it again at the twentieth anniversary service on Easter 2000. These excerpts are taken from the transcript of that service.

113 **"I think this thing is going to work":** Warren related this episode during a Saddleback staff meeting on June 6, 2007.

114 **"I could go on all day":** Halbeck, *The California Southern Baptist*, 7.

114 **Warren years later would dismiss:** Warren, interview, May 25, 2008.

114 **a national Southern Baptist publication, *Missions USA*:** Margaret McCommon, "Mail Order Church," *Missions USA*, May–June 1981, 57.

115 **"They took it to mean":** Harry Williams, interview with the author, October 25, 2007.

116 **As Williams listened he found himself thinking:** Steve Williams, interview with the author, October 23, 2007.

117 **"You're talking about a full-time position, right?":** Ibid.

120    **"We need to pray for Rick, right now":** The young pastor, Norris Burkes, who is now a chaplain and newspaper columnist in Sacramento, recalled this episode in an interview with the author on September 29, 2008.

C H A P T E R   N I N E :   *Out of the Desert*

122    **"What are you afraid of, Rick?":** Rick Warren, interview with the author, October 12, 2007.

123    **But he recognized the distinct echo of the New Testament:** Bible verses cited here are Ephesians 2:9, John 3:16, Matthew 20:28, and Romans 5:8.

127    **"Come on, Rick. Shake it off":** Steve Williams, interview with the author, October 23, 2007.

127    **Years later she would describe:** Kay Warren, interview with the author, February 27, 2008.

127    **He was reminded of the apostle Paul:** 2 Corinthians 12:7–10.

130    **Recalling that meeting later, Kreun said:** Glen Kreun, interview with the author, October 9, 2007.

131    **One Sunday during the second year:** Warren related this story at a Saddleback staff meeting on June 6, 2007.

C H A P T E R   T E N :   *Promised Land*

134    **In February 1979:** Frank Halbeck, *The California Southern Baptist*, June 5, 1980, 6.

137    **"My initial thought was":** From Warren's remarks at a Saddleback staff meeting, June 6, 2007.

138    **"I have no authority over my church":** Rick Warren, interview with the author, September 20, 2005.

138    **"to the people of the church his decisions are their decisions":** C. Peter Wagner, *Your Church Can Grow: Seven Vital Signs of a Healthy Church* (Ventura, CA: Regal Books, 1976), 75.

139    **"go . . . and make disciples of all nations":** Matthew 28:19

139    **It was not enough for churches:** Donald A. McGavran, *Understanding Church Growth*, rev. (Grand Rapids: William B. Eerdmans, 1980), 418.

140    **"Men like to become Christians without crossing":** Ibid., 223.

140    **homogeneity "encourages sinful prejudices":** Ralph H. Elliott, "Dangers of the Church Growth Movement," *Christian Century*, August 12–19, 1981, 799–801.

140    **"We focused on them because":** Warren, *The Purpose-Driven Church*, 160.

140    **"Explosive growth occurs when":** Richard D. Warren, *New Churches for a New Generation: Church Planting to Reach Baby Boomers, A Case Study: The Saddleback Valley Community Church.* Unpublished doctoral dissertation, Fuller

Theological Seminary, Pasadena, California. 1993. Retrieved December 4, 2008, from Dissertations and Theses database.

140    **Later he refined the notion of a target audience:** Warren, *The Purpose-Driven Church*, 169–71.

141    **"He made me look good":** C. Peter Wagner, telephone interview with the author, November 17, 2008.

143    **that summer Kay gave birth:** From Jimmy Warren's unpublished family history.

145    **"While you are working on the church":** Warren, staff meeting, June 6, 2007.

146    **"God, what are you doing?":** Ibid.

149    **It was an ambitious plan, to say the least:** Ronald Campbell, "Church's Vision Too Big? Debate Stirs Over Plan for 113-Acre Rural Site," *Orange County Register*, September 11, 1989, B1.

150    **"Are they saying":** Ibid.

150    **"Wait a minute":** Warren's recollections from a Saddleback staff meeting, June 6, 2007.

151    **"We didn't pay":** Campbell, "Church's Vision Too Big?"

151    **the *Orange County Register*, entered the fray:** "A Church Beset," *Orange County Register*, September 14, 1989, B10.

151    **"You've been too nice":** These comments and the following vignette are from Kay's recollections shared at a Saddleback staff meeting, June 6, 2007.

154    **"We're doing it because":** Ronald Campbell, "Saddleback Church, Developer Agree to Land Swap to Aid Both," *Orange County Register*, May 11, 1990, B5.

155    **"God knew exactly what he was doing":** Rick Warren, Saddleback staff meeting, June 6, 2007.

CHAPTER ELEVEN: *Purpose Driven*

156    **"Saddleback people do not give up!":** Rick Warren, "They Said It Couldn't Be Done: Home at Last!" Saddleback message, December 13, 1992.

156    **"Changed lives are a church's greatest advertisement":** Warren, *The Purpose-Driven Church*, 222.

157    **"We tried to appeal to everybody's musical taste":** Warren, *New Churches for a New Generation*, 281.

158    **Warren would later remark:** Warren, *The Purpose-Driven Church*, 279.

158    **(Twenty years later, that network would include):** A news release on Warren's public information website, www.rickwarrennews.com, accessed on January 7, 2009, described the network as "a global alliance of more than 400,000 pastors representing 162 countries and hundreds of denominations who have been trained by Warren and his team."

159    **"yield an evangelical harvest":** Warren Bird, "Growing Church: Get Ready for 100 New Churches!" *The Alliance Witness*, November 19, 1986, 24.

# Notes

159    **That Easter saw the launch:** Robert L. Niklaus, "Our Mandate: Managing the Impossible," *Alliance Life*, May 25, 1988, 10.

159    **"What the Christian and Missionary Alliance did":** From an interview with the author, November 3, 2008.

160    **"People really enjoyed what they heard":** Ibid.

160    **"Lasting church growth":** Warren, *New Churches for a New Generation*, 105.

161    **Out of those New Testament passages, Warren extracted four purposes:** Ibid., 113.

161    **Later he would add a fifth purpose:** Warren, *The Purpose-Driven Church*, 105.

161    **"If an activity or program fulfills":** Ibid., 103.

162    **"Saddleback is built on a system":** From an interview with the author, September 20, 2005.

163    **Zondervan, a successful Michigan-based publisher:** Zondervan began as an independent family-owned publisher in 1931. In 1988, it was acquired by New York–based HarperCollins, which had been purchased a year earlier by News Corporation, headed by Rupert Murdoch.

163    **"There's something there":** Stan Gundry, interview with the author, January 14, 2008.

165    **"Jack, you've done a wonderful job":** Ibid.

165    **To set an example, on that first Sunday:** Warren, speaking to a group of pastors at his home on May 19, 2008. The author was present.

165    **Five weeks later, some 8,800 people turned out:** Ibid.

166    **"It's an instrument, not a monument":** Stephen Lynch, "This Church Preaches to a '90s Beat," *Orange County Register*, September 18, 1995, B1.

166    **"set in a peaceful, inspiring garden landscape":** From "The Saddleback Vision," delivered by Warren in his first sermon on March 30, 1980, and appearing in *The Purpose-Driven Church*, 43.

167    **"I was the disciplinarian and the rule-maker," Kay recalled:** From an interview with the author, February 27, 2008.

167    **"never let your professional life outpace your private life," he would tell an interviewer:** *OC Metro Magazine*, December 1999.

170    **Chaundel called the hospital:** Chaundel Holladay, interview with the author, November 25, 2008.

171    **"What pastors say":** Tim Stafford, "A Regular Purpose-Driven Guy," *Christianity Today*, November 18, 2002.

171    **In 1997, the annual conference at Saddleback:** From Jimmy Warren's unpublished family history.

172    **"As I sat there by my father's bed":** From a talk at the conclusion of the "Purpose-Driven Community Gathering" at Saddleback Church, May 22, 2008. Warren relates a similar version of this story in *The Purpose-Driven Life*, 237–38.

CHAPTER TWELVE: *"It's Not About You"*

174    **"Adrenaline is a public speaker's best friend":** Rick Warren, interview with the author, September 20, 2005.

175    **"It about killed me to be alone":** Malcolm Gladwell, "The Cellular Church: How Rick Warren's Church Grew," *New Yorker*, September 12, 2005, 60.

175    **given his notoriously short attention span:** On several occasions and to various interviewers, Warren has lightheartedly referred to "my ADD" (attention deficit disorder). However, questioned about it by the author on October 12, 2007, he indicated he has not been officially diagnosed and is not being treated for the condition.

175    **"This is more than a book":** Warren, *The Purpose-Driven Life* (Grand Rapids: Zondervan, 2002), 9.

176    **"The purpose of your life":** Ibid., 17.

176    **Warren divided the book into forty relatively short, breezy chapters:** Ibid., 286.

176    **"There's nothing new in *The Purpose-Driven Life*":** Gladwell, "The Cellular Church," 60.

177    **"This is not a self-help book":** Warren, *The Purpose-Driven Life*, 19.

177    **"By the end of this journey":** Ibid., 9.

177    **"parsonage allowance":** "Appeals Court Finally Dismisses Clergy Housing Exemption Case," *Baptist Press*, August 27, 2002. Accessed online at http://www .bpnews.net/bpnews.asp?ID=14106.

177    **an IRS auditor disallowed a major portion of Warren's claimed exemptions:** Ronald R. Hiner and Darlene Pulliam Smith, "Special Report: The Constitutionality of the Parsonage Allowance," *Journal of Accountancy*, November 2002. Accessed online at http://www.journalofaccountancy.com/Issues/2002/Nov/ TheConstitutionalityOfTheParsonageAllowance.htm.

178    **the United States Tax Court ruled in Warren's favor:** Diana B. Henriques, "Religion-Based Tax Breaks: Housing to Paychecks to Books," *New York Times*, October 11, 2006, A1.

178    **the same court that . . . would rule the Pledge of Allegiance unconstitutional:** Ted Olsen, "Federal Appeals Court Says 'Under God' in Pledge of Allegiance Is Unconstitutional," *Christianity Today*, June 1, 2002. Accessed online at http://www.christianitytoday.com/ct/2002/juneweb-only/6-24-41.0.html.

178    **"any tax deduction that Rev. Warren receives":** Henriques, "Religious-Based Tax Breaks."

178    **Congress . . . quickly set about to defuse the issue:** Hiner and Smith, "Special Report."

178    **"I've always had a heart for pastors of smaller churches," he wrote:** Rick Warren, "Insuring the FAIR in Fair Market Rental Value: The Story Behind Warren vs. IRS Commissioner," a letter to pastors accessed online at http://legacy. pastors .com/RWMT/article.asp?ID=48&ArtID=1739.

179    **"You don't understand"**: Jeffrey Slipp, interview with the author, May 22, 2008.

180    **"Rick was absolutely convinced"**: Ibid.

180    **"If this appears to be a marketing program"**: Rick Warren, interview with the author, May 25, 2008.

181    **zealous "consumer evangelists"**: Greg Stielstra, *Pyromarketing: The Four-Step Strategy to Ignite Customer Evangelists and Keep Them for Life* (New York: HarperBusiness, 2005), 68.

181    **"The book had changed their lives"**: Ibid.

182    **"the fastest-selling book of all time"**: Daisy Maryles, "A Big Fete for a Big Feat," *Publishers Weekly*, September, 27, 2004.

182    **"Well, Larry, I don't know that anybody could"**: *Larry King Live*, CNN, December 25, 2002, transcript.

183    **"If I went on TV or radio"**: Rick Warren, interview with the author, September 20, 2005.

183    **"I didn't want to be a celebrity"**: Rick Warren, "Myths of the Modern Mega-Church," Pew Forum on Religion and Public Life, Key West, Florida, May 25, 2005. Accessed online at http://pewforum.org/events/index.php?EventID=80.

183    **"superstar pastor" . . . "spawning a worship sensation"**: Jim Remsen, "Marketing the Meaning of It All," *Philadelphia Inquirer*, May 25, 2003, B5.

183    **A *Charlotte (NC) Observer* columnist declared**: Ken Garfield, "Searching for Purpose, a Day at a Time," *Charlotte Observer*, April 21, 2004.

183    **the *New York Times Magazine* gave *The Purpose-Driven Life***: Rob Walker, "The Purpose-Driven Life: Book Review," *New York Times Magazine*, April 11, 2004, 24.

183    **A few months later, the *Times* carried a front-page story**: John Leland, "Offering Ministry, and Early Release, to Prisoners," *New York Times*, June 10, 2004, A1.

183    **And in the fall, a *Times* political columnist wrote that**: David Brooks, "Take a Ride to Exurbia," *New York Times,* November 9, 2004, 23.

184    **Zondervan estimated in 2004 that**: Karen Sandstrom, "Reading with God: Scores of Readers and Churches Are Embracing Book's Message of What Defines a 'Purpose-Driven Life'," *Cleveland Plain Dealer*, April 10, 2004, E1.

184    **"I asked him if I could read"**: This version of Ashley Smith's story is drawn from what she said during a news conference at her lawyer's office on March 13, 2005, and what she later wrote in her book, *Unlikely Angel: The Untold Story of the Atlanta Hostage Hero* (Grand Rapids: Zondervan; New York: William Morrow, 2005). A transcript of the news conference may be found at http://www.cnn.com/2005/LAW/03/14/smith.transcript.

184    **It was chapter 32:** In her initial account and news interviews immediately after the ordeal, Smith misidentified the chapter she read to Nichols as chapter 33. She did not expand on the content of the chapter in those interviews and later noted that she had simply confused the numbers. Based on that inadvertent error, War-

ren, in several news interviews after he returned from Africa, commented on how fitting the theme of chapter 33—the wrong chapter, a chapter on servanthood—was to Smith's situation.

184    **"God deserves your best"**: Warren, *The Purpose-Driven Life*, 249.

185    **"What do you think mine is?"**: Smith, *Unlikely Angel*, 150.

185    **"Maybe that's what God wants"**: Ibid., 222.

185    **As they talked through the night**: Although she did not mention it in her initial accounts, Smith revealed later that, in addition to breakfast and spiritual counsel, she also had given Nichols drugs, crystal methamphetamine, which she had used on and off for some time. She said he snorted some and it seemed to have a calming effect. See *Unlikely Angel*, 61–101.

185    **"Honestly, there's nothing in the book that hasn't been said"**: *Larry King Live*, CNN, March 22, 2005. A transcript may be found at http://transcripts.cnn .com/TRANSCRIPTS/0503/22/lkl.01.html.

186    **"For those who believe"**: *CNN NewsNight*, "The Phenomenon of 'The Purpose-Driven Life,'" aired March 16, 2005. A transcript of the program may be found at http://transcripts.cnn.com/TRANSCRIPTS/0503/16/asb.01.html.

186    **Predictably, the blanket news coverage sparked a sudden new surge**: Cathy Lynn Grossman, "Keeping the Faith Kept Gunman's Captive Safe," *USA Today*, March 16, 2005, 1D.

186    **Within a few days, it simultaneously hit number 1**: "Rick Warren's 'Purpose Driven Life' Achieves Unprecedented Quadruple Crown Two and One-Half Years After Release," a news release carried on PR Newswire, March 30, 2005, and written by A. Larry Ross Associates.

186    **"It changed my life"**: Stielstra, *Pyromarketing*, 63.

186    **As Warren told one interviewer**: *Larry King Live*, March 22, 2005.

187    **His customary response**: Warren, "Myths of the Modern Mega-Church."

187    **In an interview with the multifaith website Beliefnet**: David Kuo's interview of Warren, "Rick Warren's Second Reformation," may be seen at http://www.belief net.com/Faiths/Christianity/2005/10/Rick-Warrens-Second-Reformation.aspx.

187    **In 2006, *Forbes* magazine estimated**: Lea Goldman, "The Celebrity 100," posted on *Forbes* magazine's website on July 3, 2006. Accessed online at http: //www.forbes.com/forbes/2006/0703/131.html.

187    **When the list was narrowed**: Lea Goldman, "Top-Earning Authors," posted on *Forbes* magazine's website on December 8, 2006. Accessed online at http://www .forbes.com/2006/12/08/top-earning-authors-tech-media_cz_lg_books06_1208 authors.html.

188    **"When you write a book that begins"**: "The Purpose-Driven Rick Warren," *Philippine Daily Inquirer*, July 30, 2006.

188    **"All my life I planned to simply pastor"**: Warren, "Myths of the Modern Mega-Church."

188    **"Paul is talking to pastors"**: This version of the story is drawn from the Beliefnet interview in 2005, although Warren would tell it in very similar terms many
times over the years in the Saddleback pulpit, at Purpose-Driven conferences, and
in news interviews.

189    **Second, Warren stopped taking a salary**: Sonja Steptoe, "The Man with the
Purpose," *Time*, March 29, 2004, 54.

189    **"Then I added up all that the church had paid me"**: Beliefnet interview.

189    **Warren once told reporters**: Warren, "Myths of the Modern Mega-Church."

190    **"When you read this prayer"**: Warren is paraphrasing Psalm 72, which some
commentaries suggest is a prayer of King David on behalf of his son, Solomon,
perhaps at his coronation.

CHAPTER THIRTEEN: *The Road to PEACE*

192    **AIDS was not a subject that Kay cared**: Kay and Rick Warren have told this
story in a variety of interviews and venues over the years. Probably the most detailed version is contained in Kay's book, *Dangerous Surrender*, 17–35.

192    **"Twelve Million Children Orphaned"**: Warren, *Dangerous Surrender*, 18.

193    **"Why are you bothering me"**: Ibid., 19.

193    **"my heart broke and I was shattered"**: Ibid., 20.

193    **"That's great, honey"**: Kay Warren, interview with the author, February 27, 2008.

194    **Kay told him she understood**: Matthew Philips, "Why Evangelical Kay Warren
Is Fighting AIDS," *Newsweek*, a web exclusive, posted December 1, 2006, at
http://www.msnbc.msn.com/id/15993470/site/newsweek/page/2/.

194    **"Well, hallelujah, the church is finally here!"**: Ibid.

194    **Jerry Falwell had famously described AIDS as a "gay plague"**: Sue Cross, "Falwell Wants Attack on 'Gay Plague,'" Associated Press, July 5, 1983, accessed online via Lexis-Nexis, February 16, 2009.

194    **In a nationwide survey in 2001**: "Americans' Interest in Assisting the International AIDS Crisis," a national survey of U.S. adults conducted by Barna Research
Group Ltd., Ventura, California, January 2001.

195    **Kay now considered such an uncaring attitude**: Philips, "Why Evangelical Kay
Warren Is Fighting AIDS."

195    **Some 1.6 million Mozambicans**: Statistics are from a UNICEF webpage on
Mozambique accessed on February 17, 2009, at http://www.unicef.org/mozam
bique/hiv_aids_2045.html, and from a Canadian Red Cross webpage located at
http://www.redcross.ca/article.asp?id=946&tid=001.

195    **When she returned home**: Kay told the following stories during a session of
the 2007 Global Summit on AIDS and the Church, at Saddleback Church, November 28, 2007. She also wrote about them in very similar terms in *Dangerous
Surrender*, 63–67.

195    **As she would write later**: Warren, *Dangerous Surrender*, 63–64.

195 **Finally, she wrapped her arms around the woman:** Kay Warren, "Warren: Christians Must Do More to Combat AIDS, Comfort Victims," CNN.com, posted October 20, 2006. Viewed February 21, 2009, at http://www.cnn.com/2006/US/06/05/warren.aids/index.html.

196 **"Here we are preaching":** Philips, "Why Evangelical Kay Warren Is Fighting AIDS."

196 **"You never find Jesus asking":** Ibid.

197 **In Malawi, Kay was taken:** Warren, *Dangerous Surrender*, 66–67.

198 **Wilkinson had moved his family from Atlanta to Johannesburg:** Michael M. Phillips, "Unanswered Prayers: In Swaziland, U.S. Preacher Sees His Dream Vanish," *Wall Street Journal*, December 19, 2005, A1. Boston College political scientist and religion expert Alan Wolfe described the situation as "burnout" in Timothy C. Morgan, "Jabez Author Quits Africa," *Christianity Today*, February 1, 2006, which may be read at http://www.christianitytoday.com/ct/2006/february/8.76.html.

198 **"That's what I thought I was there for":** Krista Tippett, "The New Evangelical Leaders," interview with Rick and Kay Warren, *Speaking of Faith*, American Public Radio, December 6, 2007. A transcript may be found at http://speakingof faith.publicradio.org/programs/warren/transcript.shtml.

199 **"We're not helping a single orphan":** Ibid.

199 **a young African pastor came striding toward him:** Warren tells this anecdote often. This version is based on an interview with PBS's *Religion and Ethics Newsweekly*, September 1, 2006, episode 1001.

200 **He jotted them down:** Rick Warren, "Myths of the Modern Mega-Church," Pew Forum on Religion and Public Life, Key West, Florida, May 23, 2005.

201 **"You could visit millions of villages":** Rick Warren, "The Church—The Greatest Force on Earth," an article appearing on Warren's website, http://www.rickwarren.com/, viewed on February 18, 2009.

203 **Yet, unleashing that army would take time, Constantz acknowledged:** From an interview with the author on September 18, 2005.

203 **The first Reformation, Warren wrote:** Rick Warren, "PEACE plan," letter posted on the Saddleback website in November 2003. Viewed on January 28, 2009, at http://www.saddleback.com/story/6213.html.

203 **(Later Warren would sharpen his rhetoric):** "Rick Warren on Outreach," from "Rick Warren's Ministry Toolbox" on Pastors.com, posted October 11, 2006, accessed on February 23, 2009, at http://legacy.pastors.com/RWMT/?ID=280.

204 **"I'm a patient man":** Mike Constantz, interview with the author, September 18, 2005.

204 **"I now believe I know":** Ibid.

205 **The diagnosis came as a complete surprise:** Rick Warren, interview with the author, May 25, 2008.

205 **"At least it's not HIV":** Warren, *Dangerous Surrender*, 79.

205    **"Why is this happening":** Tippett, "The New Evangelical Leaders."

205    **While she felt no assurance:** Warren, *Dangerous Surrender*, 79.


CHAPTER   FOURTEEN:   *Riding Waves*

209    **Warren returned to the Saddleback pulpit:** She finished her treatments in
March 2004 and wrote later that she counts her years as a cancer survivor from
that time. See Kay Warren, "Surviving and Thriving," posted on her blog at
http://www.kaywarren.com/blogs/kaywarren/index.html?contentid=755 on March
3, 2008.

209    **"The fact that we're delaying the PEACE plan":** "Kay Warren Undergoes
Chemotherapy," Rick Warren's Ministry Toolbox, issue 130, November 26, 2003.
Posted at http://legacy.pastors.com/RWMT/article.asp?ID=130&ArtID =4940.

209    **Warren explained his personal enthusiasm for the film:** Rick Warren, "Catching the Passion Wave," *Leadership*, March 16, 2004. Accessed on March 8, 2009,
at http://www.christianitytoday.com/le/currenttrendscolumns/leadershipweekly/
cln40316.html.

210    **"That's catching a wave!":** Ibid.

210    **the movie became an instant blockbuster:** The $117 million figure derives from
David Germain, "Gibson's 'Passion' Ascends to Blockbuster Status—$117.5
Million," Associated Press Newswire, February 29, 2004. Retrieved March 8,
2009, from Factiva database. The $609 million figure was reported in Steve
Chagollan, "Special—The Contenders: *The Passion of the Christ*," *Daily Variety*,
November 9, 2004. Retrieved March 8, 2009, from Factiva database.

210    **Rick and Kay shared the pulpit and delivered a message:** Rick and Kay Warren, "God's Compassion for the Sick: Making a Difference in the Global AIDS
Pandemic," a sermon at Saddleback Church, May 22–23, 2004.

211    **"My response was not Christ-like":** Ibid.

211    **That summer the church sent sixty-four small groups:** Ibid.

212    **"It was their first experience":** Timothy C. Morgan, "Purpose Driven in
Rwanda," *Christianity Today*, September 23, 2005. Accessed on February 9, 2009,
at http://www.ctlibrary.com/ct/2005/october/17.32.html.

212    **"God makes the waves":** Warren, *The Purpose-Driven Church*, 13–14.

213    **"I know a lot of people":** This account was given to the author by a former
Saddleback staff member who was present at the meeting and who asked to remain anonymous.

214    **"There is no question":** Ibid.

215    **"The first and foremost reason Rick would do these":** From an interview with
the author, October 12, 2007.

216    **"Warren spoke at length":** Marc Bohn, "A Semester of Senate Highlights,"
posted May 30, 2006, on his weblog found at http://theworldaccordingtomarc
.blogspot.com/2006/05/semester-of-senate-highlights.html.

216    **"He just struck me at the time as":** Rick Warren, interview with the author, April 30, 2009.

217    **"Rick really got into the music":** Peb Jackson, interview with the author, December 16, 2008.

218    **Bono enlisted Warren to serve as unofficial chaplain of the Live 8 concert:** Marc Gunter, "Will Success Spoil Rick Warren?" *Fortune*, October 31, 2005, 108.

218    **"Warren disarmed the audience":** Howard Manly, "A Purpose-Driven Pastor: Warren Practices What He Preaches," *Boston Herald*, March 13, 2005, 23.

218    **He called for "more civilized dialogue":** Ibid.

219    **"I'm not here to talk about religion":** Rhoda Tse, "Rick Warren Speaks about Purpose at United Nations," *The Christian Post*, September 14, 2005, accessed online March 16, 2009, at http://www.christianpost.com/Society/General/2005/09/rick-warren-speaks-about-purpose-at-united-nations-14/index.html.

220    **"I was interested to see how the Davos community reacted":** Katherine Marshall, "Notes from Davos," posted online. Accessed March 16, 2009, at http://rru.worldbank.org/documents/psdblog/KMDavosNotes.pdf.

220    **"The contact with Warren and his team":** Katherine Marshall, memo to Jean-Louis Sarbib, World Bank senior vice president, Human Development Network, February 2, 2006. Accessed online on December 10, 2008.

221    **members of Warren's staff had met with Wolfowitz:** "World Bank OK $1.4 Billion Rwanda Debt Relief," Reuters News, April 13, 2005. Retrieved March 23, 2009, from Factiva database.

221    **"global statesman":** See http://www.rickwarrennews.com/bio_rwarren.htm. Accessed on March 23, 2009.

221    **"Rick began to struggle":** Glen Kreun, interview with the author, October 9, 2007.

223    **"My only regret, Father," Graham prayed:** The account of the prayer and of Warren's reaction to it came from one of the Saddleback staff members who was present at the meeting and who asked not to be identified.

223    *USA Today* **would note:** Cathy Lynn Grossman, "Death and Faith Intertwined: Schiavo, Pope Made Their Marks," *USA Today*, December 29, 2005, D6.

224    **"There will never be another Billy Graham":** From an interview with the author on May 25, 2008.

CHAPTER FIFTEEN: *"Global Glory"*

227    **"I felt tempted, at times":** Philip Gourevitch, *We Wish to Inform You That Tomorrow We Will Be Killed with Our Families: Stories from Rwanda* (New York: Picador, 1998), 224–25.

228    **On one visit in April 2004:** The account of the meeting between Ritchie and President Kagame was related by Ritchie's business partner, Daniel Cooper, during an interview with the author on June 5, 2008.

# *Notes*

228     **"Let us be it"**: Peb Jackson, interview with the author, December 16, 2008.

229     **"I am a man of purpose"**: Cynthia McFadden and Ted Gerstein, "Rick Warren's 'Long-Term Relationship' with Rwanda," ABC News *Nightline*, July 31, 2008. A transcript may be found at http://abcnews.go.com/Nightline/Story?id=5479972&page=1.

229     **"I could tell that this is a man who is very practical"**: Ibid.

229     **Eleven years after the genocide**: "Rwanda Poverty and Wealth," *Encyclopedia of the Nations*, accessible online at http://www.nationsencyclopedia.com/economies/Africa/Rwanda-POVERTY-AND-WEALTH.html.

229     **"The old cliché says"**: Rick Warren, interview with the author, October 12, 2007.

230     **"When Rick finished speaking"**: Jackson, interview.

231     **"The problem is not a lack of medicine"**: Warren, interview.

231     **Warren announced that "out of the ashes of evil will spring hope"**: From a transcript of the rally provided by Warren's publicity agent, A. Larry Ross, dated April 4, 2008.

231     **"Our goal is to train every church"**: The author was present at this occasion, October 13, 2007.

232     **"When you talk about spiritual emptiness"**: Paul Kagame, address, July 16, 2005. The transcript was accessed online on April 3, 2009, at http://www.gov.rw/government/president/speeches/2005/16_07_05_peace_plan.html.

233     **Warren told the cheering crowd**: Timothy C. Morgan, "Purpose-Driven in Rwanda," *Christianity Today*, http://www.ctlibrary.com/ct/2005/october/17.32.html.

233     **"I do not believe Rick Warren has a bad bone in his body"**: Alan Wolfe, "Taste—Houses of Worship: A Purpose-Driven Nation?" *Wall Street Journal*, August 26, 2005, W13.

234     **"As Warren's team disperses throughout Rwanda"**: Andrew Paquin, "Politically Driven Injustice: Fixing Global Poverty Requires More than Rick Warren's PEACE Plan," *Christianity Today*, February 1, 2006. Accessed online on April 6, 2009, at http://www.christianitytoday.com/ct/2006/february/21.88.html.

235     **"Tinhorn dictators hate the Internet"**: Gwendolyn Driscoll, "The Pastor and the President," *Orange County Register*, December 24, 2006. Accessed online April 29, 2009, at http://www.ocregister.com/ocregister/news/abox/article_1396839.php.

235     **"The PEACE plan is an amateur movement"**: McFadden and Gerstein, "Rick Warren's 'Long-Term Relationship' with Rwanda."

235     **To another interviewer, he would explain**: Timothy C. Morgan, "After the Aloha Shirts," *Christianity Today*, October 1, 2008. Accessed online on April 8, 2009, at http://www.christianitytoday.com/ct/2008/october/16.42.html?start=3.

236     **"I believe God sent me here"**: Edwin Musoni, "We're a Purpose-Driven Country—Kagame," *New Times*, March 30, 2008. Accessed online, April 8, 2009, at http://allafrica.com/stories/200803310590.html.

237    The highlight of the trip was to have been a scheduled stop in North Korea: Julia Duin, "'Purpose-Driven Life' Pastor to Preach in N. Korea," *Washington Times*, July 11, 2006, A3.

237    "If Rick Warren goes in there and preaches": Ibid.

237    "My policy has always been": Rick Warren, interview with Kim Lawton on PBS's *Religion and Ethics Newsweekly*, episode 1001, August 11, 2006. A transcript was accessed on February 21, 2009, at http://www.pbs.org/wnet/religionand ethics/week1001/interview.html.

238    "We are excited about the possibility": Rheta Murry, "Rick Warren Preaches to 100,000 in South Korea; North Korea Trip Postponed," an article appearing on Warren's Pastors.com website at http://legacy.pastors.com/RWMT/article.asp ?ID=268&ArtID=9629.

239    the state-run Syrian Arab News Agency issued a press release: "Al-Assad, US Clergyman Discuss Syrian-US Relations," Syrian Arab News Agency, November 12, 2006, as reported by the British Broadcasting Corporation Worldwide Monitoring. Retrieved April 16, 2009, from Lexis-Nexis Academic.

239    "Washington is wrong not to hold dialogue with Syria": Umar Jaftali, "Syria 'Extends Its Hand Sincerely' for Talks on Regional Issues," *Tishrin*, November 14, 2006, as reported by the British Broadcasting Corporation Worldwide Monitoring. Retrieved April 16, 2009, from Lexis-Nexis Academic.

239    Warren "had no business traveling to Syria": Joseph Farah, "The Purpose-Driven Lie," *WorldNet Daily*, November 16, 2006, accessed April 15, 2009, at http://www.wnd.com/news/article.asp?ARTICLE_ID=52969.

240    the Associated Press reported out of Athens: Brian Murphy, "Megachurch Pastor's Trip Draws Criticism," Associated Press Newswires, November 17, 2006. Retrieved February 3, 2009, from Factiva database.

240    "The official state-controlled Syrian news agency": From an electronic letter to the Saddleback congregation dated November 17, 2006, a copy of which is preserved at http://life-essentials.blogspot.com/2006/11/saddleback-in-syria-truth -about-mission.html.

240    "The Syrian government has long had a bad reputation": Press release, November 16, 2006, which was attached to Warren's electronic message to his congregation.

241    "In hindsight, I wish we'd been better prepared": Electronic letter to the Saddleback congregation, November 17, 2006.

241    "I'm a pastor, not a politician": *The Situation Room*, CNN, December 15, 2006. A transcript of the interview was accessed December 10, 2008, at http://tran scripts.cnn.com/TRANSCRIPTS/0612/15/sitroom.02.html.

CHAPTER SIXTEEN: *Made for Significance*

242    "What's up, Steve?": This and the conversation that follows, Rick Warren, interview with the author, October 12, 2007.

243     (divine punishment for "dividing God's land"): Laurie Goodstein, "Even Pat Robertson's Friends Are Wondering," *New York Times*, January 8, 2006.

244     more than eighty evangelical leaders later that year would sign a letter: David Neff, "Evangelical Leaders Reiterate Call for Two-State Solution for Israel and Palestine," *Christianity Today* (online version), posted November 28, 2007, at http://www.christianitytoday.com:80/ct/2007/novemberweb-only/148-33.0.html.

244     Twenty-two of them—including Falwell, Hagee, and a top Robertson lieutenant—had sent out a letter: Karen DeYoung, "Bush: Peace Bid Will Go Forward; President Says 'Road Map' Stands Despite Latest Attacks," *Washington Post*, May 20, 2003, A1.

244     Their view was based in part on their dispensationalist theology: During an interview with the author on May 25, 2008, Warren explained: "I'm not a dispensationalist. I am a premillennialist in that I believe that Jesus Christ will come back before the millennium. But I take everything I believe about eschatology [theology regarding end times] with a grain of humility because we don't know . . . The only sign I'm looking for right now is, as it says in Matthew, that this Gospel shall be preached in all the world to every nation, and then the end shall come. Jesus said it's not for you to know the times or the seasons . . . I believe in the people of Israel, but I do not necessarily believe 'the people' means unconditional support for the government of Israel. They are two different things. I do believe that Israel is God's chosen people. He's had a role for them in the past and he may have a role for them in the future. But I do not believe that means you just unconditionally accept what the government of Israel does. I am not a Christian Zionist, which means that Israel is the timetable for everything else. No. It may be one factor, but it's certainly not the timetable for everything else, in my opinion."

245     Public opinion surveys of evangelicals: Todd Hertz, "Opinion Roundup: The Evangelical View of Israel?" *Christianity Today* (online version), posted June 1, 2003, at http://www.christianitytoday.com:80/ct/2003/juneweb-only/6-9-31.0.html.

246     Warren briefly sketched out the Rwandan president's life story: Warren misspoke here. There was no office of vice president under the previous regime. The man Warren was referring to, Pasteur Bizimungu, had been interior minister in the previous government and was installed as president in the post-genocide Rwandan government. Kagame was named the country's first vice president. Bizimungu resigned in 2000, and Kagame became president. He then was elected to the office in 2003.

247     Israeli warplanes had staged an airstrike: David E. Sanger and Mark Mazzetti, "Analysts Find Israel Struck a Syrian Nuclear Project," *New York Times*, October 14, 2007.

247     "If we are going to team tackle these big issues": "Poverty Alleviation: Jobs, Jobs, Jobs," a panel discussion conducted at the annual meeting of the Clinton Global Initiative, September 26, 2007. A transcript is posted on the CGI's web-

site at http://www.clintonglobalinitiative.org/NETCOMMUNITY/Page.aspx?pid
=1724&srcid, accessed on March 3, 2009.

248    **"I want in on it":** Warren, interview.

249    **"I'm so glad you told him that":** Ibid.

249    **Blair would announce the launch of the Tony Blair Faith Foundation:** The Tony Blair Faith Foundation was launched on May 30, 2008. See http://tonyblairfaith foundation.org/2008/05/tony-blairs-speech-to-launch-t.html.

250    **"You're not going to believe this":** Warren, interview, October 12, 2007.

250    **Blair would become an official, although unpaid, economic adviser:** Patrick Wintour, "Blair Takes an Unpaid Role as Rwanda Advisor," *The Guardian* (London), January 18, 2008, 5.

250    **Netanyahu called Warren again:** Warren, interview.

251    **"From the time we were teenagers":** Kay Warren, interview with the author, February 21, 2008.

252    **"We started building a relationship":** Rick Warren, interview with the author, April 27, 2007.

252    **"It was a wake-up call":** From Warren's message at a memorial service for his brother on February 2, 2007, at Saddleback.

253    **"That joke bombed":** Ibid.

254    **"The other lesson of my brother's life":** Ibid.

CHAPTER SEVENTEEN: *Weathering the Storm*

255    **"Will Success Spoil Rick Warren?":** Marc Gunther, "Will Success Spoil Rick Warren?" *Fortune*, October 31, 2005. Accessed online December 10, 2008, at http://money.cnn.com/magazines/fortune/fortune_archive/2005/10/31/8359189/ index.htm.

255    **the most influential religious figure of his time:** The Barna Group, January 14, 2005.

255    **"I want evangelicals to be known not for what they're against, but what they're for":** "Interview: Rick and Kay Warren," PBS, *Religion and Ethics Newsweekly*, episode 1001. A transcript was accessed December 10, 2008, at http://www .pbs.org/wnet/religionandethics/week1001/interview.html.

256    **In a widely distributed appeal cosigned by Billy Graham:** The text of the letter was posted on Beliefnet on June 3, 2005. It was accessed on May 19, 2009, at http://www.beliefnet.com/Faiths/Christianity/2005/06/The-ONE-Campaign-An -Advocacy-Letter-From-Rick-Warren.aspx?print=true.

256    **Group of Eight leaders agreed to cancel more than $40 billion of debt:** Tony Carnes, "Can We Defeat Poverty?" *Christianity Today*, September 26, 2005. Accessed online May 29, 2009, at http://www.christianitytoday.com/ct/2005/october/ 19.38.html.

256    **a landmark statement on global warming:** Laurie Goodstein, "Evangelical Leaders Join Global Warming Initiative," *New York Times*, February 8, 2006, A12.

257    **they sent a letter . . . declaring that "global warming is not a consensus issue":** Ibid.

257    **"There is a difference between 'evangelicalism' and 'fundamentalism' and 'the Religious Right'":** Rick Warren, "Myths of the Modern Mega-Church," Pew Forum on Religion and Public Life, Key West, Florida, May 23, 2005. A transcript of the conference may be found at http://pewforum.org/events/index.php? EventID=80.

257    **"I don't think it's really good for churches to get too close to politics":** Jill Rowbotham, "Beware Politics, Pastor Urges," *The Australian*, July 4, 2006, 7.

258    **The letter, he later would insist, was "not an initiative":** From an interview with the author, May 25, 2008.

258    **evangelicals turned out at the polls in near record numbers:** These estimates came from John Green of the Ray C. Bliss Institute of Applied Politics at the University of Akron in an e-mail exchange with the author.

258    **It was inappropriate . . . he told a *Time* magazine correspondent:** Amy Sullivan, "Is the God Gap Closing?" a panel discussion conducted by the Pew Forum on Religion and Public Life, February 21, 2008. The transcript was accessed on May 31, 2009, at http://pewforum.org/events/?EventID=171.

259    **He expanded on that second point in a 2008 interview with National Public Radio:** Rick Warren, interview with Melissa Block, *All Things Considered*, National Public Radio, August 4, 2008. The transcript was accessed May 31, 2009, at http://www.npr.org/templates/story/story.php?storyId=93260209.

259    **he often would resort to a one-line quip:** Gunther, "Will Success Spoil Rick Warren?"

260    **eighteen leading abortion foes wrote:** "Rick Warren/Barack Obama AIDS Partnership Must End, Say Pro-life Groups," a statement distributed by the *Christian Newswire* on November 28, 2006. Accessed on May 30, 2009, at http://www.christiannewswire.com/news/791771591.html.

260    **Reverend Rob Schenck . . . sent e-mails to reporters:** Gwendolyn Driscoll, "Rick Warren Defends Barack Obama Invitation," *Orange County Register*, November 29, 2006. Accessed on December 10, 2008, at http://www.ocregister.com/ocregister/homepage/abox/article_1369009.php.

260    **"Of course we expect criticism":** Ibid.

260    **Saddleback Church "completely disagree with Obama's views on abortion":** Seema Mehta, "Obama an Unlikely Guest at O.C. Church," *Los Angeles Times*, November 30, 2006, B1.

261    **"I don't think that we can deny both a moral and spiritual component" to AIDS prevention:** E. J. Dionne Jr., "Message from a Megachurch," *Washington Post*, December 5, 2006, A29.

261     Warren . . . "faced down right-wing pressure": Ibid.

262     "The fight against AIDS must be done hand-in-hand": From notes of the author, who was present at the 2007 Global Summit on AIDS and the Church.

262     candidates would be allowed to "speak from the heart": From a press release from Saddleback Church dated July 21, 2008. Accessed on May 28, 2009, at http://www.rickwarrennews.com/080721_forum.htm.

263     Warren asked each candidate to reveal his "greatest moral failure": Lynn Sweet, "Faith Forum Gives Debate Preview," *Chicago Sun-Times*, August 17, 2008, A19.

264     The *New York Times* noted approvingly that it had taken "a man of God": Jim Rutenberg, "McCain and Obama Agree to Attend Megachurch Forum," *New York Times*, July 21, 2008, A14.

264     the *Los Angeles Times* added that the feat had demonstrated "the reach": Duke Helfand, "Megastar Pastor Straddles a Divide," *Los Angeles Times*, August 13, 2008, A1.

264     "I just got to thinking . . . These guys have never been together on the same stage": Ibid.

264     "You know, Rick, what we're doing here? None of this is really going to matter": Warren's recollection, from an interview with the author, October 12, 2007.

265     Roughly 74 percent of white evangelical voters had gone for McCain: Election figures based on exit polls reported by *Christianity Today* on November 5, 2008. Accessed on June 1, 2009, at http://www.christianitytoday.com/ct/2008/ november web-only/145-31.0.html.

265     he had spoken with Palin by phone: Seth Colter Walls, "Rick Warren: Sarah Palin Called Me for Advice on Tuesday," Huffington Post, posted September 10, 2008, at http://www.huffingtonpost.com/2008/09/10/rick-warren-sarah-palin -c_n_125420.html.

266     a glossy new magazine and a related online social network called the *Purpose-Driven Connection*: Press release issued on Warren's behalf by A. Larry Ross Communications on November 24, 2008.

268     Joseph Farah . . . expressed "profound and abject revulsion": Joseph Farah, "An Open Letter to Rick Warren," Worldnet Daily, posted December 22, 2008, at http://www.wnd.com/index.php?fa=PAGE.view&pageId=84211. Farah indicated in the column that he wrote the letter the previous week.

268     David Brody . . . reported that he was flooded with e-mails: David Brody, "Pro-Lifers Rip Rick Warren on Obama Invocation," The Brody File, posted December 18, 2008, at http://blogs.cbn.com/thebrodyfile/archive/2008/12/18/pro-lifers-rip-rick-warren-on-obama-invocation.aspx.

268     Warren had urged his congregation to vote for the measure: Transcript, Rick Warren statement to Saddleback congregation in late October 2008. The

transcript was created by the author from a video posted on YouTube and accessed December 21, 2008, at http://www.youtube.com/watch?v=7o4QqGbQmU0.

269   **"We feel a deep level of disrespect":** "Letter to Pres.-Elect Obama on Choice of Rev. Rick Warren to Deliver Invocation at 56th Presidential Inauguration," posted on the Human Rights Campaign website December 17, 2008, and accessed December 22, 2008, at http://www.hrc.org/11793.htm.

269   **Rea Carey . . . called on Obama to withdraw the invitation:** "Task Force Denounces Selection of Rick Warren to Give Invocation at Inauguration," a statement posted on the organization's website on December 17, 2008. Accessed on December 22, 2008, at http://www.thetaskforce.org/press/releases/pr_121708.

269   **"He doesn't need or deserve this position of honor":** "People for the American Way 'Profoundly Disappointed' that Rick Warren Will Give Invocation," a statement posted on the People for the American Way website, accessed on December 22, 2008, at: http://site.pfaw.org/site/PageServer?pagename=media_2008_12 _people_for_disappointed_rick_warren.

269   **Americans United for Separation of Church and State called the Warren invitation "disappointing news":** Rob Boston, "Inaugural Mistake: Rick Warren Is the Wrong Man for Obama's Swearing-In," a commentary posted on December 18, 2008, on the website of Americans United for Separation of Church and State. Accessed on December 22, 2008, at http://blog.au.org/2008/12/18/inaugural-mistake-rick-warren-is-the-wrong-man-for-obamas-swearingin/.

270   **it was his comments on gay marriage that would attract the most attention:** Steve Waldman, "Steve Waldman Interviews Rick Warren," Beliefnet, posted in December 2008, at http://www.beliefnet.com/News/2008/12/Rick-Warren -Transcript.aspx.

270   **"This time it is not Obama's preacher who has decided to honor a bigot," wrote Cohen:** Richard Cohen, "Warren On? Party Off," *Washington Post*, December 23, 2008, A17.

270   **Rachel Maddow described Warren as an "uncivil anti-gay religious leader":** *The Rachel Maddow Show*, MSNBC, December 18, 2008. A transcript was accessed May 27, 2009, from the Lexis-Nexis database.

271   **Sarah Posner said Warren's selection was . . . "a bow to the continuing influence of the religious right":** Sarah Posner, "What's the Matter with Rick Warren?" *The Nation*, December 17, 2008. Accessed online at http://www.thenation.com/ doc/20081229/posner.

271   **the president-elect held his ground and called on Americans to "come together":** Transcript, *Chicago Sun-Times* website, December 18, 2008, accessed at http://blogs.suntimes.com/sweet/2008/12/presidentelect_obama_ defends_i.html.

271   **Warren, meanwhile, had decided to decline all news interviews:** Rick Warren, interview with the author, April 30, 2009.

271 **he released a written statement on the same day as Obama's news conference:** Statement, released on Warren's behalf by A. Larry Ross and posted on December 18, 2008, at http://www.rickwarrennews.com/081218_statement.htm.

271 **"Rick, don't worry about the flak":** Warren, interview.

272 **Warren asserted that he had been falsely accused:** Transcript created by the author of a video message posted on Saddleback's website and accessed on May 27, 2009, at http://www.saddlebackfamily.com/blogs/newsandviews/index.html ?contentid=1723.

272 **Critics immediately pounced on the statement:** *The Rachel Maddow Show*, MSNBC, December 23, 2008. A transcript was accessed on May 27, 2009, at http://www.msnbc.msn.com/id/28425104/.

273 **Michael Cromartie . . . defended Warren as "a compassionate man":** Transcript of the program, which aired on December 18, 2008, was accessed on December 21, 2008, at http://www.pbs.org/newshour/bb/religion/july-dec08/rickwarren_12 -18.html.

273 **Melissa Etheridge described a private meeting:** Melissa Etheridge, "The Choice Is Ours Now," Huffington Post, posted December 22, 2008, at http://www .huffingtonpost.com/melissa-etheridge/the-choice-is-ours-now_b_ 152947.html.

273 **the inaugural invitation "positions Mr. Warren to succeed Billy Graham":** Katharine Q. Seelye, "Obama Selects California Evangelist for Invocation at His Inauguration," *New York Times*, December 18, 2008.

273 **61 percent of Americans supported the Warren invitation:** Jon Cohen, "61% in Poll Back Rick Warren as Invocation Pick," *Washington Post*, January 20, 2009, A11.

274 **"This means more to me personally [than praying at the inauguration]":** Erika I. Ritchie, "Saddleback Pastor Says Honoring King in Atlanta Humbles," *Orange County Register*, January 19, 2009. Accessed May 27, 2009, at http://www .ocregister.com/articles/gay-king-warren-2285107-atlanta-speak.

CHAPTER EIGHTEEN: *Higher Ground*

275 **T. D. Jakes . . . delivered a brief but spirited homily:** Holly Bailey, "At Inaugural Day Prayer Service, Advice for Obama from T. D. Jakes," *Powering Up, News Analysis of the Obama Transition*, a *Newsweek* blog, posted January 20, 2009, at http://blog.newsweek.com/blogs/poweringup/archive/2009/01/20/at -inaugural-day-prayer-service-advice-for-obama-from-t-d-jakes.aspx.

276 **"Oprah, what's going through your mind in all of this?":** Rick Warren, interview with the author, April 30, 2009.

277 **Tucked inside was a note from Billy Graham:** Warren told this story during a message at Saddleback on January 25, 2009, the weekend after the inauguration. He reiterated the story during a radio interview on April 8, and in a telephone interview with the author on April 30, 2009; Graham was one of five clergymen to

pray at Richard Nixon's first inauguration, gave both the invocation and benediction at George H. W. Bush's inauguration, and gave the invocation at both of Bill Clinton's inaugurations.

280    **"one of the greatest privileges of my life":** Rick Warren, "A Prayer for Our Nation," a sermon delivered at Saddleback on January 25, 2009. Accessed on June 3, 2009, at http://saddleback.com/mediacenter/services/currentseries.aspx?site=yDi0V4EwP58=&s=5vQH85HaZFg=.

280    **"I'm a Christian pastor," he told the Associated Press:** Rachel Zoll, "Warren's Inauguration Prayer Could Draw More Ire," Associated Press, December 30, 2008. Accessed online at http://abcnews.go.com/Politics/wireStory?id=6551684.

280    **"It was as ecumenical a prayer as an evangelical could give":** Dan Gilgoff, "Rick Warren's Inauguration Prayer Steers Clear of Controversy While Invoking Jesus," *U.S. News & World Report*, posted online January 21, 2009, at http://www.usnews.com/articles/news/national/2009/01/21/rick-warrens-inauguration-prayer-steers-clear-of-controversy-while-invoking-jesus.html.

281    **"Bad times are good times for churches":** Webcast streamed live from Saddleback Church on March 18, 2009.

281    **"Our nation, and really each of us, stands at a crossroads right now":** Warren, "A Prayer for Our Nation."

282    **appearing on *Larry King Live* on April 6, he seemed to muddy the waters:** From a transcript of CNN's *Larry King Live*, April 6, 2009, accessed on April 9, 2009, at http://transcripts.cnn.com/TRANSCRIPTS/0904/06/lkl.01.html.

282    **Larry Ross, rushed out a statement attempting to clarify Warren's clarification:** From a statement released to reporters on April 6, 2009, and e-mailed to the author on April 14, 2009.

283    **he canceled at the last minute:** Mike Allen, "Rick Warren Explains Cancellation," Politico website, posted April 12, 2009, and accessed April 13, 2009, at http://www.politico.com/news/stories/0409/21157.html.

283    **"I was asked . . . 'what would you dream of?' I said, 'To experience a repeat of Pentecost'":** Rick Warren, "News & Views," posted March 25, 2009, and accessed at http://www.saddlebackfamily.com/blogs/newsandviews/index.html.

283    **over a three-week period that April more than 2,600 people accepted Christ at Saddleback:** Warren provided these statistics to the author in an e-mail message on June 5, 2009.

284    **average weekly attendance reached a new all-time high of 25,000:** Ibid.

284    **he opened one Saddleback staff meeting in 2007 with the startling announcement:** Glen Kreun, interview with the author, October 9, 2007.

285    **"When I am sixty-five I will let go of the church":** Webcast, Saddleback Church, March 18, 2009.

# Index

# Index

# Index

# Index